Studies in Economic Transition

Series Editors
Jens Hölscher
The Business School
Bournemouth University
Bournemouth, East Sussex, UK

Horst Tomann
Department of Economic Policy and Economic History
Freie Universitaet (FU) Berlin
Berlin, Germany

This series brings together theoretical and empirical studies on the transformation of economic systems and their economic development. The transition from planned to market economies is one of the main areas of applied theory because in this field the most dramatic examples of change and economic dynamics can be found. It is aimed to contribute to the understanding of specific major economic changes as well as to advance the theory of economic development. The implications of economic policy will be a major point of focus.

More information about this series at
http://www.palgrave.com/gp/series/14147

Małgorzata Iwanicz-Drozdowska
Paola Bongini • Paweł Smaga
Bartosz Witkowski

Foreign-Owned Banks

The Role of Ownership in Post-Communist European Countries

palgrave
macmillan

Małgorzata Iwanicz-Drozdowska
SGH Warsaw School of Economics
Warsaw, Poland

Paola Bongini
University of Milano-Bicocca
Milan, Italy

Paweł Smaga
SGH Warsaw School of Economics
Warsaw, Poland

Bartosz Witkowski
SGH Warsaw School of Economics
Warsaw, Poland

Studies in Economic Transition
ISBN 978-3-030-01110-9 ISBN 978-3-030-01111-6 (eBook)
https://doi.org/10.1007/978-3-030-01111-6

Library of Congress Control Number: 2018960399

This Palgrave Macmillan imprint is published by the registered company Springer Nature Switzerland AG
The registered company address is: Gewerbestrasse 11, 6330 Cham, Switzerland

Contents

List of Figures

List of Maps

List of Tables

CHAPTER 1

Introduction

Małgorzata Iwanicz-Drozdowska

The role and market behaviour of foreign-owned banks have been analysed for both well-developed countries (e.g. Peek and Rosengren 1997, 2000; Sturm and Wiliams 2008) and emerging markets (e.g. Cull and Martínez-Pería 2013; Havrylchyk and Jurzyk 2011). The presence of foreign-owned banks as well as cross-border activity of international banks is attributable to the liberalisation of capital flows and globalisation. In this book we focus on foreign-owned banks, not the cross-border activity of international banks. However, in order to present a broader picture, we do refer, whenever needed, to studies in both veins. Financial sectors in Central, Eastern, and South-Eastern Europe (CESEE) are bank-based and the banking sector was and still is the biggest player on the CESEE markets and is of crucial importance to the national economy. A comprehensive study covering all the European countries in transition, the results of which are presented in this book, shows the impact which the openness of the banking sector to foreign investment exerted over the last two decades on financial stability, which is a public good, and on economic development, which is crucial in the further catching-up process.

After the collapse of the communism in CESEE (these countries are also called post-communist countries or countries in transition), these markets opened to international cooperation and investments restoring their links with the Western world. After the initial reforms shifting the countries towards the market economy, which were severe to their

M. Iwanicz-Drozdowska et al.,
Foreign-Owned Banks, Studies in Economic Transition,
https://doi.org/10.1007/978-3-030-01111-6_1

societies, attractiveness of the countries in transition encouraged foreign investors to explore investment opportunities in this region.[1] One of the key directions of foreign investment was the financial sector, underdeveloped in comparison with the Western countries, and potentially very attractive due to the catching-up process. International banks entered the CESEE markets by setting up their subsidiaries or taking over existing banks, fairly often through the privatisation process.

Until the outbreak of the global financial crisis (GFC) the presence of foreign-owned banks was regarded as an advantage for the national economy because foreign investors were treated as a source of stability and a helping hand for their local subsidiaries. The outbreak of the GFC and financial troubles faced by many international banks brought concerns about the transfer of shocks from the parent banks to their subsidiaries and therefore their role for the CESEE markets. These concerns were caused by the turmoil on global financial markets, the lack of trust on interbank markets, and a sudden stop of cross-border financing. Against this background, our goal is to present the role of foreign capital in the banking sector in post-communist countries with regard to financial stability and economic development over two decades. This book presents the results of the study prepared, thanks to the support of the Polish National Science Centre (UMO-2014/13/B/HS4/01619), for the project titled "Foreign capital in the Central and Eastern European banking sectors – the impact on financial stability and economic development" conducted in 2015–2018.

The analysis of the impact of foreign capital in the banking sector is important to various stakeholders, including policymakers. While assessing country's internal policy and past decisions, one can use the results of our study as a benchmark. Some CESEE countries are still on a relatively early stage of the catching-up process, mostly due to the late start of reforms and/or a long-lasting military conflict. In order to shape their economic policy properly, it is valuable to know the outcome of other countries' policies, not only from a stand-alone perspective, but on a cross-section and cross-country basis.

The book consists of seven chapters. Chapter 1 is of an introductory character, while Chap. 2 presents a brief history of the CESEE countries, with special attention paid to the process of economic and political transformation. Chapters 3, 4, 5, and 6 present the state-of-the-art research based on a review of extant literature and the empirical results of our work. Chapter 3 shows foreign bank entry in the CESEE banking sectors with different strategies, as well as the evolution of their presence and their performance. In Chap. 4, we present the credit activity of the CESEE banks for different types of owners, including state-owned banks, domestic private-owned banks, and foreign-owned banks. We analyse determinants of credit growth and its procyclicality. Bank credit plays a special role for financial stability and economic development. Both issues are thoroughly analysed in the following chapters. Chapter 5 starts with the description of the GFC impact on post-communist countries. Before presenting the determinants of financial stability in the region, we analyse different measures of financial stability, searching for the best one for post-communist countries. Chapter 6 refers to the finance-growth nexus, from both the theoretical and empirical perspectives. We analyse the determinants of economic growth expanding macroeconomic model by financial sector-specific determinants, including the role of foreign-owned banks. Conclusions are presented in the last chapter, where we attempt to identify the winners of foreign banks' presence in CESEE.

As a project leader, I would like to extend my thanks to my co-authors, Paola Bongini, Paweł Smaga, and Bartosz Witkowski, for their involvement in the project and intensive work at many stages. Moreover, I would like to thank Paweł Smaga for his valuable support in editorial works for this book and my PhD candidates (Łukasz Kurowski and Karol Rogowicz) for their support in data collection.

We hope this book will be an interesting voice in the discussion on the role of foreign capital in emerging markets and may help shape the future economic policy in the CESEE region.

Note

1. We refer to the CESEE countries as host countries, while to countries of investors as home countries.

Bibliography

Cull R, Martínez-Pería M (2013) Bank ownership and lending patterns during the 2008–2009 financial crisis: Evidence from Latin America and Eastern Europe. J Bank Financ 37(12): 4861–4878. https://doi.org/10.1016/j.jbankfin.2013.08.017

Havrylchyk O, Jurzyk E (2011) Inherited or earned? Performance of foreign banks in Central and Eastern Europe. J Bank Financ 35(5):1291–1302. https://doi.org/10.1016/j.jbankfin.2010.10.007

Peek J, Rosengren E (1997) The International Transmission of Financial Shocks: The Case of Japan. Am Econ Rev 87(4): 495–505
Peek J, Rosengren E (2000) Collateral Damage: Effects of the Japanese Bank Crisis on Real Activity in the United States. Am Econ Rev 90(1): 30–45
Sturm, J, Wiliams, B (2008) Characteristics determining the efficiency of foreign banks in Australia. J Bank Financ 32(11):2346–2360. https://doi.org/10.1016/j.jbankfin.2007.12.029

CHAPTER 2

CESEE Countries: Historical Background, Transition, and Development

Małgorzata Iwanicz-Drozdowska

2.1 A Brief History of CESEE Countries

Before World War I, Central Europe was under the rule of the Russian Tsardom, the German Empire, and the Austro-Hungarian Empire. In the Balkans, there were five separate states—Bulgaria, Romania, Albania, Serbia, and Montenegro. World War I considerably changed the geopolitical situation through, among others, the October Revolution and the post-war treaties. After three partitions and 123 years of inexistence as a state, Poland gained independence in 1918. National sovereignty was also gained by the Baltic states (Lithuania, Latvia, and Estonia), Czechoslovakia, and Hungary, while in the Balkans, Yugoslavia was established. In the eastern part of Europe, the Soviet Union emerged. The CESEE countries did not enjoy peace and freedom for a long time, as the year of 1939 brought the outbreak of World War II. Nearly six years of warfare ruined many economies in CESEE. The post-war order pushed these countries under the Soviet political and economic dominance and converted their economic systems into centrally planned economies.

A centrally planned economy lacked an effective interplay between supply and demand. In each of the countries, for a specific period of time, an extensive central plan determined what was produced and how it was distributed. The private sector was either totally squeezed out, or virtually non-existent

M. Iwanicz-Drozdowska et al.,
Foreign-Owned Banks, Studies in Economic Transition,
https://doi.org/10.1007/978-3-030-01111-6_2

or played only a minor role on the market. One of the problems that emerged during the period of communism was the shortage of supply of certain products, including necessity goods. A centrally planned economy was inefficient in solving such structural problems. Kornai (1980) called this phenomenon "the economics of shortage", indicating that this was not the result of the central planners' errors or prices set at inadequate levels, but of systemic flaws. One of the traits of "the economics of shortage" was long queues in front of shops, with people waiting for the delivery of almost all essential items. In parallel, because of these shortages, a black market for goods was flourishing (e.g. food, cigarettes, alcohol, oil, but also foreign currencies), naturally, with much higher prices than the official (regulated) ones.

After World War II, the Western Bloc was supported by the Marshall Plan (an American Recovery Plan for Europe established in 1947) to help rebuild Western European countries, as well as to protect them from the spread of communism. In order to counterbalance the results of the Marshall Plan, the Eastern Bloc (excluding Yugoslavia) established the Council for Mutual Economic Assistance (Comecon) in 1949 (which operated until 1991), with headquarters in Moscow. It was supposed to stimulate economic cooperation, speed up industrialization and technological progress, improve labour force efficiency, and boost economic development. However, in practice, these goals were not achieved. In 1962, Comecon decided upon international socialist division of labour, meaning that each country was expected to specialize in the production of certain goods.

The Eastern Bloc adopted the Soviet economic model also in its financial system. Banking and insurance sectors were state-owned, while the capital market did not exist at all. At that time, central banks played a peculiar role of a "monobank" (commercial banking and central banking activities were pursued by a single entity) and were focused on financing the central plan, for example, by annual credit plans. State-owned banks and insurers provided services to individuals and state-owned enterprises. As foreign trade posed specific requirements, some banks were specialized in foreign-trade transactions, including deals with countries from the Western Bloc. There was no financial supervision and no deposit protection schemes, because under the communist system no bankruptcies were allowed. Kornai (1979), who also introduced the concept of "soft budget constraints" for socialist countries, showed that socialist firms were bailed out by state agencies when their revenues did not cover costs.

Starting in the mid-1950s, after the death of Stalin, social unrest frequently sparked off in the region as a result of, for instance, price increases, food shortages, or the lack of civil liberties. This region's history is marked by events of social disturbance in the following years: 1956 (Hungary and Poland), 1968 (Czechoslovakia), 1970 (Poland), and 1980 (Poland). In the mid-1980s the "wind of change" started to blow as a result of "perestroika" initialized in the Soviet Union by Mikhail Gorbachev. Due to the innate inability to reform the centrally planned economy and increasing social unrest, in 1988 the region faced a period of forthcoming changes later referred to as "the Autumn of Nations". It started in Poland in February 1989 and spread to Hungary, East Germany (with the fall of Berlin Wall; formally German reunification took place in October 1990), Bulgaria, Czechoslovakia, and Romania. In 1991 Yugoslavia collapsed as a federal state, which was followed by the declaration of independence by former Yugoslav republics. Severe ethnic tensions led to a war in this part of the Balkans. The Soviet Union collapsed on 26 December 1991, finalising the fall of communism in CESEE and ending the ideological separation between the Eastern and Western Blocs in Europe.

2.2 Economic and Political Transition

After the collapse of communism, the CESEE countries started, sooner or later, the transformation from centrally planned economies, or "economies of shortages", in fact, into market economies. Some of them even declared economic reforms as early as in 1988 (Hungary and Poland). Democratic reforms led to multi-party systems and the establishment of democratic institutions. In parallel, a legal framework for economic freedom was established, including the freedom to set up a private firm, the level of prices, the right to choose the type of goods produced, or the services provided. The start of the transformation very much resembled "a shock therapy" for the societies in individual countries due to the changing social and economic rules. This therapy started later in most of the post-Soviet republics. It was not a mild change, as the region faced a significant decline of GDP, struggled with hyperinflation and growing unemployment rate caused by collapsing state-owned enterprises, unable to function effectively in free market conditions. Kornai (1994), using Hungarian experiences, pointed out the main causes of the so-called transformational recession, that is, "*(1) the shift from a sellers' to a buyers' market, (2) the transformation of the real structure of the economy, (3) the disturbances in the coordination mechanisms, (4) the macroeconomic consequences of the hardening of financial discipline, and (5) the backwardness of the financial system.*"

For several consecutive years in the 1990s, there was a significant drop in GDP (fairly frequently a double-digit figure) reported in the following countries[1]: Bulgaria (8 years), Ukraine (at least 7 years), Hungary (4), Moldova (at least 4), Albania and Romania (3), Belarus and Macedonia (at least 3), and Poland (2). For several years, the inflation rate exceeding 100% was observed in Albania (1), Belarus (3+), Bulgaria (3), Croatia (2+), Macedonia and Moldova (3+), Poland (1), Romania (3+), and Ukraine (3+). As Polijaniuk and Obal (2002) presented, year 1992 was difficult particularly for the Baltic states, where the rate of inflation revolved around 1000% and the GDP declined from 15% (Estonia) to 35% (Latvia). Both the deep GDP decline and hyperinflation brought about a shock to CESEE societies and economies. Moreover, state-owned enterprises, which faced financial troubles, laid off their employees and unemployment was a new phenomenon in the transforming states, because during communism "full-employment policy" was imposed. During the first stage of the transition process—as Baltowski and Mickiewicz (2000) noticed—the governments had to focus on stabilization (including state budget deficit, inflation), internal and external liberalization, but not on the ownership transformation.

The transition towards market economy required spectacular changes in international relations, including directions of the foreign trade (import and export) and foreign direct investments (FDIs). As Bitzenis and Marangos (2007) concluded, the International Monetary Fund (IMF) and the World Bank "*also contributed to the of transition economies [into the international political economy] by enforcing shock therapy policies upon transitioning economies through conditionality. The shock therapy policies ensured that these economies were integrated in the globalized world to facilitate the easy penetration of multinational enterprises.*" They call this phenomenon an "integration-assisted transition". Although this statement may be regarded as controversial, there is no doubt the CESEE markets were attractive to multinational companies, not only because of their vast populations and thus potentially huge demand for goods, but also because of potential opportunities to buy state-owned enterprises, including financial companies, at attractive prices. The CESEE governments were open to offer attractive prices as the sale of state-owned assets enabled reduction of the state budget deficit. The huge demand for goods stemmed from the previous shortages. At the beginning, there was no initial potential of the CESEE economies alone to meet this demand and it had to be satisfied by importing goods from market economies.

The stock of FDIs in the region, including the former Soviet republics, increased from 2828 million USD in 1990 to 263 billion USD in 2003, while the ratio of FDI inflows to GDP grew from 1.3% to 23.7% within the same time range (Bitzenis and Marangos 2007). The inflow of FDIs was very important to the CESEE economies due to the lack of local capital available for investments. The insufficient local capital constituted an obstacle to the privatization of state-owned enterprises, with the use of local capital alone or to a prevailing extent. In most, cases local investors represented, at the beginning of the transformation, one of the following groups (Baltowski and Mickiewicz 2000): former *Nomenklatura* members (i.e. top representatives of the communist regime), shadow economy, or old licenced private sector. Therefore, the methods of privatization became one of tough political issues, as not all citizens could participate on equal terms. As Brucker (1997) summarized (cited after Baltowski and Mickiewicz 2000), "this reallocation of property rights is regarded as unjust by broad segments of population, because the acquisition of competence, information and assets by former members of *nomenclature* is not perceived as *legitimate.*"

At the beginning of the transformation, the private sector generated only a small part of GDP. For example, in 1989 in Poland it was about 20%, in Hungary 15%, and in Czechoslovakia less than 5% (Bornstein 1999). Since Poland was the most liberal in this respect during the communist time, one might assume that in the other CESEE countries the role of the private sector was similar to the one in Czechoslovakia. State-owned enterprises had (as during communism) no incentive to operate efficiently. Therefore, it was necessary to reorganize the framework for their operations. It is crucial to indicate that former Yugoslav republics represented a different ownership type, which was called social ownership combined with workers' self-management (Slaveski 1997). This type was also inefficient due to the workers' pressure to increase wages and the number of employees. A typical path towards market-oriented solutions, as described by Bornstein (1999), was as follows: (1) corporatization—converting a state-owned enterprise into a joint-stock company; (2) commercialization—running a profit-seeking business; and (3) privatization—selling shares to private investors using different methods (e.g. initial public offerings, public tenders, management and employee buy-outs, auctions of shares with the use of vouchers[2]). The same author presented different characteristics of branches of industry which should be considered while conducting a privatization process. Four branches which are not so much capital-consuming already existed as partly private, that is, retail trade, consumer services, housing, and agriculture. The last one, however, needed significant restructuring due to a peculiar organization of agriculture under communism. Agriculture, to a large extent, was based on big state-owned farms. The branches for which FDIs were supposed to play a vital role in a need of restructuring were as follows: light and heavy industries, banking, energy sector, and telecommunication. It is worth adding that the heavy industry was in focus during the communist times. Most of the branches requiring FDIs are strategic to a national economy, as well as require dedicated regulations (banking, energy, telecommunication).

Banks in the transitioning countries were state-owned and operated in the so-called monobank structure, promoted in the Soviet Union. After the collapse of communism, their activities were separated and central banks focused on their core activities. Their commercial banking parts were transferred to state-owned banks, which were quite often new-established. Assets of the former monobanks and other state-owned banks included substantial stock of loans provided to state-owned enterprises. As they were collapsing, banks faced significant predicaments related to the burdening stock of bad loans (non-performing loans, NPL). This problem was not recognized immediately, because there was no framework capable of identifying and dealing with bad loans. The proper accounting standards and/or prudential regulations were implemented gradually around the mid-1990s. Also new banks set up at the beginning of the transformation period did not possess adequate know-how to run banking businesses and plunged into financial troubles. During the mid-1990s, many banks in the CESEE countries fell into financial turmoil and most countries suffered banking crises (e.g. Baltic states, Bulgaria, Croatia, Czech Republic, Macedonia, Poland, Ukraine) as a result of large portfolios of bad loans. The change of the set-up and the development of the banking sector are presented in Chap. 3 in detail.

The privatization process in the CESEE countries is not evaluated *unisono*. Our purpose is to present the transformation process in a concise way, so we do not elaborate on each country's privatization approach. The features and the assessment are provided broadly in numerous studies, for example, Hashi and Xhillari (1999) for Albania, Mygind (1999) for Baltic states, Prohaski (1998) for Bulgaria, Čučković (1993) for Croatia, Louzek (2009) for the Czech Republic, Slaveski (1997) for Macedonia, Baltowski and Mickiewicz (2000) for Poland, Thompson and Valsan (1999) for Romania, Radiçová (1993) for Slovakia, Yekhanurov (2000) for Ukraine, and Bornstein (1999) for the Czech Republic, Hungary, and Poland. Still, after around 25 years of transformation, the outcome of privatization is in many of these countries deemed a controversial, political issue.

2.3 How Developed Are CESEE Countries?

After the period of transformational recessions, the CESEE countries started a process of catching-up with advanced economies. Still, after more than 25 years of transition, there is a huge gap in the level of economic development between the CESEE countries and advanced economies.[3] The trend of GDP per capita and GDP (in current prices) for the period of our analysis is presented in Fig. 2.1 GDP per capita quadrupled in CESEE, while in advanced economies it doubled. Almost the same was observed for the average level of GDP. The GDP growth rates were higher among CESEE countries for the most part of this period (see Fig. 2.2 for details).

As a study by Próchniak and Witkowski (2014) confirmed, there is a convergence among 27 EU countries over the period of 1993–2010. The annual rate of convergence is 6%, while for the "old" EU member states, only 3%. This means that thanks to "new" EU members, convergence process was faster as they managed to catch up with their advanced peers.

Two other macroeconomic variables, namely the rate of inflation and the rate of unemployment, also underline the existing differences (Fig. 2.3). The inflation was higher in CESEE, especially until 2001, then—on average

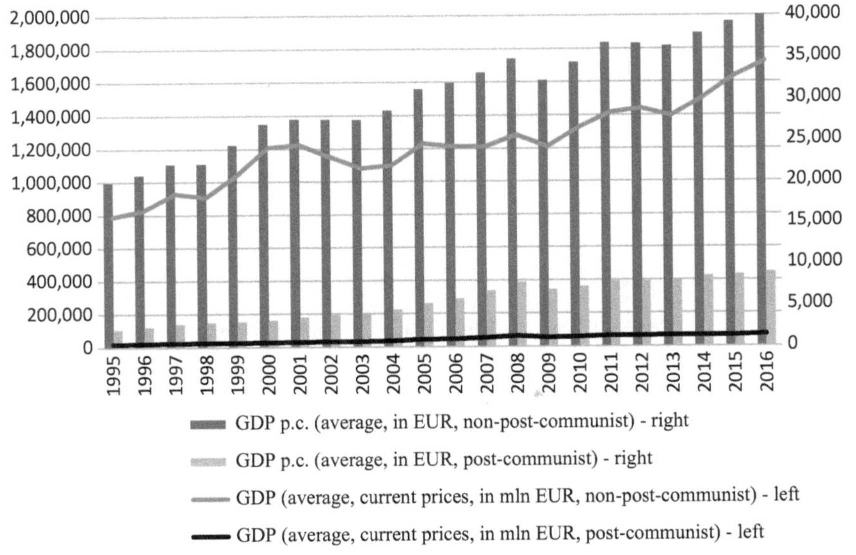

Fig. 2.1 GDP and GDP per capita (1995–2016). (Note: Arithmetic averages in both groups; Source: Based on data from European Central Bank (ECB) and World Bank)

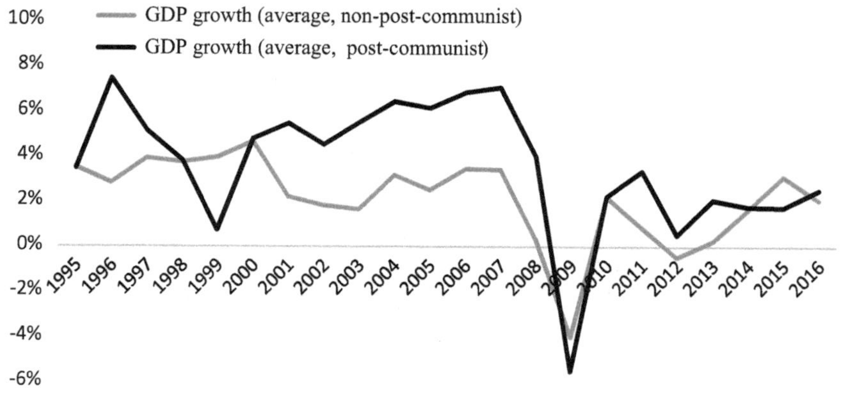

Fig. 2.2 GDP growth (1995–2016). (Note: Arithmetic averages in both groups; Source: Based on data from ECB and World Bank)

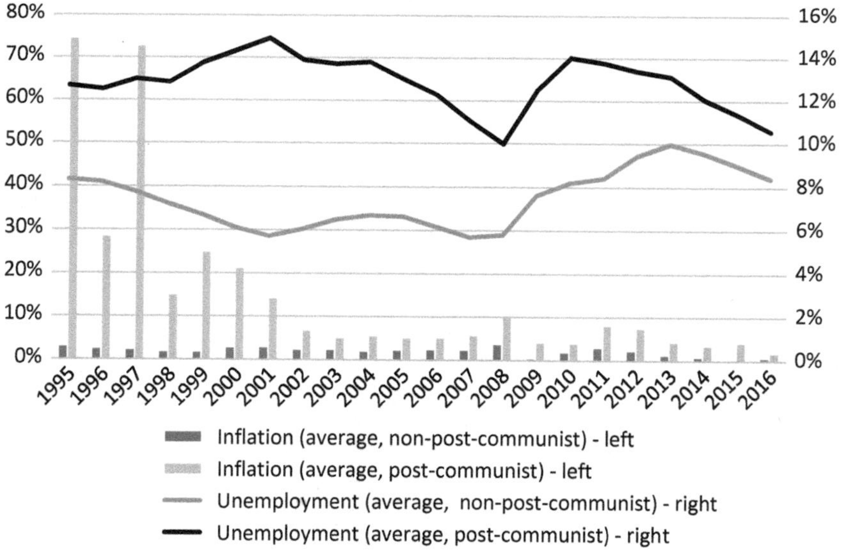

Fig. 2.3 Rate of inflation and unemployment rate (1995–2016). (Note: Arithmetic averages in both groups; Source: Based on data from ECB and World Bank)

it declined. Due to structural problems with labour force, the unemployment rate—though declining—was higher than in advanced economies. This is an example of the communist legacy—the importance of professions and jobs diminished after the collapse of the centrally planned economy and not everyone was able to adjust their skills to new demands of the labour market. This situation has been changing gradually ever since as new cohorts arrived to the labour market. Moreover, after joining the EU, people from many post-communist countries decided to "go West" to make their living and exited the local labour market. This phenomenon, however, has drawbacks from the long-term perspective of the population's age structure, dependency ratio, and potential labour force shortages in the CESEE countries in the future, which may slow down their growth potential.

As presented in the previous section, one of the necessary reforms of the centrally planned economies was external liberalization. The CESEE countries began to open to FDIs and expanded their trade relations (see Fig. 2.4 and refer to maps in Chap. 3 for detail on foreign trade geographical structure).

Trade openness, measured as the ratio of exports and imports to GDP, reveals the same pattern as in advanced economies. This means that trade

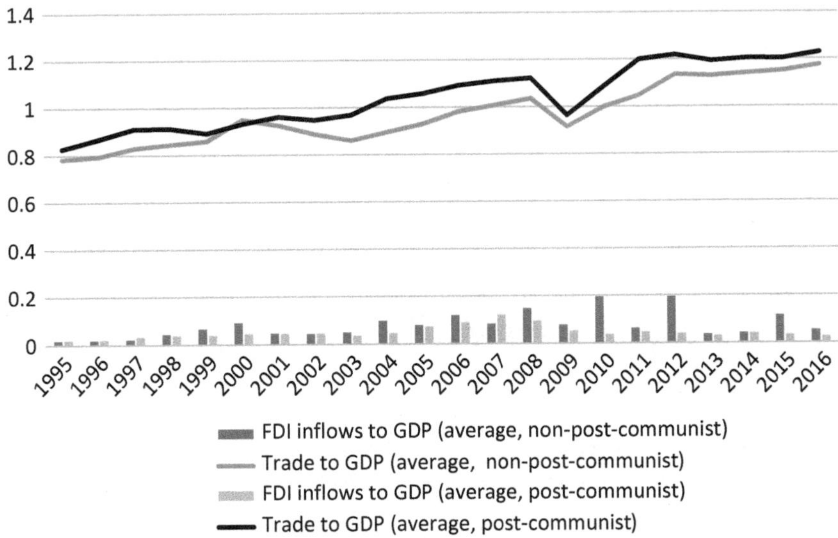

Fig. 2.4 FDI inflow to GDP and openness to trade (1995–2016). (Note: Arithmetic averages in both groups; Source: Based on data from World Bank)

liberalization was fair enough. The main trade partners across the CESEE region are Germany and Italy and for the Eastern countries—Russia. The FDI inflow to GDP since the mid-1990s is lower than in the advanced economies. However, at the beginning of the transformation period the role of FDIs in the CESEE countries was significant to their development and catching-up process due to the shortage of local capital available for investment.

Similar to overall economic development, the financial market in CESEE is less developed than in advanced economies (see Fig. 2.5). Typical measures used for that purpose (see Chap. 6 for more information) are (1) domestic credit to private sector to GDP, showing the role of the banking sector in the economy and (2) stock market capitalization to GDP, indicating the role of the stock exchange in the provision of financing to the economy. Stock markets in CESEE were built in the early 1990s from scratch and played a significant role in some countries during the privatization process. As a study by Iwanicz-Drozdowska et al. (2016) confirmed, there is a strong convergence of the financial sector (i.e. the banking sector and the stock market) among post-communist and advanced economies

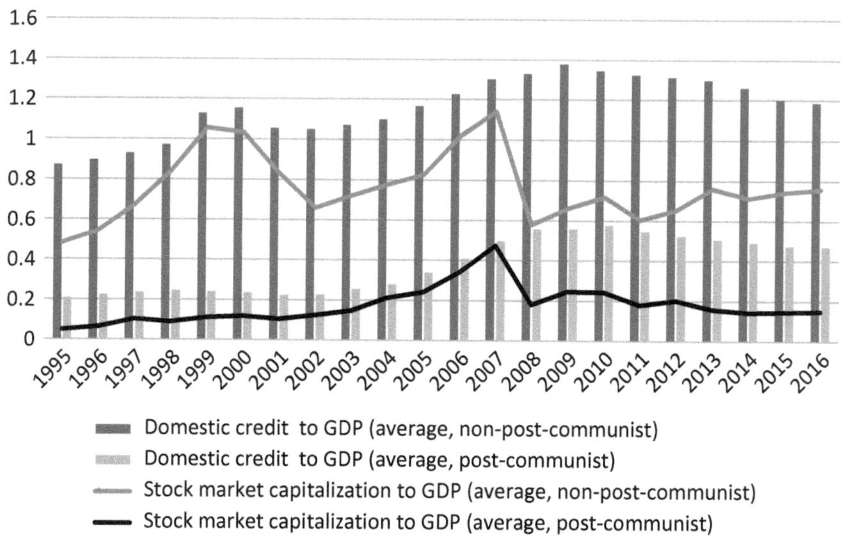

Fig. 2.5 Domestic credit to private sector to GDP and stock market capitalization to GDP (1995–2016). (Note: Arithmetic averages in both groups; Source: Based on data from World Bank)

over the period of 1995–2014. However, the post-communist countries do not constitute one convergence club which is reflected in different paces of their transition. The GFC helped reduce the gap in the financial sector development between these two groups of countries.

Iwanicz-Drozdowska (2016) underlined that the financial safety net in post-communist countries developed very well and in certain respects is even more advanced, that is, (1) in the case of deposit protection schemes, the schemes are better capitalized and therefore show higher capacity to meet commitments in case of a bank failure and (2) position of a central bank is stronger, which helps in safeguarding financial stability. The supervision authorities and the deposit protection schemes were built from the scratch after the collapse of communism.

The role of the financial sector, especially banking, for the financial stability and the economic development with special attention paid to its size and the role of foreign-owned banks, will be presented in Chaps. 5 and 6, respectively.

2.4 What Are the Development Driving Forces?

When discussing development driving forces in transition economies, one should differentiate between an early transition period, associated with a transformational recession, and the period afterwards. In the case of the early period, as already discussed, the CESEE countries faced shock therapies. As Fidrmuc and Tichit (2009) indicated, patterns of growth changed at least three times between 1990 and 2007 in transition economies. In the same vein, Popov (2007) estimated models for "transformational recession" (from 1989 to 1996 or 1998) and "post-recession recovery" (1995–2005). In the next chapters we tackle this problem by somehow starting our empirical analyses from 1995.

Da Rocha (2015) studied, for an early period, the impact of the interplay between liberalization of prices and large-scale privatization on economic growth in post-communist countries. The number of countries included in his study was larger than in our research, as most post-Soviet republics were included. Da Rocha (2015) concluded that "piecemeal" reforms, that is, price liberalization without privatization or privatization without price liberalization, may have negative effects on economic growth, while only joint implementation of both (with large-scale privatization, as opposed to a small-scale privatization) is growth-proactive. In almost all the countries, price liberalization was implemented before privatization.

The growth-enhancing impact of price liberalization, combined with a large-scale privatization, was confirmed by different specifications in da Rocha's study. Positive impact was confirmed for trade liberalization and the implementation of regulations on competition interacted with the liberalization of prices. The dummy variable indicating a war showed negative impact on GDP growth.

After finalising a crucial part of reforms towards the market economy, the CESEE countries became a competitive place for investment due to, for example, cheap and well-qualified labour force and openness to foreign capital. The countries which applied for EU accession started to receive from 1998 financial support to improve their infrastructure (Da Rocha 2015). Year 1998 was marked, however, also by the Russian financial crisis which had a negative contribution to many post-Soviet republics, including Belarus, Lithuania and Ukraine (Polijaniuk and Obal 2002).

Cieślik and Tarsalewska (2013), in their study, covered 24 transitioning countries from 1993 to 2006 (post-recession recovery), concluding that privatization was growth-enhancing if it was a small-scale privatization, while the role of country's external openness was mixed (opposed to Da Rocha 2015). The differences may be explained by application of a different methodology, the number of countries, and the period, underlining how different the initial stage of transformation was.

Around the half of the first decade of the twenty-first century, the CESEE countries marked another milestone. From 1 May 2004 eight CESEE countries joined the EU (Czech Republic, Estonia, Hungary, Lithuania, Latvia, Poland, Slovakia, and Slovenia). Two more countries joined the EU on 1 January 2007, while the last one (Croatia)—on 1 July 2013. The EU accession process integrated, into the single European market, those countries which represent the highest level of economic and institutional development across CESEE. The EU accession proved that the transformation process, in at least these 11 countries, was successful. It is worth stressing that some other CESEE countries are on their way to join the EU.

To sum up, the driving forces of economic development in the CESEE countries differ in time and across countries. At an early stage, after the initial shock, privatization combined with price liberalization was an important driving force for their development. Later on, external support for EU accession countries, helped stimulate their development and integrate to a larger extent into the European market. We will present the results of our research on economic development in CESEE in Chap. 6, covering a period of 20 years (1995–2015) to explore the growth-enhancing factors, including the role of foreign-owned banks in national banking sectors.

Notes

1. Starting in 1990; based on IMF data from World Economic Outlook. Due to the lack of historical data for some Balkan states and former Soviet Union republics, we are not able to present a complete picture.
2. Vouchers were distributed under mass privatization programmes to citizens free of charge.
3. Advanced economies are represented in our study by EU "old" Member States, Norway, Switzerland, USA, and Japan.

Bibliography

Baltowski M, Mickiewicz T (2000) Privatisation in Poland: Ten Years After Privatisation in Poland: Ten Years After, Post-Communist Econ 12(4):425–443. https://doi.org/10.1080/14631370050216498

Bitzenis A, Marangos J (2007) Globalization and the Integration-Assisted Transition in Central and Eastern European Economies. J Econ Issues 41(2):427–434. https://doi.org/10.1080/00213624.2007.11507030

Bornstein M (1999) Framework Issues in the Privatisation Strategies of the Czech Republic, Hungary and Poland. Post-Communist Econ 11(1):47–77. https://doi.org/10.1080/14631379996048

Brucker H. (1997) Privatisation in East Germany. A Neo-Institutional Analysis. London, Frank Cass

Cieślik A, Tarsalewska M (2013) Privatization, Convergence, and Growth. Eastern Eur Econ 51(1):5–20. https://doi.org/10.2753/EEE0012-877551010

Čučković N (1993) Privatisation in Croatia: What went wrong? Hist Eur Ideas 17(6):725–733. https://doi.org/10.1016/0191-6599(93)90095-8

da Rocha BT (2015) Let the markets begin: The interplay between free prices and privatisation in early transition. J Comp Econ 43(2):350–370. https://doi.org/10.1016/j.jce.2014.10.003

Fidrmuc J, Tichit A (2009) Mind the break! Accounting for changing patterns of growth during transition. Econ Sys 33(2):138–154. https://doi.org/10.1016/j.ecosys.2009.02.002

Foster N, Stehrer R (2007) Modeling transformation in CEECs using smooth transitions. J Comp Econ 35(1):57–86. https://doi.org/10.1016/j.jce.2006.10.002

Hashi I, Xhillari L (1999) Privatisation and Transition in Albania. Post-Communist Econ 11(1):99–125. https://doi.org/10.1080/14631379996066

Iwanicz-Drozdowska M (2016) Sieć bezpieczeństwa finansowego. Gdzie szukać liderów? In: Karmańska A, Ostaszewski J (ed) Przełamywanie dysonansów poznawczych jako czynnik stymulowania rozwoju nauk o finansach. SGH, Warsaw

Iwanicz-Drozdowska M, Smaga P, Witkowski B (2016) Financial Development. Have Post-Communist Countries Converged? Trans Bus Econ 15(2A)(38A):389–414
Kornai J (1979) Resource-Constrained versus Demand-Constrained Systems. Econometrica 47(4):801–819
Kornai J (1980) Economics of Shortage. Amsterdam: North Holland
Kornai J (1994) Transformational Recession: The Main Causes. J Comp Econ 19(1):39–63. https://doi.org/10.1006/jcec.1994.1062
Louzek M (2009) The Czech privatisation after 20 years. Post-Communist Econ 21(3):345–359. https://doi.org/10.1080/14631370903090065
Mygind, N (1999). Privatisation, governance and restructuring of enterprises in the Baltics, OECD
Polijaniuk H, Obal T (2002) Kraje nadbałtyckie In: Iwanicz-Drozdowska M (ed) Kryzysy bankowe. Przyczyny i rozwiązania. PWE, Warsaw
Popov V (2007) Shock Therapy versus Gradualism Reconsidered: Lessons from Transition Economies after 15 Years of Reforms. Comp Econ Stud 49(1):1–31. https://doi.org/10.1057/palgrave.ces.8100182
Próchniak M, Witkowski B (2014) On the Stability of the Catching-Up Process Among Old and New EU Member States On the Stability of the Catching-Up Process Among Old and New EU Member States. Eastern Eur Econ 52(2):5–27. https://doi.org/10.2753/EEE0012-8775520201
Prohaski G (1998) A review of Bulgarian privatisation. OECD and Bulgarian Centre for Economic Development
Radiçová I (1993) Privatisation: The case of Slovakia. Hist Eur Ideas 17(6):735–740. https://doi.org/10.1016/0191-6599(93)90096-9
Slaveski T (1997) Privatization in the Republic of Macedonia Privatization in the Republic of Macedonia Five Years After. Eastern Eur Econ 35(1):31–51. https://doi.org/10.1080/00128775.1997.11648611
Thompson G, Valsan C (1999) Early Privatization in Romania Early Privatization in Romania. Eastern Eur Econ 37(6):35–53 https://doi.org/10.1080/00128775.1999.11648704
Yekhanurov Y (2000) The Progress of Privatization The Progress of Privatization. Eastern Eur Econ 38(1):71–93. https://doi.org/10.1080/00128775.2000.11648712

CHAPTER 3

Foreign Bank Entry into CESEE Countries in the 1990s and Afterwards

Paola Bongini

3.1 Why Did Foreign Banks Decide to Enter?

The decision to expand abroad is the outcome of a multifaceted process consisting of the following steps: (i) define which business(es) to conduct in the host country (what to do); (ii) outline the mode(s) of conducting these businesses (how to do it); and (iii) delineate the organizational forms of operations in the host country.

Within the first step, banks need to specify which businesses are involved in the three main business areas in which they operate: wholesale banking, retail banking, or universal banking. This decision will affect subsequent steps, as each business has its own specific mode of operations and its preferred organizational form.

Wholesale lending typically involves direct lending to large-scale borrowers (states and multinational companies); as such, this does not require physical presence in the host country and is considered a cross-border, and also cross-currency, activity of international banks. An international bank is a financial entity that offers financial services, such as payment accounts, lending opportunities, trade financing, or foreign exchange operations, to foreign clients. It involves the least investment intensity from the parent bank, which can set up corresponding banking agreements or representations in the host country. Correspondent banking represents the lowest

M. Iwanicz-Drozdowska et al.,
Foreign-Owned Banks, Studies in Economic Transition,
https://doi.org/10.1007/978-3-030-01111-6_3

exposure to the foreign market, involving the use of a bank located in the host market to provide services to the foreign bank. The sort of services offered via a correspondent banking relationship comprises the offer of payment services and other transaction services, as well as trade credit facilities. Via their representative offices, banks can obtain a slightly greater exposure to the foreign market, although these structures are usually small and cannot take deposits or grant loans. They usually act as marketing offices for the parent bank and are typically set up in risky markets where the prospects of doing banking business are still to be probed and a negligible investment project, such as a representative office, can easily be absorbed in case of losses and closure if commercial prospects are not good. It can also be used to test the possibility of further engagement in the host country (Goldberg 1992).

On the opposite side stands the decision to offer retail banking services (loans and deposits to businesses and household customers) or universal banking services, which, along with retail banking services and the wholesale business, also include asset management services. In these two cases, the bank's foreign activity involves foreign direct investments in the host country, via greenfield or merger and acquisition operations. As such, it is defined as multinational banking, as opposed to the simple form of international banking.

Physical presence abroad may take two diverse organizational forms: branches or subsidiaries/affiliated banks. Establishing a branch office or a subsidiary indicates a higher level of commitment to the foreign market compared to cross-border activities or setting up a representative office.

Foreign branches constitute integral parts of the parent bank and may offer a broad range of banking services to both domestic and foreign customers. A branch acts as a legal and functional part of the parent's head office. Branches can perform all the functions allowed by the banking authorities of the host country, namely, take deposits and grant loans as well as sell other types of banking and financial services. Branches are rather easy form of foreign bank expansion, especially in EU, where the Second Banking Directive introduced the freedom of establishment for banks from Member States (so-called single European passport). A subsidiary, however, constitutes a legal entity separate from its parent bank—one that has its own capital and is organized and regulated according to the laws of the host country. As such, subsidiaries have identical banking powers as domestic-owned banks, that is, they have an independent legal status. The subsidiary's risk exposure is limited by its own capital, which is legally separated from the parent bank's own capital. Other differences between branches and subsidiaries involve supervision, risk and business focus. Branches are supervised by the supervisors of the parent's home country, while the host country's supervisors have direct responsibility for subsidiaries, which also have to comply with the host country's regulatory framework, which could be quite different from what is in place at home. The subsidiaries' operations (lending, for instance) are constrained to the level of their own capital, while foreign branches rely on the capital of the foreign parent bank. As to business orientation, while foreign branches are more focused on wholesale and corporate banking operations, subsidiaries or affiliated banks are typically retail-oriented (Focarelli and Pozzolo 2005). Indeed, up until the recent spread and importance of online banking, physical presence was considered a prerequisite for developing personal relationships, which are at the core of the most traditional banking activities, especially in value added operations, such as lending to businesses or providing portfolio management services to households.

The development of multinational banking was particularly intense in the 1990s and directed both to emerging or transition economies and advanced economies.

As a matter of fact, the main mantra of the 1990s was the following. "If a country (whether emerging or transition) seeks to create an efficient market-oriented banking system, three strategic options are available": (1) to transform existing state-owned banks into private market-oriented banks; (2) to offer banking licences to newly created local banks; (3) to favour foreign banks' performance of business operations in the country.

The third option was considered the most promising: "importing" a portion of the banking system from abroad was deemed to deliver the desired result—an efficient banking system—within a reasonable period of time. Indeed, at that time, both the academia and international institutions, such as the World Bank and the International Monetary Fund, were unanimously highlighting the positive roles which foreign banks' presence may play in any economy which strives at catching-up soon with the advanced economies, as it was the case of transition economies trying to rapidly transform their economies from the centrally planned ones, with very low levels of intermediation, to catch up with the rest of the EU. These positive roles may be briefly summarized as bringing valuable bank management know-how to those countries which would otherwise need to take a long time to accumulate expertise and develop specialized human capital competent at risk management techniques and promoting efficiency in the overall banking system. Foreign banks operating abroad are usually the largest and the most efficient in their domestic markets and as such they have the potential to transmit best practices while bringing the element of stability to the financial system as their exposure to the host country is only a small proportion of their overall balance sheet position. Further, they are more resistant to political pressures while pursuing their business, particularly lending, and may be less susceptible to local euphoria leading to excessive lending (Llewellyn 2004).

The question why, when and how banks go abroad has been thoroughly analysed as an empirical issue by the extant literature, which mainly during the 1990s and the first quinquennial of the new millennium[1] witnessed and tried to explain the surge of multinational banking activities directed to both emerging and advanced economies, for example, Goldberg and Johnson (1990), Goldberg and Grosse (1994), Buch (2000), Williams (2002), Clark et al. (2003), and Focarelli and Pozzolo (2001, 2005).

There is no single explicit theory explaining why a bank would go abroad. Williams (1997) still represents the most comprehensive survey of positive theories of multinational banking which treat the decision of a bank to invest abroad as a subset of the study of multinational enterprises (MNEs). The two key paradigms in this field are the internationalization theory, originally elaborated on by Buckley and Casson (1976) and the eclectic theory, as developed by Dunning (1980). The former stresses that the advantages of MNEs come from the firm's ability to internalize market failures so as to reduce its transaction costs. In other words, the firm prefers outright ownership of complementary assets rather than bearing the costs of contracting in the open market: the internalization of intermediate products is the key element of the multinational firm. Information is the typical intermediate product that could lead a firm (and particularly a bank) to a decision to organize its activities internally in order to develop and exploit its specific advantages in the knowledge domain. The knowledge advantage becomes a public good within the firm, which can be best exploited by expanding off-shore (Williams 1997).

On the other hand, the eclectic theory considers the decision to expand abroad to be driven by three fundamental factors or advantages (OLI): (i) ownership; (ii) location, and (iii) internalization. Ownership advantages are typically intangible assets which refer to the possession of proprietary technology, ability to innovate, better management skills, favoured access to inputs, and economies of scope. Location advantages involve the characteristics of both the home country of the MNE and the host country of investment. Examples are input prices, barrier to trade, tax regimes, institutional arrangements, the prospects of the economy, and socio-political environments. Location factors help explain the site of the internalization once the decision has been made on the basis of ownership advantages, and the mode of entry, once internalization-specific advantages have been taken into consideration. The latter stems from market imperfections and failures which make more convenient internalizing risks and the risk management process or exploiting economies of scale and scope. As Dunning (1980) highlights, market failures lead to internalization (and expansion abroad), while the ownership of a particular asset explains why identical firms may differ in their propensity to become and be multinational.

Starting from these two overarching paradigms and the subsequent different theories conceived to explain and interpret, within the domain of industrial organization theory, the specific motives of foreign bank entry (see Fig. 3.1), a substantial empirical literature, starting from the 1990s,

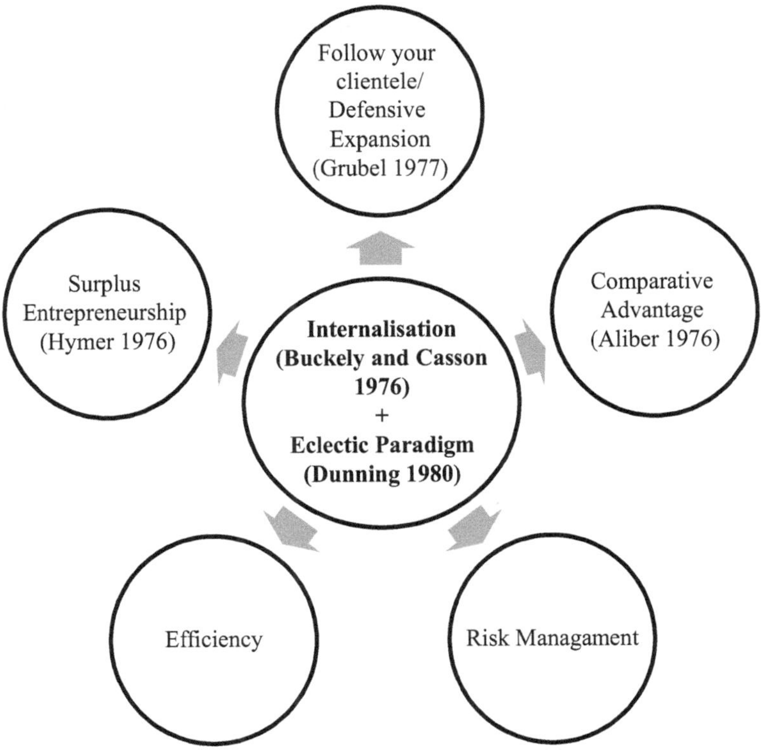

Fig. 3.1 Theories of multinational banking. (Source: Based on Rajan and Gopalan (2014))

has generated some testable hypotheses levering on the theories just discussed. As Rajan and Gopalan (2014) point out, notwithstanding the framework used to theorize the drivers of multinational banking, the question of why banks go abroad is essentially an empirical issue.

Indeed, as banking is typically a profit-oriented business, the main reason behind the decision to take on the multinational course is to generate profits. In this sense, the host market could appear to be a place for increasing, safeguarding, and stabilizing homemade profits, where "and" and "or" could simultaneously apply.

Three main drivers have been identified in the empirical literature to explain the decision to set up affiliates in a foreign market (see Fig. 3.2): microeconomic factors, institutional factors, and "macro-economic" characteristics of both the home and host countries.

The microeconomic drivers, derived from the internalization theory, include the defensive expansion motive and the benefits from (geographical) diversification of the business activity. The first motivation is to assist home country customers in their international transactions ("follow the customer" or "defensive expansion hypothesis"; see Williams 2002). According to this view, a bank follows its clients abroad to support the

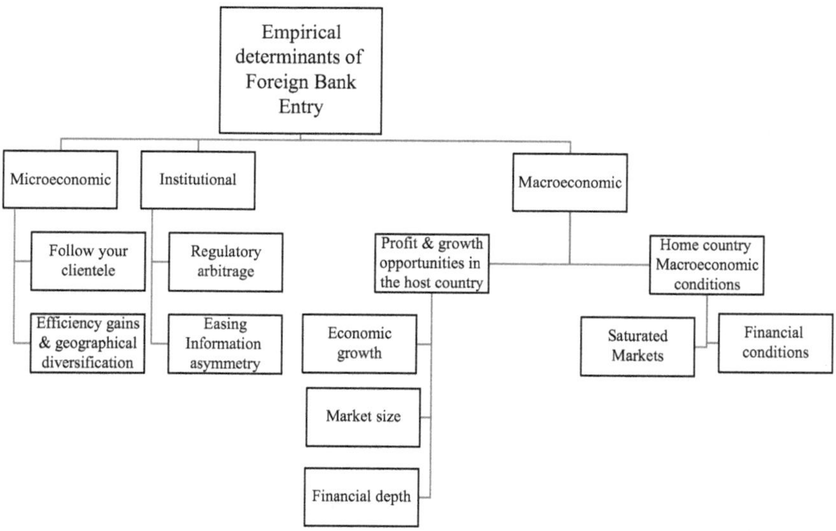

Fig. 3.2 Empirical determinants of foreign bank entry. (Source: Adapted from Rajan and Gopalan 2014)

existing bank-customer relationships also in the host country, where the bank customer has a specific interest (trade relations or FDIs). The main idea is to follow international retail and corporate customers abroad to exploit informational advantages of long-term bank-customer relationships established at home and not to dissolve them because of the international activity of their customers. Indeed, a high number of empirical studies found a positive correlation between the pattern of bank internationalization and the degree of economic integration between the home and the host countries (Buch 2000; Williams 2002). Banks follow their clients to foreign markets to provide seamless financial services. A proxy for economic integration is the level of non-bank FDI and trade flows. The empirical literature is biased towards the US, where the evidence is unanimous in confirming the "follow your customer" hypothesis (Goldberg and Saunders 1980, 1981; Goldberg and Johnson 1990; Miller and Parkhe 1998). Outside the US, less clear evidence is present. Brealey and Kaplanis (1996), in a sample of advanced economies and emerging market economies, find that countries with the highest foreign bank presence were those with the greatest trade and non-bank FDI links. On the other hand, Seth et al. (1998), having examined the lending patterns of foreign banks, found no support for the "follow your customer" hypothesis, as the majority of lending was not directed at borrowers from the same home country. However, the direction of the causal relationship, which may go the other way round, from bank FDI to non-bank FDI and trade flows, still remains unclear. Clark et al. (2003) suggest that foreign bank entry may lay the groundwork for greater non-bank FDI.

The second obvious motive for foreign expansion is the desire to reap the gains from the diversification of activities, which stabilize the flow of earnings while reducing risk and delivering efficiency-gain potentials. By expanding into different markets, banks capitalize on geographical diversification, enhancing their risk-reward trade-off and profitability the less correlated the earnings in the foreign market are to those in the home market. Besides, geographical diversification may bring efficiency gains through economies of scale, scope or the product mix (Soussa 2004).

The second set of determinants refers to the institutional environment of the host country, namely the presence of regulatory opportunities and/or the presence of factors limiting information asymmetries, which can act as external favourable (unfavourable) conditions facilitating (deterring) foreign bank entry.

Foreign bank entry can be eased or impeded by regulatory and legislative attitudes towards foreign ownership. Unsurprisingly, foreign banks are more likely to enter markets with fewer regulatory restrictions and a local authorities' more positive attitude towards foreign bank's operations (Papi and Revoltella 1999; Focarelli and Pozzolo 2001; Barth et al. 2001; Buch and DeLong 2004). Foreign bank entry was allowed in European transition economies only from the mid-1990s, when the authorities began to actively pursue policies to privatize the ailing banking systems, which included and supported foreign direct investments to help fast restructuring of failing banks (Soussa 2004; Mathieson and Roldos 2001). Lensink and De Haan (2002) provide strong evidence that foreign bank entry in CESEE positively responded to economic reform measures, including privatization of the financial and manufacturing sectors and measures of the financial sector liberalization. Among the institutional characteristics that can help multinational banks to decide to establish presence abroad is the potential for easing informational costs that afflict any market entrant who wishes to compete with market incumbents (Sharpe 1990; Petersen and Rajan 1994). The empirical literature identifies three dimensions of overcoming the information asymmetry in the host country, specifically: geographical proximity, cultural proximity, and the presence of credit bureaus. The lack of these characteristics boosts informational costs and reduces the likelihood of foreign bank entry. As such, geographical and cultural links may be considered more as an explanation of the location decision of foreign banks, once the decision to go abroad is undertaken. Banks have an incentive to enter those markets with better informational quality (for instance, for the presence of well-functioning agencies which collect and research individual credit information to share or to sell for a fee to creditors, so they can make decisions to grant loans) and/or a largely similar institutional and cultural environment, thanks to a common language, a comparable legal system, akin social norms or common colonial links (Galindo et al. 2003; Buch and DeLong 2004). The importance of geographical proximity between the bank head office and its branches has been thoroughly investigated by the literature on bank-firm relationships. The distance is considered as a characteristic capable of influencing the ways in which the bank-customer relationship develops and above all, the possibility for banks to acquire an informational advantage, through the acquisition of soft information that could be available only to proximate lenders. What is relevant is not only the distance between the customer and the bank branch, but the distance between the customer and the "brain" of the bank, that is, the head office or the physical place where credit decisions are actually undertaken. As such, the technological advances in information transfer cannot diminish the importance of "distance" in acting as a barrier to foreign bank entry, though a recent study by Claessens and Van Horen (2014) shows that not only the absolute distance matters in location decisions, but also the distance of the competitor countries.

Finally, the third cluster refers to the quest for pursuing new growth opportunities abroad with higher profit margins and more favourable risk-adjusted returns, especially when domestic markets become more saturated. The market of the host country may offer new opportunities to make money, depending on the characteristics of the host economy (like size and potential for growth, political and macroeconomic stability of the host country, features of the local financial sector). In this case relevant pull factors are the search for new clients and the unused potential of household and businesses in local credit markets, combined with higher profit opportunities (proxied by higher interest rate margins) of the local banking market. A number of studies offer support for this view, particularly when considering foreign bank entry in emerging and transition economies: foreign banks are attracted to markets with low taxes, high per capita income or higher per capita GDP as well as higher expected rate of economic growth (Brealey and Kaplanis 1996; Papi and Revoltella 1999; Buch 2000; Claessens et al. 2000; Focarelli and Pozzolo 2005; Kraft 2004). Cerutti et al. (2007), studying the determinants of foreign banks' organization forms, notice that branches are a less likely option when entering relatively poorer countries. Two non-mutually exclusionary explanations are provided. First, subsidiaries are often the result of crisis-related acquisitions that are more likely to occur in poorer countries. Second, foreign banks enter as subsidiaries in markets where they believe there is ample room for expansion and these are typically poorer economies, where the local banks are less developed and capitalized, and hence easier to compete against.

Multinational activity can deliver diversification benefits and enhance risk-adjusted returns to the parent bank and such a result is extremely valuable when limited growth opportunities are present at home due to the already significant market shares and/or high levels of credit penetration. In other words, the combined situation of limited diversification opportunities at home and being a "giant" in the home market urge the bank to exploit its comparative advantages in other markets.

In both situations, the size is an important factor behind the decision to go abroad. Larger banks are much more international than smaller ones, most likely because they have more internationally diversified customers (Berger et al. 1995); larger banks have stronger incentives to internationally diversify their portfolios and smooth the effects of asynchronous fluctuations in loans and deposits (Focarelli and Pozzolo 2005). Besides, given their size, they are more likely to become involved in asset management and investment banking activities that, due to their inner nature, are typically undertaken at the international level (Ball and Tschoegel 1982).

The empirical literature that specifically focuses on the decision to entry the CESEE markets (see Table 3.1) highlights that foreign banks did not pursue the follow your client (FYC) strategy, they rather competed with domestic-owned banks in retail and wholesale markets (Lensink and de Haan 2002; Kraft 2004; Wezel 2004; de Haas and van Lelyveld 2006; Naaborg 2007; Hryckiewicz and Kowalewski 2010). According to Haselman (2006), the decision of foreign banks to enter the CESEE economies seemed to be driven by long-term strategic goals in countries where they could exploit their relatively higher efficiency. In a similar vein are the findings of Kraft (2004) and Hryckiewicz and Kowalewski (2010), who showed that following the client relationship was only important in the first years of the transition process in the CESEE countries, while later on exploiting opportunities in those markets was the main motivation for foreign bank's entry. Concrete evidence for the importance of profitability in foreign bank entry is available for the Czech Republic, Hungary and Poland (Konopielko 1999), Croatia (Kraft 2004), Estonia (Kowalski et al. 2002), Lithuania (Dubauskas 2002) and Romania (Florescu 2002). Foreign bank entry in CESEE was not largely motivated by the perceived need to support the existing client base; on the contrary, it was mainly motivated by the expected profitability of banking abroad relative to banking at home. In particular, Naaborg (2007) reports that for the big regional foreign banks the high competition in the home country played a far more important role in explaining their decision to entry the CESEE economies, especially in the light of the prospect of EU accession, which helped governance and laws to be improved and modernized. The peculiar research strategy used by Naaborg (2007) to assess the reasons for foreign bank penetration in the CESEE countries, that is, by means of structured interviews to heads of foreign parent banks, local foreign-owned banks and financial supervisory authorities helped to detect new reasons not yet been mentioned in the literature. Indeed, the majority of foreign banks interviewed—Western

Table 3.1 Review of empirical literature focusing on CESEE markets

Authors	*Dependent variable*	*Period*	*Methodology*	*CESEE*	*Theories tested*	*Determinants of foreign bank entry in CESEE*	*Comments*
Konopielko (1999)	Binary variable given the value 1 for banks which are present in at least one of the three countries examined and 0 otherwise	1996	OLS and logit	CZ, HU, PO	Follow customers, business opportunity, …	Imports (+ for CZ, – for PL), exports (+), FDI (+), size (+)	Follow your client is the prevailing determinant in PL and CZ, while in HU the prevailing one is search for new opportunities (survey data)
Papi and Revoltella (1999)	N. of investment initiatives from a foreign to a host country (distinguishing majority and minority of control)	1992–1996	GLS	CZ, EE, HU, LV, LT, PO, RO, SK, SI	Pull and push factors	Trade relations (+); stability of the host banking system (+); host country macro (+) and political stability (+); distance (−)	Trade relations and distance more relevant when foreign banks have a minority stake
Lensink and de Haan (2002)	Ratio of the total value of assets of foreign banks and the value of assets of all deposit money banks; total number of foreign banks divided by the total number of banks	1992–2000	Factor analysis and OLS regression	HR, CZ, EE, HU, LV, LT, PO, SI	Reforms and political freedom as important pull factors; follow your customer; economic attractiveness of host market foreign bank entry	Economic reforms (+); political freedom (+)	Strong evidence for the importance of reforms for foreign bank entry. Political freedom also seems to be important. No support for the view that the size of financial sector or openness of a country

(*continued*)

Table 3.1 (continued)

Authors	*Dependent variable*	*Period*	*Methodology*	*CESEE*	*Theories tested*	*Determinants of foreign bank entry in CESEE*	*Comments*
Kraft (2004)	n.a.	2002	Survey questionnaire and face to face interviews with bank managers	HR	Pull and push factors	Interest rate margins (++); search for new clients (++); unused credit potential (+) of households and businesses; competition in host credit market (+); geographic proximity (+)	Pull factors are more important than push factors; do novo foreign banks stand out for cost efficiency, asset quality and credit expansion
Wezel (2004)	FDI flows of the German banking sector to 24 EME across all regions	1994–2001	Pooled OLS	CZ, H, P (plus other regions)	Follow your client, market risk,…	Host country economic growth, GDP (+); banking sector fragility M2/RES (−)	Follow your client not important determinant
Haselman (2006)	Difference of loans provided by bank *i* in period t and t-1 divided by Total assets	1994–2002	Fixed effect model	BU, HR, CZ, EE, HU, LV, LT, PO, RO, SK, SI Ukraine	Efficiency gains; tech advantages over information disadvantages	Cost efficiency of foreign banks (+); host country GDP (+)	Foreign banks move to the CEE markets to compete with their domestic counterparts for markets shares

de Haas and van Lelyveld (2006)	(A) Percentage growth in total credit of bank *i* in year t; (B) the percentage change in the credit market share of bank *i* in country *j* in year t	1993–2000	Random effect model, FGLS with heteroscedastic error structure; IV estimator	HR, CZ, EE, HU, LV, LT, PO, RO, SK, SI	Host and home country business cycle (pull and push factors); differences between modes of entry (greenfield versus take-overs)	(A) HOST-HOME GDP (+); weakness parent bank (−); bank solvency (+); B) home lending rate (+); interest rate margin (+); for greenfields: home GDP (−); weakness of parent bank (−); liquidity (−); size (+)	Take-overs may be preferred to greenfield when there is more emphasis on the need to be a real local bank
Lanine and Van der Vennet (2007)	Binary value that takes the value one for banks that are engaged in a cross-border acquisition	1995–2002	Logit model	BK, BU, HR, CZ; EE; HU; LV; LT; MK; SI; PO; RO; SK	(1) the efficiency hypothesis and (2) the market power hypothesis	Target bank size (+); market shares of targets in the loan market (+) and in the deposit market (+)	The main motivation of Western European banks is neither the efficiency hypothesis nor profitability. Evidence support market power hypothesis

(*continued*)

Table 3.1 (continued)

Authors	*Dependent variable*	*Period*	*Methodology*	*CESEE*	*Theories tested*	*Determinants of foreign bank entry in CESEE*	*Comments*
Fritsch et al. (2007)	CAR of M&As	1990–2005	Event-study	AL; BK; BU; HR; CS; CZ; EE; HU; LT; LV; MK; PL; RO; SI; SK	Determinants of successful M&A activities in emerging markets, with a focus on the bidder bank	Country-specific conditions: growth (−); economic freedom (−)	Drivers for successful M&A in emerging CEE markets are primarily country-specific characteristics: a high degree of regulation and thus a low degree of economic freedom in the target countries market as well as a low GDP growth. Further, bidders that bought their targets in governmental auctions were more successful than those that acquired their target in private negotiations
Naaborg (2007)	–		Structured interviews to head of Erste Bank, KBC; Raiffeisen International; ING; HVB group; ABN Amro; SEB, Swedbank, Sampo plc; host country supervisors	CZ; SI; HR;HU; RS; PL; Al; SK; Bosnia; UK; LT; LV; RO;EE	Determinants of entry	Host country markets profitability prospects (+); Follow Your Client (+); bank reputation and status (+)	High profit expectations were key determinants, followed by competitors' pressure to follow them in CESEE markets. Going with the crowd sometimes was more important than the results of an NPV analysis based on expected revenues, costs and risks

Poghosyan and de Haan (2008)	A dummy that takes the value of one when bank *i* in country *j* was acquired at time *t*	1992–2006	Multilevel mixed effect logit model	BU, CZ; EE; HR; HU; LV; LT; PO; RO, SI; SK	Importance of bank-level factors conditional on country-level determinants	Market power (+); target bank characteristics: capital adequacy (+); intensity of loan provisioning (−); deposit funding (+)	Target banks have a high level of efficiency and a large share in the loan and deposit markets. For countries with a better institutional environment and significant progress in economic reforms, the primary motivation for the entry was to upgrade the efficiency of the acquired bank
Hryckiewicz and Kowalewski (2010)	Number of foreign banks by country of origin. Mode of entry investigated (branch, subsidiary, greenfield)	1994–2004	Poisson and bi-variate probit regression	CZ, H, P and Sl	All motivations	Inflation (+); country risk (−); bank regulation (+); stock market cap (−); differences in growth rates (+); income per capita (+); trade (−); creditor rights (−); distance (−); common origin (+); EU dummy (+); crisis dummy (−)	Macroeconomic and institutional determinants significantly influence a foreign bank's decision to expand into a specific emerging market. Foreign banks were mostly attracted by the potential of the emerging markets. Foreign bank's choice of organizational structure strongly depends on the economic characteristics and risk of the host country

Source: Own work

Notes: *AL* Albania, *BH* Bosnia and Herzegovina, *BG* Bulgaria, *HR* Croatia, *CS* Serbia and Montenegro, *CZ* Czech Republic, *EE* Estonia, *HU* Hungary, *LT* Lithuania, *LV* Latvia, *MK* Macedonia, *PL* Poland, *RO* Romania, *SI* Slovenia, *SK* Slovakia

European banks—and their supervisors reported that bank reputation and status triggered their decisions to enter the CESEE economies. For instance, it was reported that the positive experience by Austrian Raiffeisen inspired its home competitor, Erste, to enter CESEE. In addition, Western European banks wanted to test the possibility of further involvement in the region. This motive was important especially for early entrants, like Raiffeisen.

Other studies emphasized the role and importance of economic reforms and, to a certain extent, political freedom in attracting financial FDIs in the region (Lensink and de Haan 2002). More recent studies highlight also the importance of the "market power" motivation, showing that foreign banks were targeting relatively large and efficient local banks in economies with weak institutions (Lanine and Van der Vennet 2007; Poghosyan and de Haan 2008). Indeed, empirical studies showed that the modes of entry by foreign banks strongly depended on the economic, institutional and risk conditions of the host country. According to Hryckiewicz and Kowalewski (2010), foreign banks tended to locate their branches in more developed CESEE countries and only during the periods of global economic expansion, preferring greenfield investments or acquisitions as an entry mode during periods of high global uncertainty.

In sum, the bulk of empirical research on foreign bank entry into CESEE markets is unanimous, with the exception of Papi and Revoltella (1999) and partially Naaborg (2007) who discard the FYC motivation and highlight the relevance of macro pull factors (profit and growth opportunities in the host country).

On Maps 3.1, 3.2, and 3.3 we present the geographical structure of foreign trade and home countries of foreign-owned banks (as of the end of 2000, 2008, and 2015). In the year 2000, when Western European and US banks had already started their move into the region, only Estonia showed a clear strong relationship between trade relationships that the country had with the rest of the world and the country of origin of the more locally active foreign banks. Poland, Croatia, Hungary and Macedonia showed a positive correlation between trade links and foreign banks ownership, though the higher market share was held by banks whose home country was not the main trade partner of the host country. In 2008 however, in three countries there was strong relationship, namely in Croatia, Estonia, and Ukraine, while the positive links were observed for Bulgaria, Czech Republic, Hungary, Kosovo, Macedonia, Poland, and Slovenia. In the final year of the analysis (2015) the number of countries

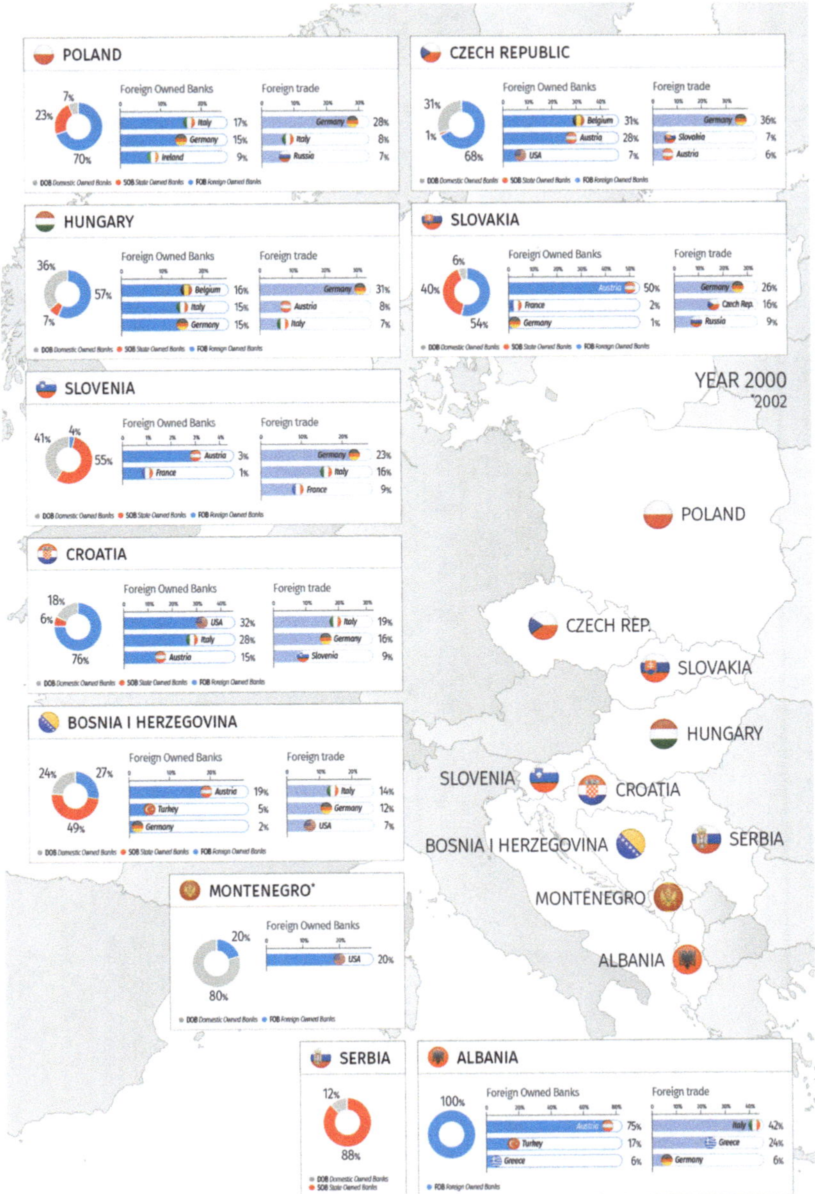

Map 3.1 Geographical structure of foreign trade vis-à-vis home countries of foreign-owned banks-year end 2000. (Source: Maps produced using IMF trade statistics, BankScope data and hand-collected data)

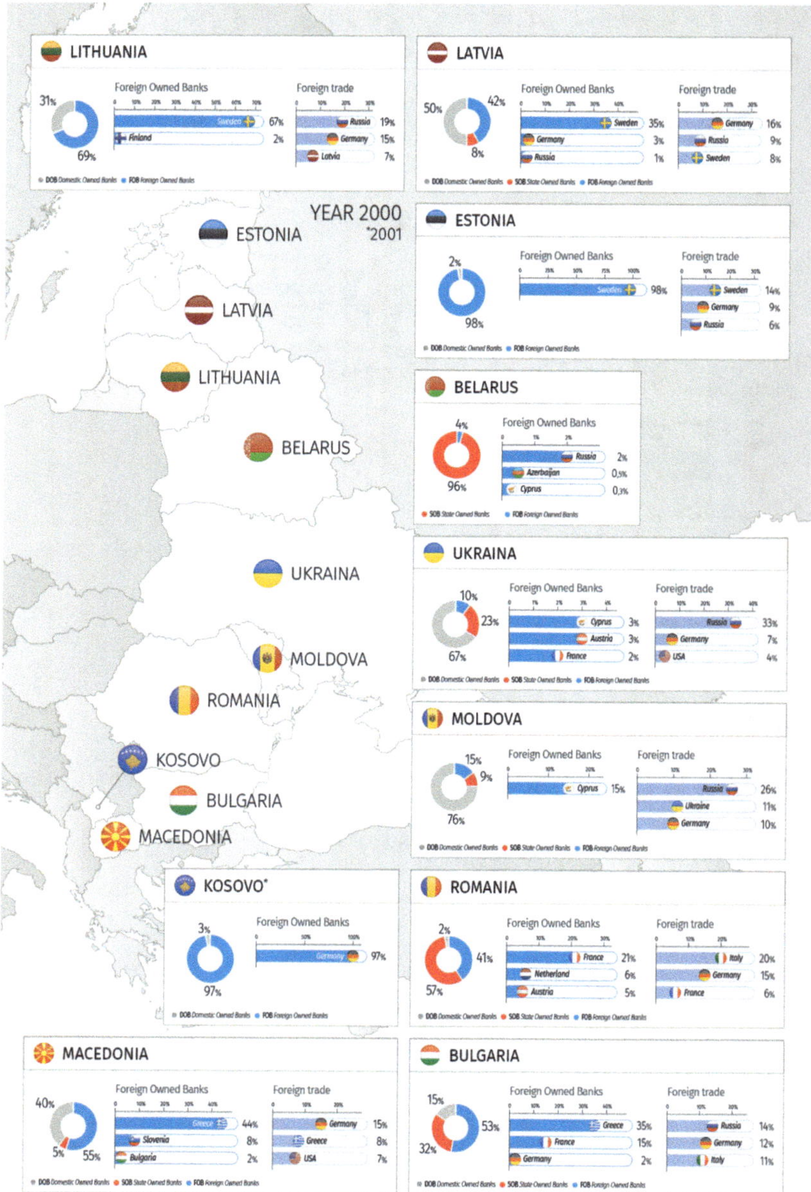

Map 3.1 (continued)

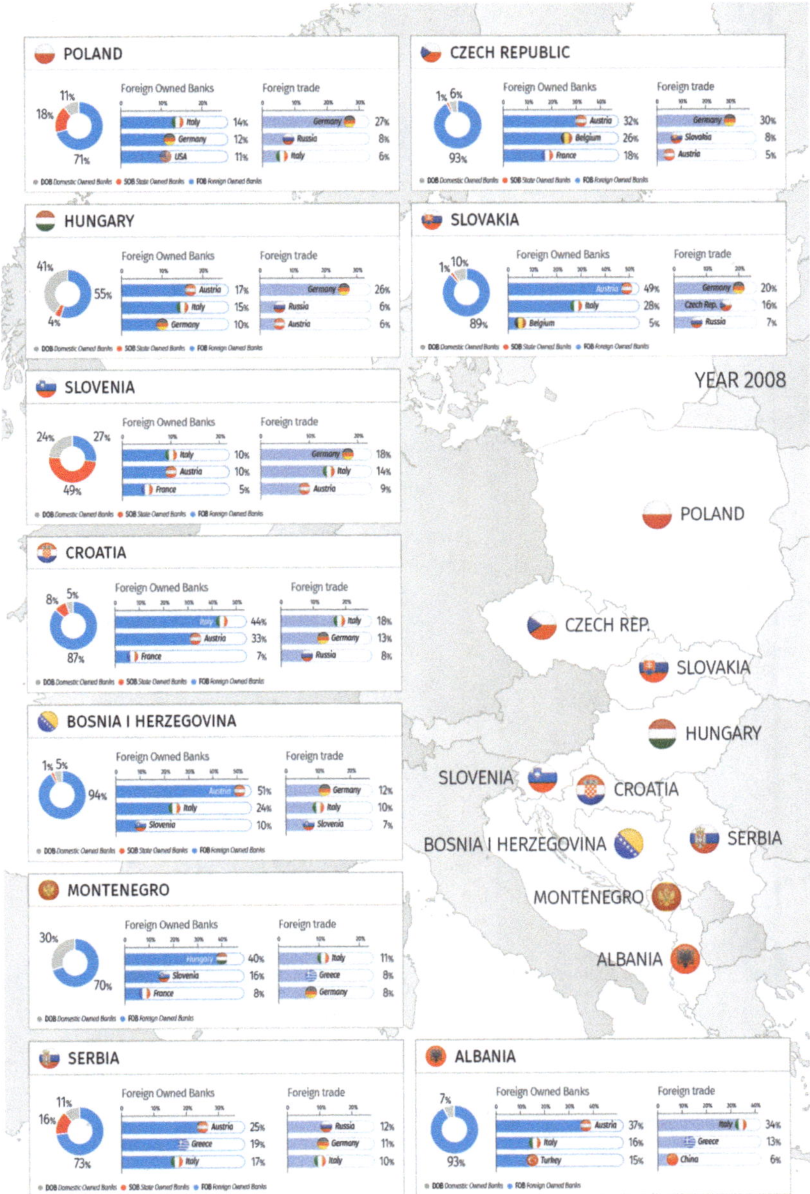

Map 3.2 Geographical structure of foreign trade vis-à-vis home countries of foreign-owned banks-year end 2008. (Source: Maps produced using IMF trade statistics, BankScope data and hand-collected data)

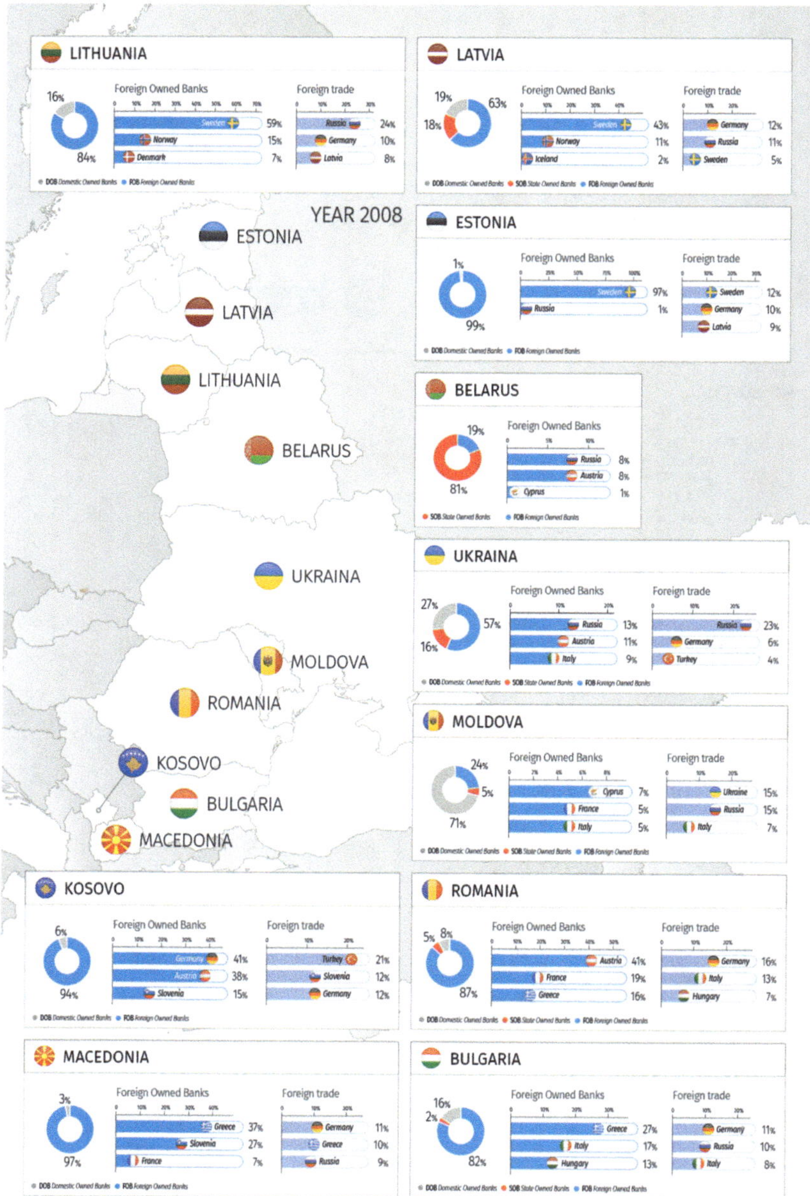

Map 3.2 (continued)

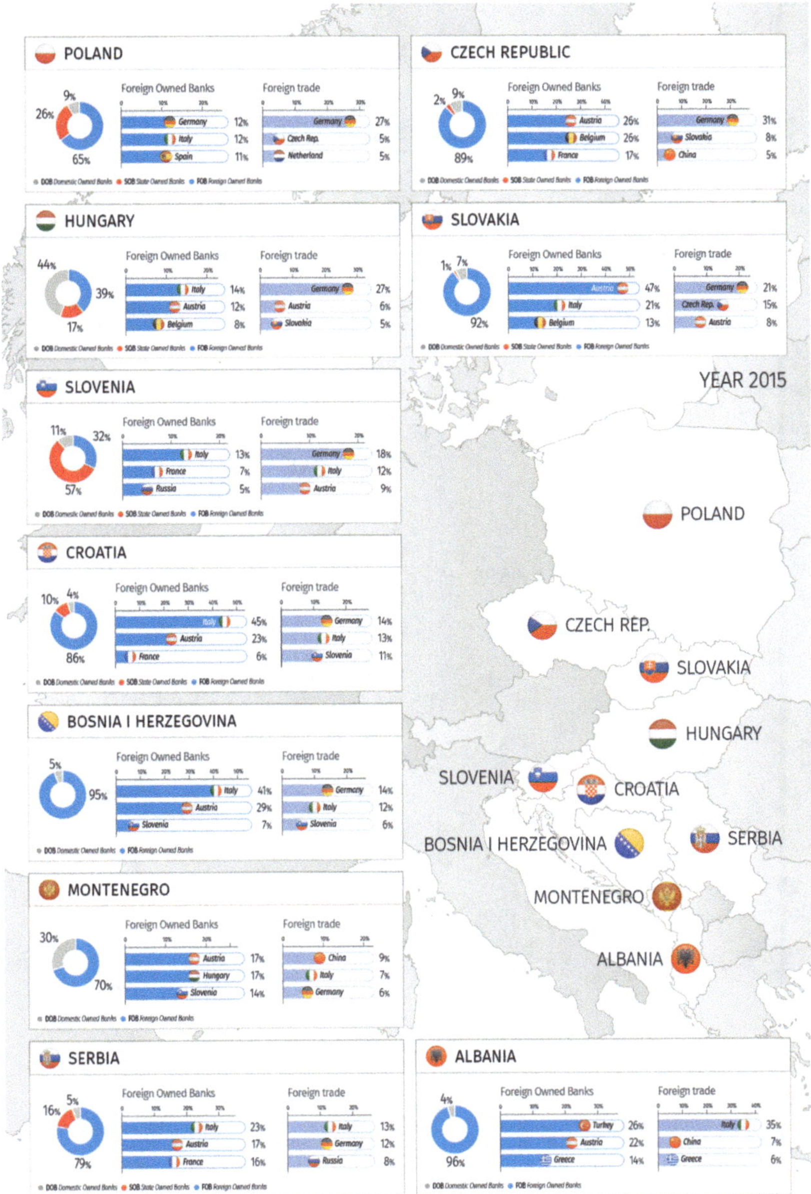

Map 3.3 Geographical structure of foreign trade vis-à-vis home countries of foreign-owned banks-year end 2015. (Source: Maps produced using IMF trade statistics, BankScope data and hand-collected data)

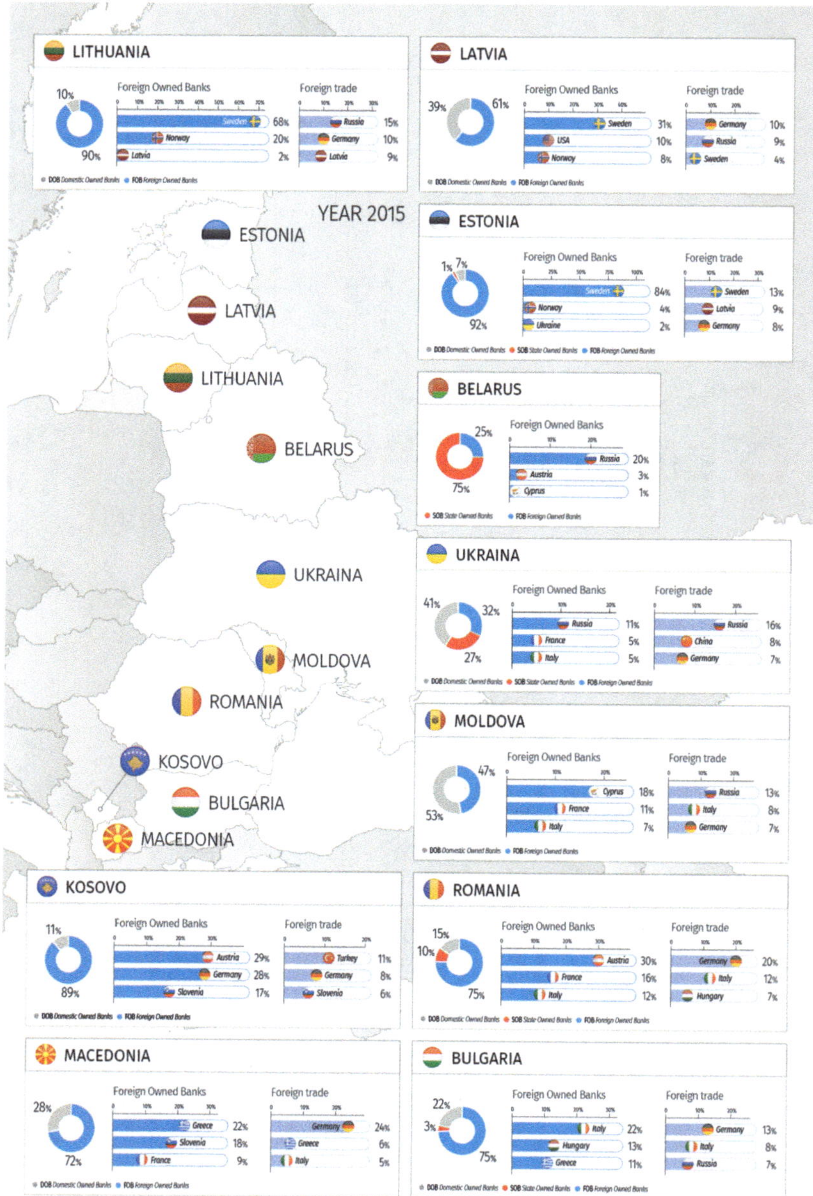

Map 3.3 (continued)

confirming this relationship did not change considerably, but the list of the countries has changed, showing strong link between foreign trade and foreign-owned banks in Balkans.

3.2 Entry Strategies and Organizational Forms

The entries of foreign banks occurred at the time when the CESEE countries were transitioning to market economies; this was the reason why they significantly contributed to the development of these countries' banking sectors (Casu et al. 2006).

Figure 3.3 shows the evolution of foreign bank participation starting from 1995 until 2015, in our sample of countries, clustered into three macroregions, Central Europe (CE) (Czech Republic, Hungary, Poland, Slovakia, Slovenia), Eastern Europe (EE) (Belarus, Estonia, Lithuania, Latvia, Moldova, Ukraine), and South-East Europe (SEE) (Albania, Bosnia Herzegovina, Bulgaria, Croatia, Kosovo, Montenegro, Macedonia, Romania, Republic of Serbia).

At the beginning of our investigation period, 1995, state ownership was predominant. At that time, foreign participation was in its infancy, with only CE economies attracting or allowing a mere 11% of total assets to be in the hands of foreign investors. Indeed, at the start of the transition process, policies towards foreign ownership, in all its possible modes of entry (establishing de novo subsidiaries or branches, purchasing equity stakes in domestic-owned banks) differed considerably across EE countries, although nearly all governments viewed foreign participation in the banking sector as a mean for quickly importing the needed banking expertise. In some countries, specific policies, such as tax holidays, were put in place to attract greenfield operations; in others (such as the Czech Republic or Poland), foreign owners were invited to take minority stakes in existing (ailing) domestic-owned banks, both state-owned and privately owned while greenfield ones were limited or even restricted.

By the year 2000, state ownership was reduced to almost one third of total banking assets in EE and SEE, and to a mere 20% in CE, in favour of foreign participation, which exceeded 50% of the total banking assets in the majority of economies. The process evolved during the last 15 years, with foreign banks holding the majority of the banking assets in CE and SEE, while reaching well-nigh 50% of the total in EE, where the state still holds a significant stake in the banking sector (on average 20% or above, with Latvia and Ukraine leading the way).

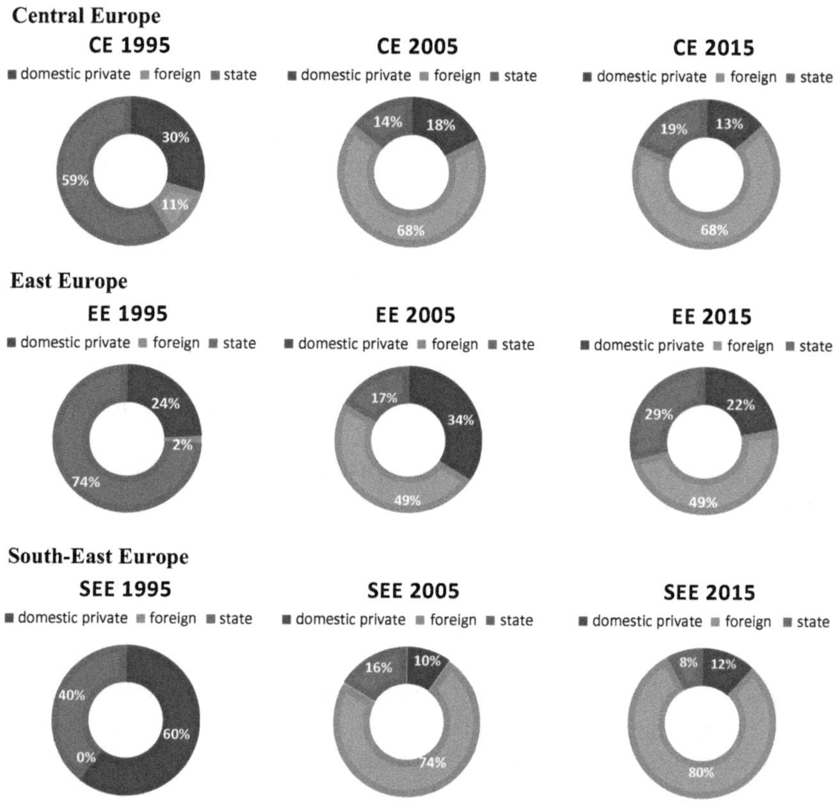

Fig. 3.3 Evolution of foreign bank participation in 1995–2015, by macroregions. (Source: Own calculation)

However, the year 2016 witnessed noteworthy changes in market structures throughout the entire region driven by a general downtrend in the foreign banks' involvement (with Unicredit disposal in Poland being the most striking one) and the increasing (mirroring) market share of state-owned banks (see for instance the nationalization of Privatbank in Ukraine).

This trend is particularly important in Central Europe, where the market shares in the region have been pushed down over the past few years, following the de-risking policy of major foreign incumbents and their business optimization, through refocusing on core/home markets (Raiffeisen Research, June 2017 CEE Banking Sector Report).

Western European countries were the most active in the CESEE banking market entry process, with Austrian banks leading the way, being involved almost in the whole region, followed by German banks, Swedish and Finnish financial institutions and Italian banks.

Austrian banks had a strategic interest in Visegrad countries (Czech Republic, Hungary, Poland, Slovakia); German banks were the first to participate in the privatization process, especially in those countries where strong trade relationships were in place; Swedish and Finnish banks expanded into the proximate Baltic region where they had historical trade links. Finally, Italian banks were initially attracted by the need to follow their customers (which had been relocating their manufacturing activities in the CESEE markets) and later on by the profit opportunities offered by these fast-growing markets (Casu et al. 2006). It is also true that the pattern of foreign banks' entry varied across the region, with the Baltic states almost exclusively benefiting, until the very recent years, from Swedish investments, while other Central European states (Poland, primarily) were host to a more diversified group of countries, including the US, which also played a role here.

As of 2014 (Roaf et al. 2014) both globally active banks, with established worldwide operations, like ING and SocGen, are present along with a prominent group of commercial banks having a strategic regional focus on CESEE, which accounted for about 70% of the total Financial Sector FDI. This group of banks was mainly attracted by both economies of scale considerations and the lack of opportunities to expand in their home markets (Domanski 2005).

There are three interrelated peculiarities of foreign banks' presence in CESEE: (1) a large part of foreign ownership came from the privatization of state-owned banks; (2) there was a predominance of subsidiaries over branches as a form of entry; (3) foreign-owned banks did not limit their operations to the wholesale business, but rather aimed at developing retail business.

Studies on banks' choices of their modes of entry in the host country (i.e. greenfield or acquisition of a local bank) are scarce and mainly devoted to analyse the effects of such a decision on subsequent performance. According to Buch (2000), the costs of these two modes of entry are the same as long as perfect information about future business conditions is guaranteed; on the contrary, under uncertainty, a greenfield investment is likely to require higher costs. Indeed, as Lenher (2009) shows, acquisitions dominate the entry model in less developed markets, which are characterized by higher uncertainty about the country's economic conditions and the health of its financial system, while developed markets attract greenfield investments. Besides, the author demonstrates that there is a tendency towards acquisition entry in smaller host countries and greenfield entry in larger host states. As Naaborg (2007) argues, the choice for an acquisition is positively related to the level of information asymmetry between the bank and its preferred customer in the host country and negatively related to the (in)direct costs of an acquisition. These costs sum up to the direct costs of the purchase and the post-acquisition expenses (i.e. due diligence costs to review the loan portfolio and its quality, restructuring and integration of the subsidiary in the parent-bank group, which involves overcoming cross-cultural differences and technological mismatches). On the other hand, greenfield investments take a longer time to grow and reach break-even and involve risks relating to the unfamiliarity with local market conditions and knowledge (Pomerleano and Vojta 2001), the lack of skilled labour in the host country and the impossibility to benefit from an existing customer base, as in the case of acquisitions (Buch 2000). As Naaborg (2007) highlights, major Western European players in the region were found to have a preference for acquisitions arguing that a greenfield investment was more costly because of the time it takes to develop.

Indeed, as large privatization programmes took place in the mid-1990s and were precisely organized to favour foreign bank entry, the acquisition of local banks was the preferred mode of entry with respect to greenfield, though a number of foreign banks also set up "de novo banks" in order to avoid inheriting the stock of NPLs legacy of the communist era. Having acquired local subsidiaries and their local market knowledge, foreign banks were less exposed to the typical "new entrant winner's curse" (in the credit market) and therefore, were more prone, once the restructuring of the inefficient local bank was completed, to reap the benefits of developing the retail banking business, more profitable and less exposed to international competition.

In truth, apart from Raiffeisen Bank, which only used de novo banks to enter CESEE banking markets, all other foreign players used a mix of greenfield and de novo bank entry mode, according to the specific situation they were facing. As purchasing costs play an important role in the decision, when the price quoted for the privatization or the listed price was considered "reasonable", then acquisitions were the preferred mode of entry. For instance, in the Baltic states, acquisitions became more attractive during the Russian crisis of 1998, as listed banks became cheaper; similarly,

HypoVereinsbank (HVB) entered the Czech Republic through greenfields and Poland via an acquisition, as "the price in Poland was more reasonable than what was quoted for the former state banks in the Czech Republic" (Naaborg 2007).

Besides, the level of competition in the host market has an impact on the mode of entry: greenfield becomes less attractive as competition increases. In the initial season of entry (end of 1980s—early 1990s), the first movers tended to prefer greenfield investments, following their home country large customers and concentrating on servicing big local companies. As newcomers were approaching CESEE banking markets in the midst of the large privatization processes, the growing number of banks offering wholesale activities (investment and corporate banking services) led to decreasing margins in this segment and to the surge of an interest for retail banking, also thanks to the fact that the privatization process dealt with former state saving banks.

In fact, next to the level of competition and the costs of entry, the third variable that affects the mode of entry as well as the organizational form of foreign presence (i.e. branch or subsidiary) is the customer focus. If the targeted market is the retail segment, then the choice will lead towards the acquisition of a local bank, for its ability to bring valuable information on the existing clientele; in other words, the choice for an acquisition is positively related to the level of information asymmetry between the bank and its target customers.

As regards the organizational form, the targeted market also matters. Subsidiaries are the preferred organizational form when seeking to penetrate local markets establishing retail banking while foreign branches are more oriented to the investment and corporate banking operations (Focarelli and Pozzolo 2005; Naaborg 2007). Therefore, if the organizational form of foreign banking is not exogenously determined by the local regulation, the choice for the branch or subsidiary format depends respectively on the focus on wholesale or retail banking in the host country.

Table 3.2 shows the relative importance of different lines of business carried out by the accession countries' banking sector, as of 2001. In most countries, there was a preference for developing retail and commercial banking (accounting for more than 60% of the total) rather than wholesale activity. This preference still characterizes these banking systems in more recent years (see Fig. 3.4): the retail ratio—calculated as the ratio of customer deposits plus (net) customer loans over total assets—is above 100% for all the CESEE banking systems with no relevant decreasing pattern to be detected, in line to the recent development of EU bank business models and their higher reliance on retail activities (ECB 2016).

Table 3.2 Relative importance of lines of business in CESEE banking sectors (2004)

% of the total	*Corporate finance*	*Trading and sales*	*Retail banking*	*Commercial banking*	*Asset Management*	*Others*
BG	0.00	0.00	60.00	40.00	0.00	0.00
CZ	10.30	20.70	31.00	31.00	3.40	3.40
EE	10.00	10.00	30.00	30.00	20.00	0.00
HU	9.50	9.50	33.30	38.10	0.00	9.50
LT	0.00	0.00	42.90	42.90	14.30	0.00
LV	0.00	0.00	42.90	42.90	14.30	0.00
PL	13.90	13.90	25.00	25.00	5.60	16.70
RO	14.30	14.30	28.60	42.90	9.00	0.00
SK	7.70	7.70	30.80	38.50	15.40	0.00
All accession countries	**9.80**	**11.20**	**32.20**	**33.60**	**8.00**	**6.30**

Source: ECB (2014), DG-I/MAW/04 78

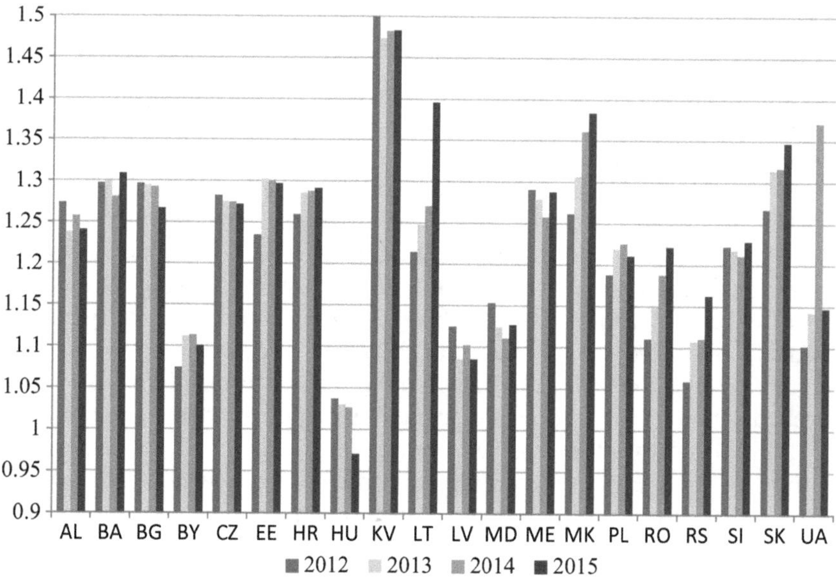

Fig. 3.4 The relative importance of the retail business. (Note: Retail business = ratio of customer deposits plus (net) customer loans over total assets; Source: Own calculation from Bankscope data)

3.3 Performance of Foreign-Owned Banks

This paragraph takes a microeconomic approach and analyses foreign-owned banks on the basis of information contained in their financial statements. The analysis is founded on more than 7000 observations from the balance sheet of commercial, savings and cooperative banks in the period 1995–2015 extracted from BankScope database. The ownership information was hand-collected from several sources, from the banks' annual statements and partly, from the Bankscope database.

In the last 20 years, the number of banks has doubled in CE,[2] increased by eight times in EE[3] and six times in SEE.[4] However, we are aware that the actual number of banks may differ from the number of banks available in the BankScope database. Considering bank ownership, in 11 countries from all the three regions foreign-owned banks outnumber domestic-owned banks, in 6 countries (Hungary, Belarus, Estonia, Moldova, Bulgaria, Croatia and Montenegro) the banking system is evenly distributed among these two types of banks, while only in 3 cases (Slovenia, Latvia, Ukraine) domestic-owned banks outnumber foreign-owned ones. However, the distribution in the number of banks by type of ownership is not a complete picture of the relevance of foreign-owned banks, which in 2015 account for the majority of total banking assets also in those countries where they are numerically lower than or similar to domestic-owned banks, namely in Latvia, Montenegro, Bulgaria, Croatia and Estonia.

Banks in the three regions differed and still differ considerably in size. An average CE bank was bigger than an EE/SEE bank in 1995 and grew considerably relative to it. In 1995, it was only less than twice as large as a SEE bank; in 2015 this multiple rose to 4.5. SEE banks were mostly affected by bank crises at the beginning of the 2000s and shrank in size accordingly. Figure 3.5 relates this general growth in bank size in CESEE banking systems to bank ownership: in all the three regions foreign-owned banks grew considerably in size relative to domestic-owned banks, especially in SEE, where domestic-owned bank growth is virtually absent. The development of foreign-owned banks' average size starts in 2000, that is, it coincides with the period of privatizations and favourable political and economic conditions that fostered foreign bank entry.

In support of the conclusions drawn in the previous paragraph, that is, that foreign banks entered CESEE banking systems to develop retail banking, Figs. 3.6 and 3.7 show the growth of customer loans and customer deposits by bank ownership: as before, much of the growth in credit and

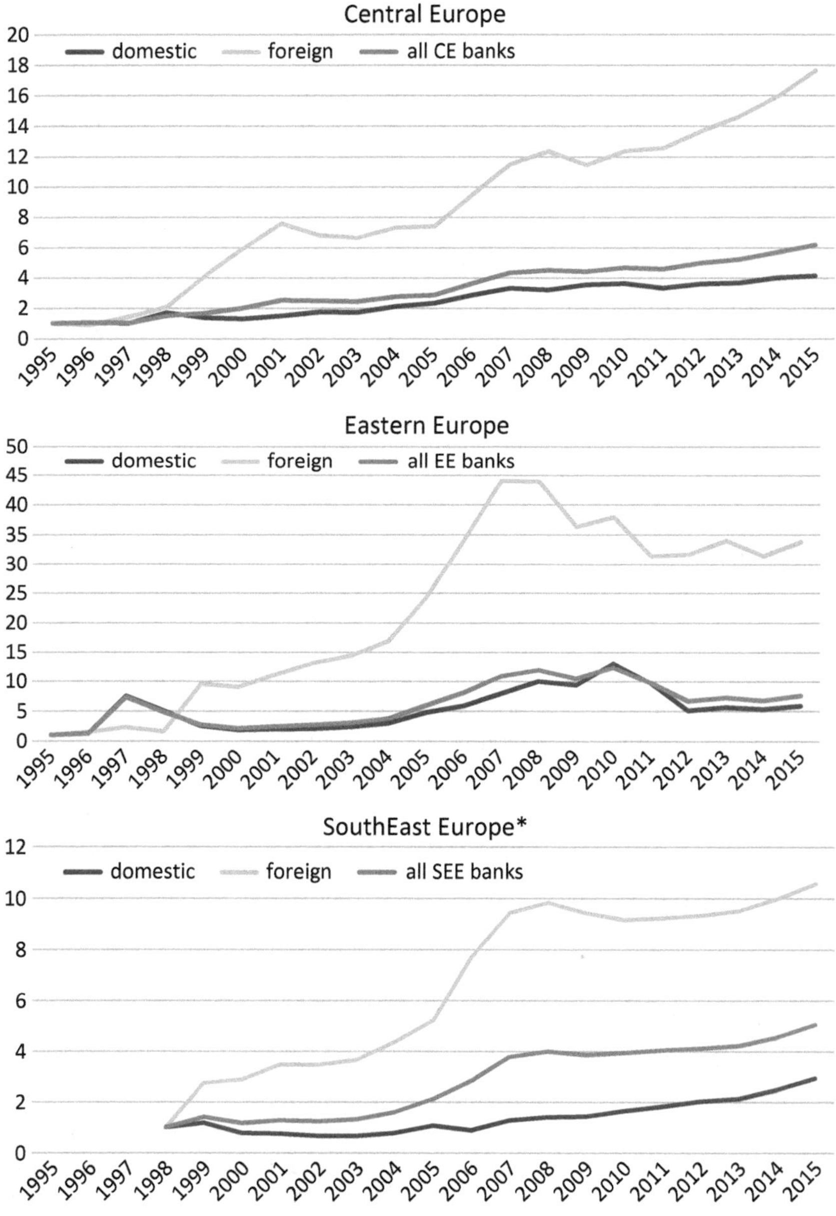

Fig. 3.5 Average growth in bank size (1995 = 1), by bank ownership. (Note: *Starting point is year 1998, as before 1998 the presence of foreign banks was so negligible, it would reduce comparability of growth rates; Source: Own calculation)

deposit taking, that is a traditional intermediation business, is attributable to foreign-owned banks. This is also explained by the fact that during the first years of transition many state-owned banks changed proprietorship and fell into the foreign sphere.

Figure 3.8 reports selected financial indicators, which help compare the behaviour and performance of foreign-owned banks vis-à-vis domestic-owned banks, during our sample period.

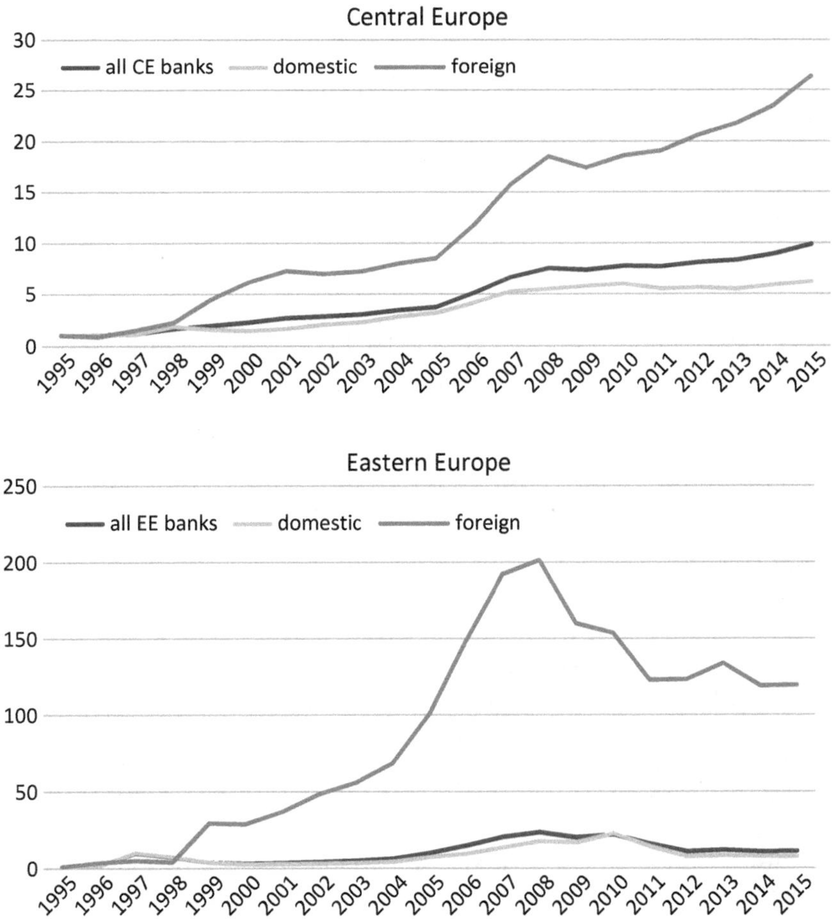

Fig. 3.6 Average growth in credit (1995 = 1), by bank ownership. (Note: *Starting point is year 1998, as before 1998 the presence of foreign banks was so negligible, it would reduce comparability of growth rates; Source: Own calculation)

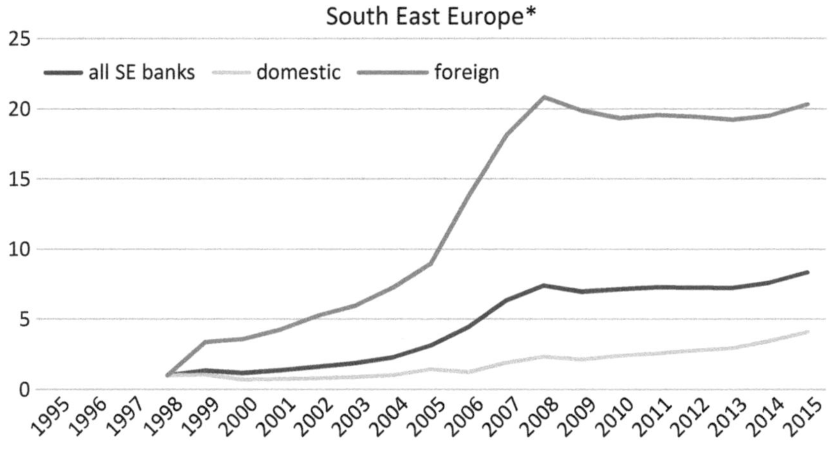

Fig. 3.6 (continued)

As foreign-owned banks started to gain market shares in total banking assets and credit markets, their loan portfolio made the most of their total banking assets, exceeding, in many cases, those of their domestic-owned counterparts. Unfortunately, we do not have complete data on credit portfolio composition. However, it has been acknowledged by for example EBRD (2006), Haselman and Wachtel (2009), Bonin et al. (2010) that this credit deepening came into the form of rapid growth in household credit, both mortgage lending and other forms of consumer credit. Lending to households has grown rapidly in many transition countries. In 2005 it was more than a half of total bank lending in Croatia and in the Czech Republic (EBRD 2006); in 2014, it reached 20% and over in Poland, Czech Republic, Slovakia and Latvia (Léon 2018). Using the 2009 EBRD survey on Banking Environment and Performance (BEPS), Haselman and Wachtel (2009) showed that foreign-owned banks in particular were more active in increasing household lending, while maintaining the existing level of lending to enterprises. In fact, foreign-owned banks might be more tempted to primarily lend to households rather than to businesses, given the well-known asymmetric information problems that affect new entrants in the credit markets. Without access to valuable information about local markets stemming from repeated lender-borrower interactions (i.e. relationship lending), entrant banks are susceptible to the so-called winner's curse problem, in which they face the risk of attracting poor-quality borrowers that were previously rejected by local banks. Therefore, foreign competitors are expected to focus on those market segments in which the knowledge of the borrower is less important and loan conditions are easily standardized, such as lending to households.[5] Yet, by

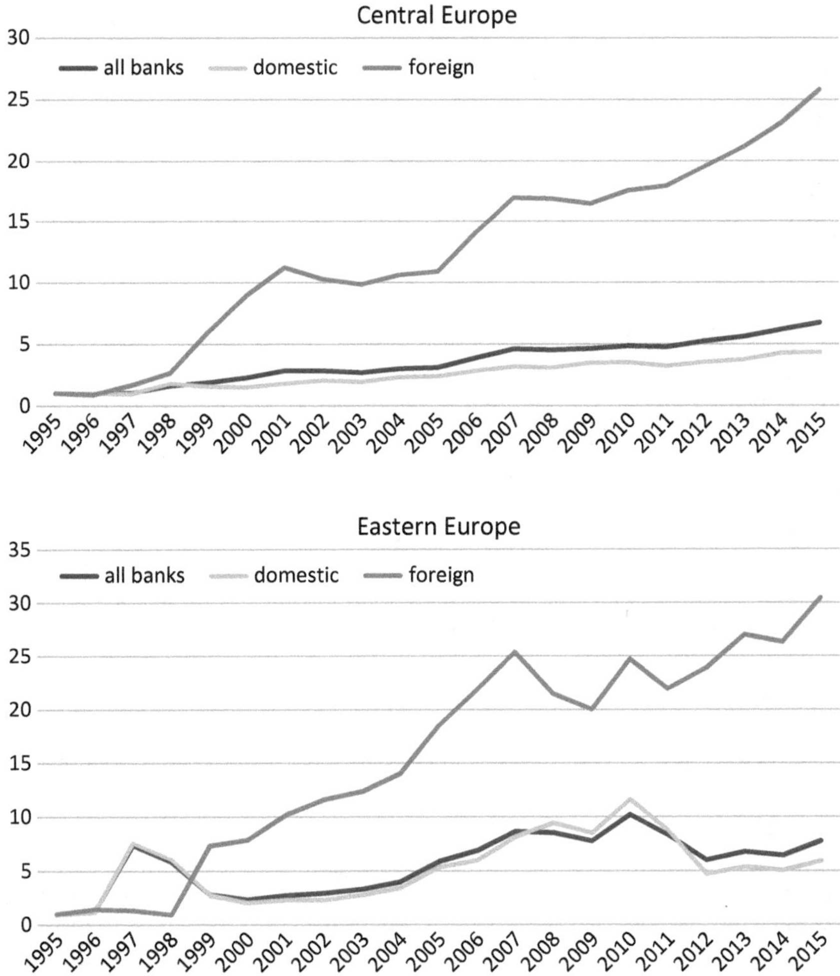

Fig. 3.7 Customer deposits growth by bank ownership (1995 = 1). (Note: *Starting point is year 1998, as before 1998 the presence of foreign banks was so negligible, it would reduce comparability of growth rates; Source: Own calculation)

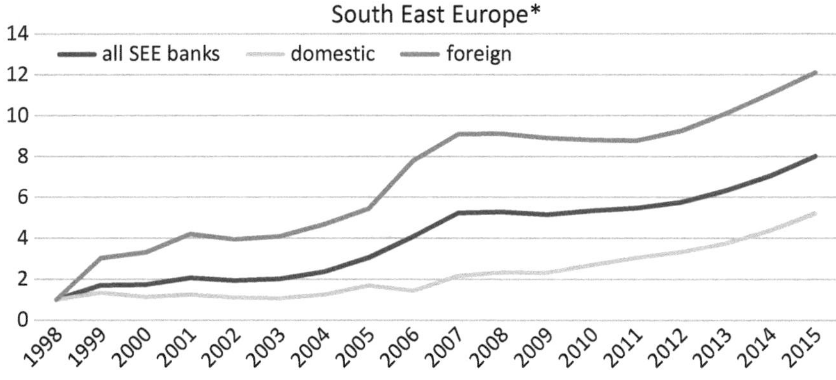

Fig. 3.7 (continued)

doing so, foreign banks' greater efficiency and profitability (with respect to local banks) is not translated into—through for example, lending to enterprises—improved economic performance of the host country, as an issue that we will tackle in Chap. 6.

As both foreign-owned and domestic-owned banks are commercial banks involved in the traditional banking business, the majority of their funding base comes from customer deposits (60% or more). Even in this market, foreign-owned banks gained grounds, though never surpassing their domestic peers. A recent study by the EBRD (2017) shows that even in areas where a number of foreign-owned banks are already competing with each other, some household segments may still remain underserved because they do not meet the strict requirements (in terms of documentation and job status) typically imposed by foreign-owned institutions.

However, the ratio of loans to customer deposits and short-term funding highlights that there is still a low degree of intermediation in CESEE, especially when compared to Western Europe, where this ratio, though decreasing because of the financial crisis, is greater than 1. Again, even in this respect, foreign-owned banks were able to catch up with their domestic peers by the mid-2000s and close the intermediation circuit the most.

As far as the quality of credit, domestic-owned banks started with a handicap given the stock of NPLs heritage of the planned economy period. As the process of selling domestic-owned banks to foreign investors continued

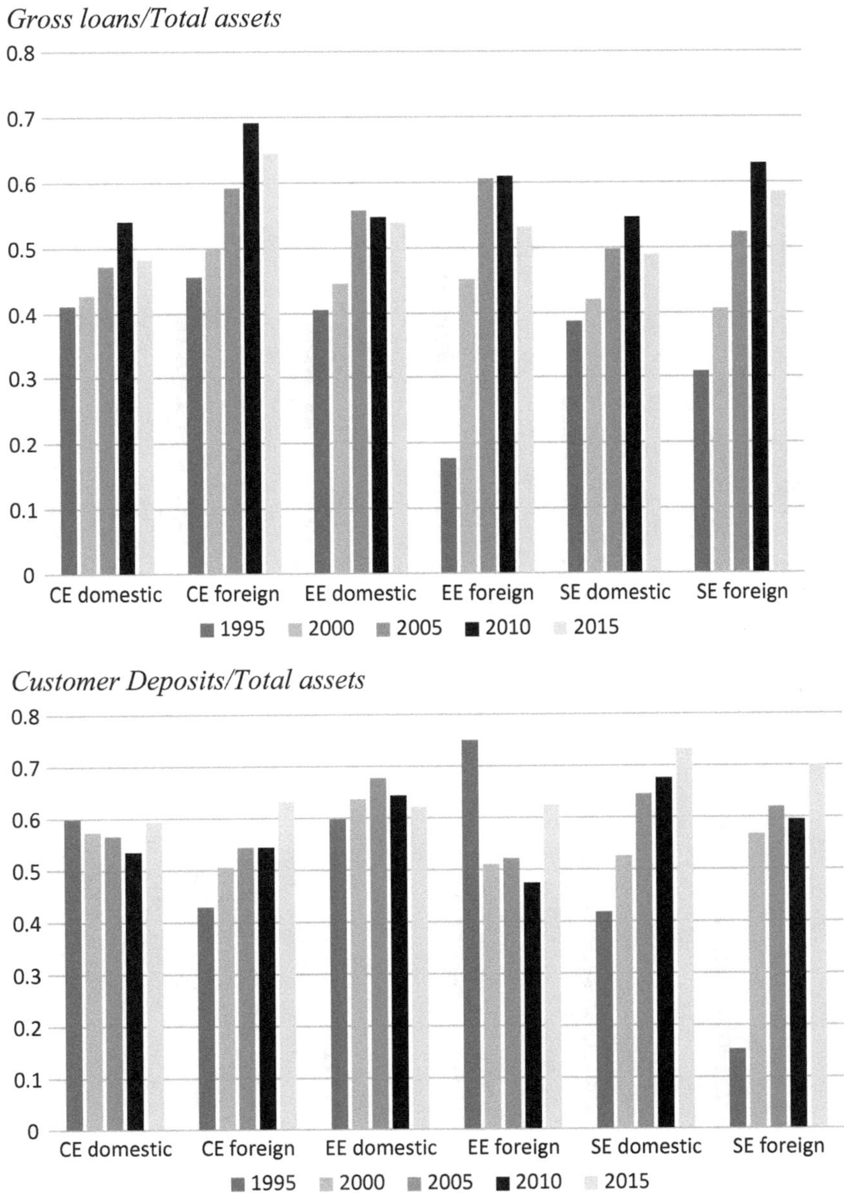

Fig. 3.8 Selected performance indicators (1995–2015) by bank ownership and regional decomposition. (Source: Own calculation using BankScope data)

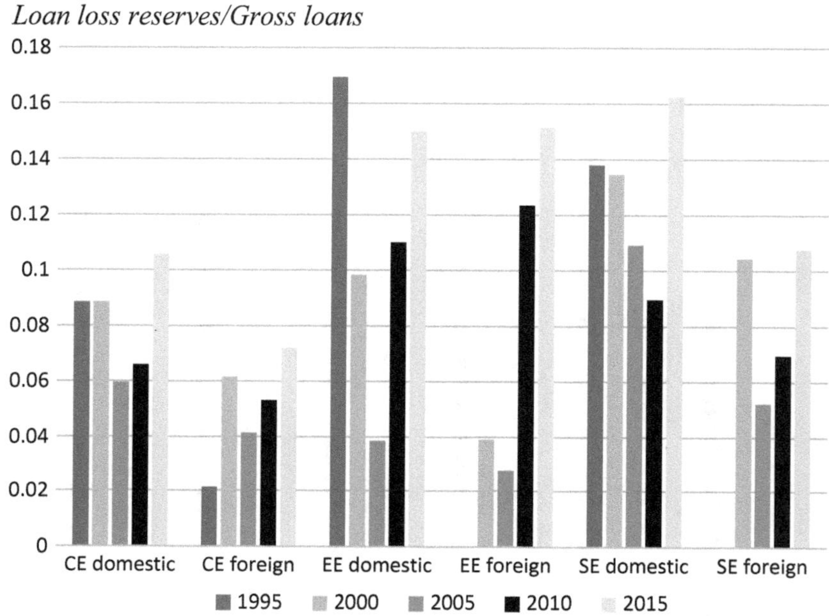

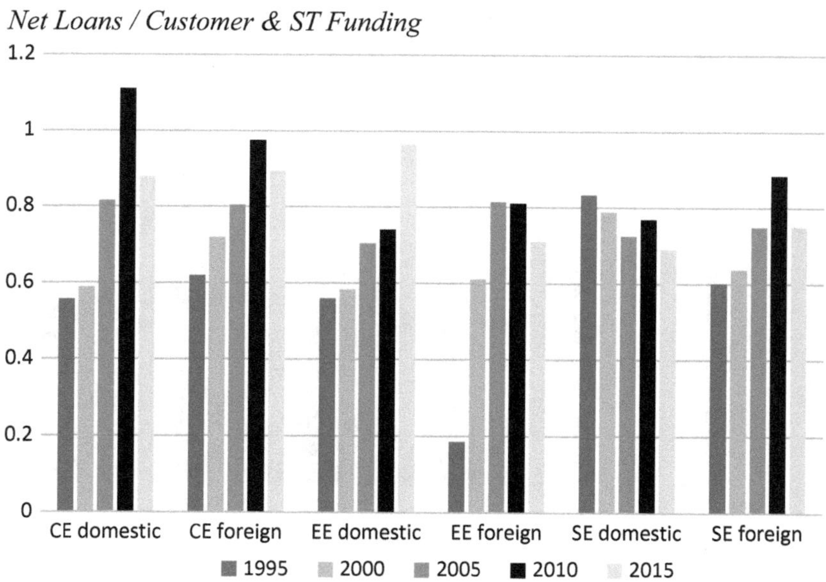

Fig. 3.8 (continued)

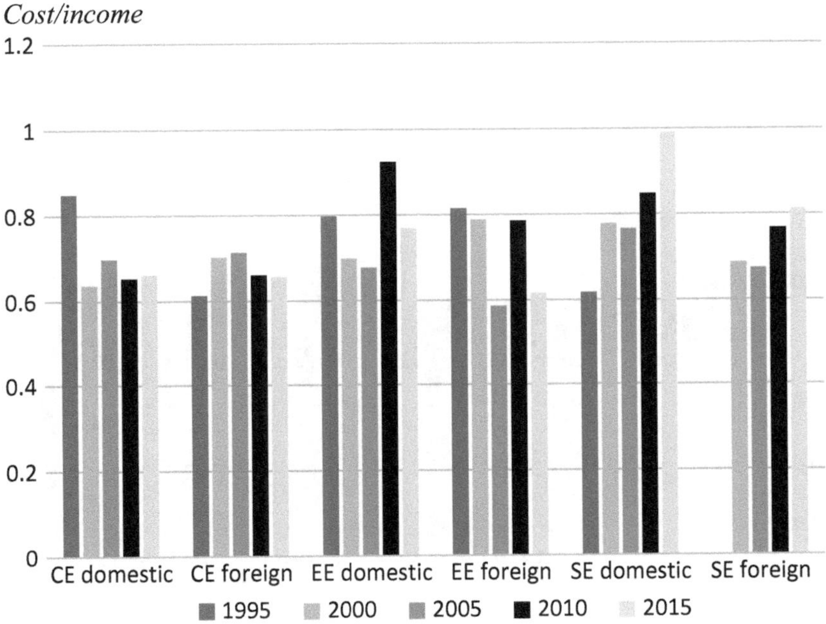

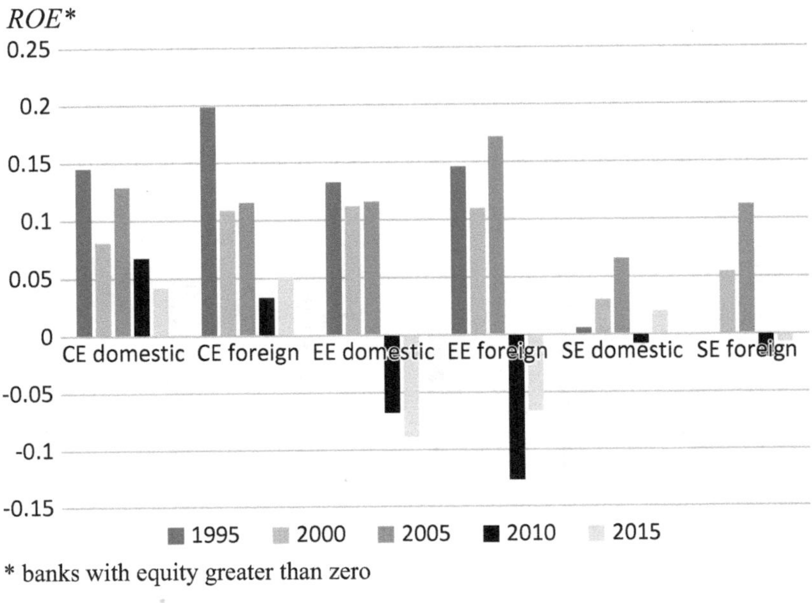

Fig. 3.8 (continued)

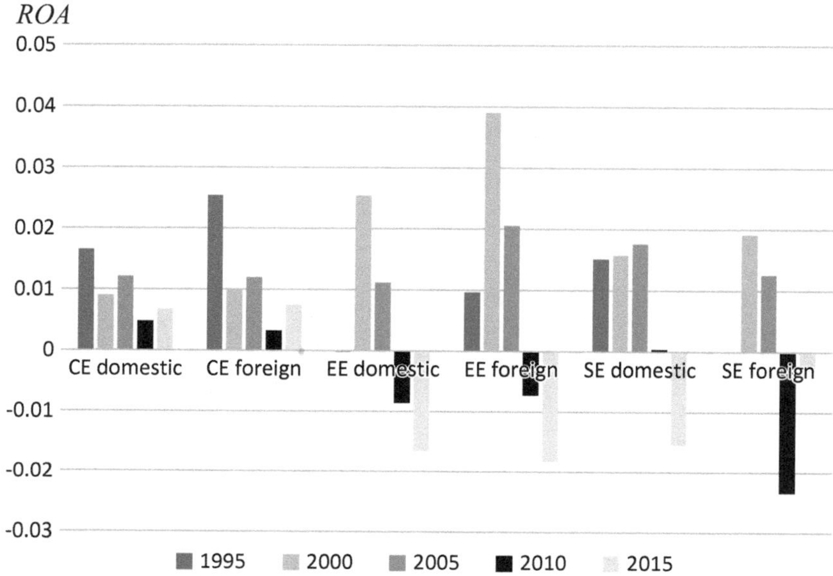

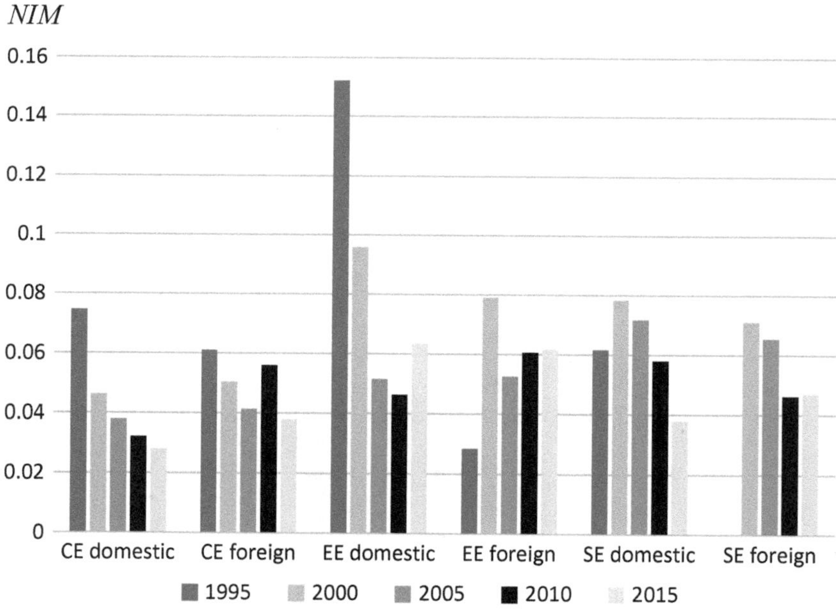

Fig. 3.8 (continued)

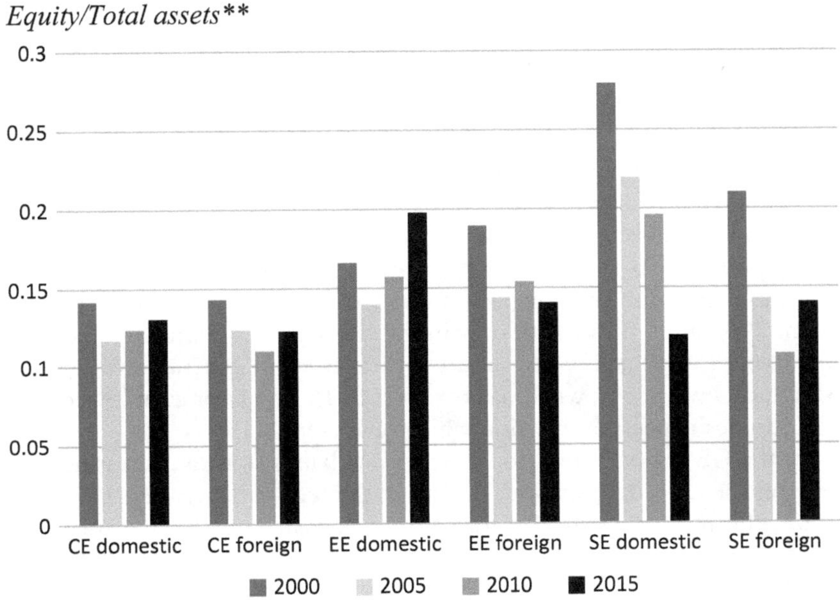

** data on 1995 not reliable (too few observations)

Fig. 3.8 (continued)

and the involvement of these banks in the credit market increased, also the quality of their portfolios diminished, showing deterioration in the ratio of NPLs to gross loans, especially in 2005 and 2010. However, in 2016 the loan portfolio's credit quality turned out to be higher in all three regions for foreign-owned banks.

As regards profitability of the intermediation business, domestic-owned banks enjoy a higher net interest margin at the beginning of the opening up of their banking markets, in 1995. This could be explained by two not mutually exclusive reasons. First, at that time, domestic-owned banks were not facing higher or fiercer competitive pressure from foreign-owned banks and given their limited number were operating in an oligopolistic market, where they could set higher prices. Second, since domestic and foreign-owned banks were not initially competing for the same kind of customers at the foreign banks' entry, domestic-owned banks were left with smaller, opaque businesses and households, and as such could set higher prices and had to do so in consideration of their higher risk. Changes start to arise starting from 2000, when net interest margins of domestic-owned banks decrease to a higher extent relative to the same decrease experienced by foreign-owned banks. This could be interpreted as an increased participation of foreign banks in domestic credit markets and the effect of a higher competition.

The overall profitability of the banking business as measured by the return of total assets (ROA) and the return on equity (ROE) show interesting patterns. As for ROA, until 2005 foreign-owned banks were more profitable than domestic-owned banks in all the three regional partitions. From 2005 and up to 2010, only in the EE region foreign banks continued to enjoy higher efficiency in using their assets to generate earnings. In SEE and CE foreign-owned banks report ROA similar or even lower than their domestic peers, a situation which reverts in 2015.

In the CE region, while domestic-owned banks enjoy a decreasing pattern on the ratio of costs over income in the ten years between 1995 and 2005, the reverse is true for foreign-owned banks, which see this ratio increasing and stabilize at levels close to their domestic peers. The process of integration of acquired banks proved to be costly and slow. Similarly, in the EE region, foreign-owned banks started to enjoy higher efficiency since 2005, when the process of entry was completed in the bigger countries of this group. In the SEE region, although the ratio shows an increasing pattern for both clusters of banks, most probably due to decreasing margins which cannot be compensated for by cost tightening, foreign banks benefit from higher efficiency during the whole period under scrutiny.

As far as ROE is concerned, the picture is more blurred than with respect to return on assets. Only in Central Europe, foreign-owned banks are strikingly more profitable than domestic peers; in the other two regional segmentation of the CESEE sample, the picture is less obvious, with foreign-owned banks suffering more in 2010 to regain better positioning in 2015.

Finally, even with respect to the level of capitalization, our clusters of banks behave differently according to the region under consideration. In Central Europe, no striking differences can be detected in the gearing ratio and to some extent in the regulatory capital level of foreign-owned and domestic-owned banks. In EE and SEE foreign banks have a higher leverage ratio and lower regulatory capital mirroring a less risky credit portfolio (NPL ratio).

3.4 Conclusions

In this chapter we analysed the role of foreign-owned banks in CESEE in several ways.

We first tackled the question of why a bank should go abroad, investigating the issue on the basis of the extant theoretical and empirical research, and examining foreign bank entry in European transition economies. In the case of CESEE, the conventional hypothesis that banks follow their customers abroad did not find support while our analysis reveals that for the majority of the banks involved in the process, high profit expectations were the key determinant, along with the "follow your competitor" reason. Indeed, for Western European large regional commercial banks the "follow the leader" strategy was as important as pull factors (Naaborg 2007).

The mode of entry was mainly through acquisition of local banks for three main reasons. First, greenfield investments are typically the choice of the first movers, as they entail less risk of inheriting the stock of bad loans of the planned economy era, and are set up to follow large customers from home and host country; however, the rush to enter this region started quite immediately, increasing competition, which reduced the attractiveness of concentrating on the wholesale business. Third, the large privatization process resulted in facilitation and reduction of costs of the decision to enter through the acquisition of a local bank. Besides, as we showed that the targeted market was the retail segment, the choice leaned towards the acquisition of a local bank, for its ability to bring valuable information on the existing client base.

This peculiar trait is supported by our final analysis on micro data: the growth in total banking assets, customer credit and customer deposits in the last 15 years has to be attributable to foreign banks, which entered CESEE to compete with local domestic-owned banks. The effect of this choice on the overall performance is less clear, or in other words, the supposed superiority of foreign-owned banks (given their higher know-how in risk management practices and skilled labour) is less evident when comparing profitability and efficiency of domestic and foreign banks.

Notes

1. In the 1980s only with reference to US banking market, see Goldberg and Saunders (1980, 1981).
2. Czech Republic, Hungary, Poland, Slovenia, Slovakia.
3. Belarus, Estonia, Lithuania, Latvia, Moldova, Ukraine.

4. Albania, Bosnia Herzegovina, Bulgaria, Croatia, Kosovo, Montenegro, Macedonia, Romania, Republic of Serbia.
5. However, as we saw in paragraph 3.2, foreign banks mainly entered transition economies by means of mergers and acquisitions of local banks so that this knowledge should not have been so difficult to acquire. Another reason for this preference is the attractiveness of this market segment (households) relative to enterprises in periods of economic growth and low banking penetration in the household market. In fact, the initial phase of expansion of a new market/business area is the one that delivers the highest margin at the lowest level of risk (cream skimming).

Bibliography

Ball CA, Tschoegel A (1982) The decision to establish a foreign branch or subsidiary: an application of binary classification procedures. J Financ Quant Anal 17(3):411–424

Barth JR, Caprio G, Levine R (2001) The regulation and supervision of banks around the World. A new database. World Bank Policy Research Working Papers, No. 2588

Berger AN, Kashyap AK, Scalise JM (1995) The transformation of the US banking industry: what a long, strange trip it's been. Brookings Pap Eco Ac 2:55–218

Bonin JP, Hasan I, Wachtel P (2010) Banking in transition countries. In: Berger AN, Molyneux P, Wilson JOS (ed) The Handbook of Banking. Oxford University Press, Oxford

Brealey RA, Kaplanis EC (1996) The determination of foreign banking location. J Int Money Financ 15:577–597. https://doi.org/10.1016/0261-5606(96)00022-8

Buch CM (2000) Why do banks go abroad? – Evidence from German data. Financial Markets, Institutions and Instruments 9(1): 33–67.

Buch CM, DeLong G (2004) Cross-border bank mergers: What lures the rare animal? J Bank Financ 28:2077–2102. https://doi.org/10.1016/j.jbankfin.2003.08.002

Buckley PJ, Casson M (1976) The future of the multinational enterprise. Macmillan, London

Casu B, Girardone C, Molyneaux P (2006) Introduction to Banking. Pearson Education Limited, London

Cerutti E, Dell'Ariccia G, Martínez Pería MS (2007) How banks go Abroad: branches or subsidiaries?. J Bank Financ 31:1669–1692. https://doi.org/10.1016/j.jbankfin.2006.11.005

Claessens S, Van Horen N (2014) Foreign banks: trends and impact. J Money Credit Bank 41(1): 295–326. https://doi.org/10.1111/jmcb.12092

Claessens S, Demirgüc-Kunt A, Huizinga H (2000) The role of foreign banks in domestic banking systems. In: Claessens S, Jansen M. (ed) The internationalisation of financial services: Issues and lessons for developing countries. Kluwer Academic, Boston

Clark G, Cull R, Martínez Pería MS, Sanchez SM (2003) Foreign bank entry: experience implications for developing economies, and agenda for further research, World Bank Res Obser 18(1):25–59.

De Haas RTA, van Lelyveld IPP (2006) Foreign bank penetration and private sector credit in Central and Eastern Europe. Journal of Emerging Markets Finance 3(2):126–151. https://doi.org/10.1177/097265270400300203

Domanski D (2005) Foreign banks in emerging market economies: changing players, changing issues. BIS Quarterly Review, December

Dubauskas, G. (2002) Motivation of foreign banks entry into the emerging economies: the case of Lithuania. Working papers TTUWPE No 02/69, Tallinn

Dunning JH (1980) Towards an Eclectic Theory of International Production, The International Executive 22:1–3

EBRD (2006) Transition Report 2005, London

EBRD (2017) Transition Report 2016, London

ECB (2014) Financial FDI to the EU Accession Countries, DG-I/MAW/04 78, https://www.bis.org/publ/cgfs22ecb.pdf

ECB (2016) Financial Stability Review. May, Frankfurt

Florescu, G. (2002). Foreign banks entry into Romania, Working Paper TTUWPE, No. 02/71, Tallinn.

Focarelli D, Pozzolo AF (2005) Where Do Banks Expand Abroad? An Empirical Analysis. J Bus 78(6):2435–2464. DOI: https://doi.org/10.1086/497052

Focarelli D, Pozzolo AF (2001) The patterns of cross-border bank mergers and shareholdings in OECD countries. J Bank Financ 25:2305–2337. https://doi.org/10.1016/S0378-4266(01)00192-3

Fritsch M, Gleisner F, Holzhäuser M (2007) Bank M&A in Central and Eastern Europe. SSRN: https://ssrn.com/abstract=966294

Galindo A, Micco A, Serra C (2003) Better the devil that you know: evidence on entry costs faced by foreign banks, InterAmerican Development Bank Working Paper, No. 477

Goldberg, L.G. (1992) The competitive impact of foreign commercial banks in the United States. In Gilbert, R.A. (Ed.) The Changing Market in Financial Services, Proceedings of the Fifteenth Annual Economic Policy Conference of the Federal Reserve Bank of St. Louis. Kluwer Academic, Norwell.

Goldberg L.S, Grosse R (1994) Location choice of foreign banks in the United States. J Eco Bus 46(5):67–79

Goldberg LG, Johnson D (1990) The determinants of US banking activity abroad, J Int Money Financ 9:123–137

Goldberg LS, Saunders A (1980) The causes of US bank expansion overseas: the case of Great Britain. J Money Credit Bank 12:630–643
Goldberg LS, Saunders A (1981) The determinants of foreign banking activity in the United States, J Bank Financ 5:17–32
Haselman R (2006) Strategies of foreign banks in transition economies. Emerg Mark Rev 7:283–299
Haselman R, Wachtel P (2009) Bankers' perceptions of the legal environment and the composition of bank lending: evidence from the transition countries. New York University Stern School of Business Working Paper Series, No. EC06-16
Hryckiewicz A, Kowalewski O (2010) Economic determinates, Financial Crisis and Entry Modes of Foreign Banks into Emerging Markets. Emerg Mark Rev 11:205–228. https://doi.org/10.1016/j.ememar.2010.05.003
Konopielko L (1999). Foreign banks entry into Central and East European markets: Motives and activities. Post-Communist Eco 11:463–485. https://doi.org/10.1080/14631379995841
Kowalski T, Uiboupin J, Vensel V (2002) Motives of foreign banks entry into the transitional economies: the comparative empirical evidence from Estonia and Poland. Working Paper TTUWPE, No. 02/78
Kraft E (2004) Foreign banks in Croatia: reasons for entry, performance and impacts. J Emerg Mark Financ 3:153–174. https://doi.org/10.1177/097265270400300204
Lanine G, Van der Vennet R (2007) Microeconomic determinants of acquisitions of Eastern European banks by Western European banks. Eco Trans 15(2): 285–308
Lenher M (2009) Entry mode choice of multinational banks. J Bank Financ 33(10): 1781–1792. https://doi.org/10.1016/j.jbankfin.2009.03.009
Lensink BW, de Haan J (2002) Do reforms in transition economies affect foreign bank entry? Int Rev Financ 3:213–232. https://doi.org/10.1111/j.1369-412X.2002.00039.x
Léon F (2018) Convergence of credit structure around the world. Econ Model 68:306–317. https://doi.org/10.1016/j.econmod.2017.07.021
Llewellyn, DT (2004) Competition and profitability in banking: are there lessons from the UK?. In: Eijffinger SCW, van Gemert HG, van Roij GPL (ed) Intermediair tussen Wetenshap en Onderwijs. Gianotten, Tilburg
Mathieson DJ, Roldos J (2001) The role of foreign banks in emerging markets. In: Litan R, Masson P, Pomerleano M (ed) Open doors: foreign participation in financial systems in developed countries. Brooking Institution Press
Miller SR, Parkhe A (1998) Patterns in the expansion of US banks foreign operations. J Int Bus Stud 29:359–390. https://doi.org/10.1057/palgrave.jibs.8490040
Naaborg I (2007) Foreign Bank entry and performance with a focus on Central and Eastern Europe. University of Groningen

Papi L, Revoltella D (1999) Foreign Direct Investments in the Banking Sector: a Transitional Economy Perspective. In: Claessens S, Jansen M (ed) The internationalization of financial services. Kluwer, The Hague

Petersen MA, Rajan R (1994) The Benefits of Lending Relationships: Evidence from Small Business Data. J Financ 49(1):3–37

Poghosyan T, de Haan J (2008) Determinants of Cross-Border Bank Acquisitions in Transition Economies: A Latent Class Analysis. CESifo Working Paper Series, No. 2372. Available at SSRN: https://ssrn.com/abstract=1259643

Pomerleano, M, Vojta GJ (2001) What do foreign banks do in Emerging Markets? An institutional study. In: Litan ER, Masson P, Pomerleano M (ed) Open Doors: Foreign Participation in Financial Systems in Developing Countries. Brookings Institution Press, Washington DC

Rajan RS, Gopalan, S (2014) Economic Management in a Volatile Environment: Monetary and Financial Issues. Palgrave Macmillan, Basingstoke

Roaf J, Atoyan R, Joshi B, Krogulski K (2014) 25 years of transition. Post-communist Europe and the IMF, Regional Economic Issues Special Report, IMF, Washington DC

Seth R, Nolle DE, Mohanty SK (1998) Do Banks Follow Their Customers Abroad? Financial Markets, Institutions, and Instruments 7(4):1–25

Sharpe SA (1990) Asymmetric Information, Bank Lending, and Implicit Contracts: A Stylized Model of Customer Relationships. J Financ 45(4):1069–1087

Soussa F (2004) A note on banking FDI in Emerging Markets: literature review and evidence from M&A data. Bank of England, London

Wezel T (2004) Foreign bank entry into Emerging Economies: an empirical assessment of the determinants and risks predicated on German FDI data. Studies of the Economic Research Center, Discussion paper 01/2004, Deutsche Bundesbank

Williams B (1997) Banking: Eclectic theory versus Internalisation theory, J Econ Surv 11(1): 71–100

Williams B (2002) The defensive expansion approach to multinational banking: Evidence to date. Financial Markets Institutions & Instruments 11(2): 127–203. https://doi.org/10.1111/1468-0416.00008

CHAPTER 4

Credit Activity of Foreign-Owned Banks in CESEE

Małgorzata Iwanicz-Drozdowska, Paweł Smaga, and Bartosz Witkowski

4.1 What Drives Credit Growth in CESEE?

4.1.1 Credit Growth: The Pre- and Post-crisis Picture

The banks operating in CESEE represent a traditional banking model, based on taking deposits and granting credits. The goal of this section is to find out to what extent local conditions, namely macroeconomic and bank-specific factors of the host countries, have a consistent impact on banks with different owners. Moreover, in the case of a foreign-owned bank, we take into account its parent bank and home country traits to control for the impact of factors originating outside the host country. We pay special attention to foreign-owned banks due to their significant market shares. In this chapter we use a large set of bank-level and country-level data for both host and home countries.

Credit growth is stimulated by many factors on both micro- and macroeconomic levels. However, in the case of foreign-owned banks there is an additional set of factors playing a role in subsidiaries' credit growth. As Houston et al. (1997) and Houston and James (1998) pointed out, there is an "internal capital market" which operates between the parent company and

M. Iwanicz-Drozdowska et al.,
Foreign-Owned Banks, Studies in Economic Transition,
https://doi.org/10.1007/978-3-030-01111-6_4

its subsidiaries. This internal market may not only promote expansion on local markets, but also transmit financial shocks from parent banks to subsidiaries, for example, Peek and Rosengren (1997, 2000), Jeon et al. (2013). The impact of the parent bank and its home country situation is known as a parent-subsidiary nexus. After the outbreak of the GFC, a sudden stop of credit activity was observed among subsidiaries and a stronger competition for liquidity on internal capital market impacting lending activities. Numerous parent banks faced financial problems and foreign-owned banks reduced their lending more than domestic-owned and state-owned banks. There was a threat in the CESEE region that foreign-owned banks might have "cut and run" because of the liquidity constraints and deleveraging process; however, this has not materialized. State ownership in the banking sector was fairly often criticized in countries in transition; however, several studies indicate that state-owned banks proved to be a stable source of financing, especially during the GFC, for example, Micco and Panizza (2004), Bertay et al. (2015).

The impact of foreign ownership was regarded as an advantage before the outbreak of the GFC, because foreign investors from industrialized countries were treated as a source of stability for their local subsidiaries. This was the case, for instance, in the study by De Haas and van Lelyveld (2006). This stream of research expanded significantly after the outbreak of the GFC, for example, Cull and Martínez-Pería (2013), De Haas and van Lelyveld (2014), Epstein (2014), De Haas et al. (2015), Dekle and Lee (2015), Festić (2015), Frey and Kerl (2015), Iwanicz-Drozdowska and Witkowski (2016), Allen et al. (2017), Bonin and Louie (2017), Temesvary and Banai (2017), showing, however, a different picture of the parents' role.

Cull and Martínez-Pería (2013), De Haas and van Lelyveld (2014), Allen et al. (2017) indicated the negative impact of deteriorating home country and parent bank situation on the subsidiary's credit growth. Moreover, a survey conducted by De Haas and Naaborg (2006) among bank managers revealed that subsidiaries were strongly integrated with their parents in terms of capital allocation and credit steering and therefore, the impact of the parent bank was extensive. An interesting issue was analysed by De Haas and Van Horen (2013), who—using data on cross-border lending after the collapse of Lehman Brothers (LB)—check whether the bank-borrower's closeness is related to the lending stability. They found a strong negative link between geographical distance and the lending stability in cross-border lending. This perspective, though, differs from ours.

One of the grounds for cutting lending was reduced access to liquidity. Ivashina and Scharfstein (2010) analysed this phenomenon for the US corporate lending after the collapse of LB. The decrease in loan supply occurred in the case of banks with narrower access to deposit funding and higher exposures to credit-line drawdowns, putting some pressure on loan spreads. The borrowers were not able to switch easily to other lenders with more stable financing. In contrast, in CESEE the corporate lending is less developed than lending to individuals, so the overall decline (if observed) was not so significant. A study based on a unique dataset of German multinational banks and their subsidiaries by Frey and Kerl (2015) concluded that local deposit funding attracted by subsidiaries was stabilizing, while reliance on short-term wholesale funding was a destabilizing factor for their lending after the collapse of LB. However, high ROE of subsidiaries protected them from deleveraging within the banking group due to profitability-seeking. Moreover, there was an increase in competition for liquidity on the internal market because German banks focused on stabilizing lending on their home market. In times of crisis, the parent banks adjusted their business strategies and affected the lending behaviour within the whole group.

Although the impact of the parent bank and its home country during the GFC on subsidiaries' credit growth was negative, there was no "cut and run" situation on the CESEE markets. This phenomenon will be presented in detail in Chap. 5 from the financial stability perspective. In general, there are two reasons here. First, the Vienna Initiative (VI) was set up at the end of 2008 to stabilize the situation in some CESEE markets. Second, the CESEE markets themselves were attractive and stable and therefore, it was rational and efficient to remain in those markets. The VI's impact was analysed by De Haas et al. (2015) and Temesvary and Banai (2017). De Haas et al. (2015) confirmed that foreign-owned banks reduced their lending more than domestic private-owned banks, but subsidiaries of the parent banks participating in the VI were more stable lenders than other banks in the same country. Moreover, the VI parent banks did not withdraw their exposures from non-VI countries. Temesvary and Banai (2017), except for the VI, put stress on lending in foreign currencies (especially Swiss francs) and the location (EU vs non-EU) of the subsidiaries' countries. In their analysis, the authors covered 26 parent banking groups and 63 subsidiaries in 11 transitioning countries over 2002–2013. In conclusion, the crisis effect in the VI countries was lower than in other countries. Throughout the sample and the period, lower capital adequacy (measured by capital to assets ratio) and higher NPLs ratio, either in the subsidiary or the parent bank, destimulated credit growth of the subsidiaries.

Moreover, Bonin and Louie (2017) stressed that the behaviour of foreign-owned banks was not the same. They differentiated between "Big 6" parent banks (i.e. Raiffeisen, Erste, Intesa Sanpaolo, Unicredit, Societe Generale, and KBC), which find the CESEE region the second home market, and other parent banks in the region. In their analysis, they covered eight countries from emerging Europe over 2005–2010. Subsidiaries of "Big 6" were stable lenders, while other foreign parents reduced their lending via subsidiaries after the GFC outbreak. In the same vein, Iwanicz-Drozdowska and Witkowski (2016) showed that foreign ownership could not be treated as a monolith, because there were differences in the parents' bank policies depending on whether the parent company was a G-SIB or just a multinational bank.

4.1.2 Empirical Analysis of Credit Growth

In this empirical study, we use bank-level and country-level data over the period of 1995 through 2015. The bank-level data were extracted in euro from the Bankscope database and supplemented by hand-collected data on banks' owners (divided into: development banks, state, foreign and domestic private). There are about 5200 bank-year observations in our sample, including approximately 2200 observations for foreign-owned banks operating as subsidiaries. The country-level data were extracted from the World Bank database and central banks' websites. For the crisis and bailout dummies we used papers by Laeven and Valencia (2008), Costa-Navajas and Thegeya (2013) and Iwanicz-Drozdowska et al. (2016).

The sample includes banks from the following countries: Albania, Belarus, Bosnia, Bulgaria, Croatia, Czech Republic, Estonia, Hungary, Kosovo, Latvia, Lithuania, Macedonia, Moldova, Montenegro, Poland, Romania, Serbia, Slovenia, Slovakia, and Ukraine. In order to analyse the impact of parent companies of foreign-owned banks, we used adequate data for parent banks and their home countries. The sample includes such home countries as: Austria, Belgium, China, Cyprus, Denmark, Finland, France, Germany, Greece, Ireland, Israel, Italy, Japan, Lebanon, Netherlands, Norway, Portugal, Russia, Spain, Sweden, Switzerland, Turkey, the UK, and the US.

In certain cases, foreign-owned banks have parents from other transitioning countries, since some domestic private-owned or state-owned banks decided to expand internationally. Such cases include the following (parent) banks from CESEE: First Investment Bank (Bulgaria), Home Credit (Czech Republic), MKB Bank and OPT Bank (Hungary), Ukio Bank (Lithuania), Mortgage and Land Bank and its successors (Latvia), Getin Bank and PKO BP (Poland), Komercijalna Banka (Serbia), NLB and Nova KBM (Slovenia), JT Finance (Slovakia), Pivdennyi and Privatbank (Ukraine).

Countries covered by the VI (Bosnia and Herzegovina, Hungary, Latvia, Romania and Serbia) and parent banks participating in the VI (Alpha Bank,

Bayerische Landesbank, Erste, Intesa Sanpaolo, KBC, Raiffeisen, Unicredit, Eurobank EFG, National Bank of Greece, Societe Generale, Volksbank, Piraeus, Hypo Alpe-Adria, NLB Group, DnB Nord, Nordea, Swedbank, SEB)[1] are marked as VI in some regressions from 2009, when the VI arrangements were actually implemented.

We model the credit growth in real terms. Independent variables are divided into three groups: host country and host bank-level variables, home country and parent bank variables and group- and market-specific variables to control for the subsidiaries' position within the group and on the host market. The list of regressors is presented in Table 4.1, while their descriptive statistics are available from the authors on request.

Table 4.1 Regressors

Notation	*Definition*
Host country and host bank-level variables	
ΔZ-Score	Proxy for financial position; if $\text{Z-Score}_t - \text{Z-Score}_{t-1} > 0$, then dummy = 1; Z-Score is defined as: $\text{Z-Score} = \frac{ETA_t + ROA_t}{\sigma_{ROA}}$, where ETA—equity to total assets ratio; ROA—return on assets (see formula for Z-Score_2 in Sect. 5.3.1)
ΔD_L	Funding proxy; change year over year of deposits from customers to loans to customers ratio $(D\_L_t - D\_L_{t-1})$
Size	The natural logarithm of total assets (million EUR)
ΔGDP	Growth of GDP year over year in real terms; $(GDP_t - GDP_{t-1}) / (1+INF)$; INF—Rate of inflation
ΔNIR	Change in nominal interest rates; $NIR_t - NIR_{t-1}$
CRISIS	Dummy CRISIS = 1 if there was a crisis in a given year
Home country and parent bank-level variables	
ΔZ-Score_P	Proxy for financial position; if $\text{Z-Score\_P}_t - \text{Z-Score\_P}_{t-1} > 0$, then dummy = 1
ΔD_L_P	Funding proxy of; change year over year of deposits from customers to loans to customers ratio $(D\_L\_P_t - D\_L\_P_{t-1})$
Size_P	The natural logarithm of total assets (million EUR)
ΔGDP_P	Growth of GDP year over year in real terms; $(GDP\_P_t - GDP\_P_{t-1}) / (1+INF\_P)$; INF—rate of inflation
ΔNIR_P	Change in nominal interest rates; $NIR\_P_t - NIR\_P_{t-1}$
CRISIS_P	Dummy CRISIS_P = 1 if there was a crisis in a given year
Group- and market-specific variables	
SHARE_G	The share of subsidiary in assets of parent group
ROE_G	Dummy ROE_G = 1 if ROE of subsidiary is higher than ROE of parent group
DISTANCE	The distance between the capital cities of host and home countries (km)
SHARE_M	The share of subsidiary in host market in terms of assets
ROE_M	Dummy ROE_G = 1 if ROE of subsidiary is higher than ROE of banking sector in host country

Source: Own work

The data used in the analysis constitute a bank-level panel with annual frequency. We apply a linearized form

$$\Delta \text{loans}_{it} = x'_{it}\beta + \varepsilon_{it}, \tag{4.1}$$

where Δloans_{it}, the dependent variable, is the change of the loans granted to customers (in real terms) for the i-th bank in period t, x'_{it} is the vector of independent variables, β is the vector of parameters, and ε_{it} is the error term. Following appropriate tests and previous research, we allow for the first order autocorrelation. Additionally, given the heterogeneity of the considered sample, we allow for heteroskedasticity of the error term. The model can thus be estimated with the use of a feasible generalized least squares estimator. Most of the time series of the loans granted are non-stationary. The use of the first difference as the dependent variable eliminates the risk of attaining spurious regressions while the dependent variable is I(1). Consequently, the first differences of the independent variables are also included.

The regressors in the x'_{it} vector include characteristics of both the bank itself and its parent as well as macroeconomic characteristics of the host and home countries. In particular, we capture the effect of financial crises by including an appropriate dummy variable. In consequence, there is no possibility—though no need, as well—to include fixed time effects. Due to the short-termism in banks' policies, stimulated by the pressure from regulators and owners, banks adjust their policies to the current market situation. Therefore, we resigned from using lagged bank-level variables. In additional estimated models, we did, however, use lagged macroeconomic variables, assuming that banks may react to the changes in the macroeconomic situation with a certain delay. These models confirmed our results and are available from the authors on request.

Model (4.1) represents a general functional form that is estimated and discussed in our analysis. However, we estimate a number of models, which differ in terms of the exact list of regressors and the population the sample of which comes from. This has been done for two reasons. Firstly, we verify whether the estimated relation is the same or similar across different bank groups. The considered groups differ in their ownership (domestic-owned, foreign-owned, etc.), as well as country-level characteristics (whether the host country is a member of the VI or not). At the same time, we draw conclusions regarding robustness of the results. Those are based on models estimated on different samples as described above, as well as a modified set of regressors. In the discussion, wherever we use the concept of significance of a variable, we assume 10% level of significance for brevity.

Table 4.2 Estimates of model (1.1) in different samples according to host bank ownership structure

Variables	*All banks (1.1.1)*	*Banks in VI countries (1.1.2)*	*Domestic-owned (1.1.3)*	*State-owned (1.1.4)*	*Foreign-owned & development (1.1.5)*
ΔZ-Score	−0.0698***	−0.0780***	−0.1141***	−0.1035***	−0.0698***
	(−12.30)	(−5.25)	(−10.31)	(−6.73)	(−9.68)
ΔD_L	−0.0457***	−0.0572***	−0.2648***	−0.1484***	−0.0389***
	(−22.31)	(−22.36)	(−22.00)	(−9.19)	(−20.70)
Size	−0.0129***	−0.0556***	0.0028	−0.0103***	−0.0224***
	(−5.73)	(−7.29)	(0.63)	(−2.78)	(−7.88)
ΔGDP	2.1827***	2.6224***	1.8162***	2.1333***	2.4972***
	(26.49)	(11.17)	(11.69)	(10.55)	(22.26)
ΔNIR	−0.3854***	−0.4266	−0.5817***	−0.0131	−0.5354***
	(−5.59)	(−1.54)	(−5.92)	(−0.16)	(−3.94)
CRISIS	−0.0468***	0.0631 (1.52)	−0.0938***	−0.1250***	0.0018 (0.09)
	(−3.57)		(−4.18)	(−5.76)	
Constant	1.1869***	1.4922***	1.1328***	1.1361***	1.2584***
	(72.07)	(26.23)	(41.11)	(36.80)	(57.49)
n	5219	856	1661	496	3023

Notes: Based on the WB and IMF database, Bankscope, central bank websites, banks annual statements and hand-collected data

t statistics are in parentheses. $^{*}p < 0.1$, $^{**}p < 0.05$, $^{***}p < 0.01$

In Table 4.2 we provide estimates of regressions estimated on the sample of host banks with the inclusion of host country variables (model 1.1). The average loan growth for all banks was higher than for banks in the VI countries. The average for domestic-owned banks was the highest, while of state-owned and foreign-owned banks was among the lowest. One may identify differences in determinants of loan growth for banks in various settings: all banks in the sample, banks with different owners (private domestic-owned, state-owned, foreign-owned, including owned by foreign commercial banks, i.e. having a bank as an owner), or domiciled in the VI countries. In all the cases the models suggest a positive impact of the GDP growth on loan growth and a negative impact of other factors. The role of GDP is in line with long-term observations of the banks' behaviour on the market (including procyclicality, which is discussed in the next section), as well as the results of previous studies, for example, De Haas et al. (2015), Bonin and Louie (2017), Allen et al. (2017). The actual GDP growth and its forecasts positively affect both the credit supply and credit demand sides. The current and forecasted macroeconomic situation is included in the banks' financial plans and provides guidelines on how to operate on the market.

Two bank-level variables negatively impact the growth of credit, namely the change in the Z-Score and the change in the deposit to credit ratio. The increase in the Z-Score means that the bank has become safer. Looking at the definition of this measure, we regard its negative impact as the result of a tighter policy towards the level of capital (a typical crisis and post-crisis reaction of supervisors and banks). A higher ratio of equity to total assets increases the Z-Score, but reduces the leverage and thus, the space for credit expansion. The deposits to loans ratio demonstrates to what extent the deposits attracted from customers are sufficient to finance loans to customers. The ratio being equal to or higher than 1 means that the bank is able to finance its credit portfolio with customer deposits. A decrease of this ratio means that the funding deteriorated, while its increase shows improvement in funding. Looking at the deposits to loans descriptive statistics, one finds that its mean nominal level in the CESEE banks was high (1.7366) in comparison with the parent banks (0.8803). The mean of its change was −0.1509, showing that the banks in the region reduced the level of this ratio. One may thus conclude that initially a very conservative level of the deposits to loans ratio was reduced over time in order to use the attracted funding for credit expansion. The banks in the CESEE region were able to use their liquidity stocks in order to increase the role of credit in the economy, still keeping the ratio above 1.

One can observe differences in the impact of the interest rates, crisis events and size. The growth of the interest rates is in general found to negatively impact credit growth, as expected, because it significantly lowers the demand for credit, given the dominance of variable-rate loans in the CESEEs, but for banks in the VI countries and state-owned banks, this impact is not statistically significant. They are found to be less dependent on the local central bank policy and able to attract alternative funding or to get support from the state or their foreign owner, respectively. In other studies, for example, Bonin and Louie (2017) and Allen et al. (2017), the inflation rate was used instead of the interest rates, showing a negative impact of the Consumer Price Index (CPI) increase on loan growth. Given that changes of the central bank interest rates and the rate of inflation are interrelated, our results are in line with previous studies.

During the crisis periods, the lending was significantly less intense in the group of all banks and the domestic-owned (private and state) ones, while no significant difference could be spotted in the groups of banks in the VI countries and the foreign-owned banks. The influence of the size on credit growth has not been confirmed in the group of domestic private-owned banks, while it is found to have had a significantly negative influence in the case of other banks, for example, De Haas et al. (2015), Bonin and Louie (2017). These results underline the differences between a foreign-owned bank and other banks in the CESEE region, as well as between banks in the VI countries and banks in other countries.

In Table 4.3 we present estimates of regressions based on the sample of foreign-owned banks, which have banks as their parent companies. We use a wider set of regressors in the estimated regressions and additional independent variables including parent bank characteristics (model 2.1). The first four models (2.1.1–2.1.3) were estimated with the use of the sample which covers all the foreign-owned banks in the CESEE region and they differ in the sets of regressors. Only those foreign-owned banks whose parents participated in the VI (starting from 2009) were included in the sample used to estimate model 2.1.4, while only foreign-owned banks located in the VI countries, which have VI parent banks, were used to estimate model 2.1.5. Moreover, we estimated two models for two different groups of parent banks, namely G-SIBs (2.1.6) and non-G-SIBs (2.1.7). We use 2.1.1 as a baseline model for further discussion.

As the statistically significant results suggest, credit growth in foreign-owned banks is stimulated by the host and home countries' GDP growth, while it is destimulated by a wide set of other factors, including subsidiary characteristics, the size of the parent company, its funding policy and a crisis event in the home country. The occurrence of crises in the host country has not been found to significantly affect the loan growth, which is in line with full sample results. These results confirm the role of the parent bank and its macroeconomic conditions. The parent's Z-Score used as a proxy for its financial condition is not statistically significant, while the change in the deposits to loans ratio of a parent company is found to have a statistically significant negative effect. In contrast to banks from the CESEE countries, the mean of the deposits to loans ratio was below 1 (0.8803), showing a more aggressive lending policy. The credit portfolio was not only financed with customers' deposits, but also with other types of liabilities. The mean change of this ratio over the considered period was slightly above zero (0.0002). When the balance sheet

Table 4.3 Estimates of model (2.1) in different samples according to type of parent with different set of regressors

Variables	*All foreign-owned banks*			*Parents VI*		*G-SIBs vs other parents*	
	Baseline (2.1.1)	*Role in group (2.1.2)*	*Role on market (2.1.3)*	*All countries (2.1.4)*	*VI countries (2.1.5)*	*G-SIBs (2.1.6)*	*Other (2.1.7)*
ΔZ-Score	−0.0585***	−0.0617***	−0.0579***	−0.0251***	−0.0092	−0.1137***	−0.0605***
	(−7.92)	(−7.75)	(−7.11)	(−3.91)	(−0.47)	(−3.73)	(−6.72)
ΔD_L	−0.0860***	−0.0853***	−0.0833***	−0.0573***	−0.0555***	−0.7964***	−0.0806***
	(−15.49)	(−15.16)	(−14.96)	(−25.52)	(−32.92)	(−8.88)	(−14.34)
Size	−0.0133***	−0.0138***	−0.0189***	−0.0225***	−0.0591***	0.0073	−0.0197***
	(−3.28)	(−2.95)	(−3.93)	(−6.5)	(−4.05)	(0.57)	(−3.82)
ΔGDP	1.5827***	1.7367***	1.7102***	0.6733***	0.1998	1.1057*	1.8894***
	(10.74)	(11.46)	(11.02)	(4.59)	(0.37)	(1.69)	(11.08)
ΔNIR	−0.0907	−0.1118	−0.1203	−0.6259*	−2.1534**	1.1346	−0.1139
	(−0.48)	(−0.58)	(−0.62)	(−1.95)	(−2.18)	(1.48)	(−0.56)
CRISIS	0.0053	0.0142	0.0014	−0.0548***	0.0091	−0.1578	0.0257
	(0.22)	(0.58)	(0.06)	(−4.0)	(0.16)	(−1.57)	(0.88)
ΔZ-Score_P	0.0089	0.0111	0.0051	−0.0138**	−0.0157	0.008	0.0044
	(1.25)	(1.43)	(0.65)	(−2.28)	(−0.82)	(0.27)	(0.51)
ΔD_L_P	−0.1836***	−0.1882***	−0.1787***	0.0484	−0.0997	−0.1238	−0.1809***
	(−4.67)	(−4.67)	(−4.38)	(0.86)	(−0.56)	(−0.77)	(−4.24)
Size_P	−0.0106***	−0.0119**	−0.0099**	0.0319***	0.036***	0.0253	−0.0082*
	(−2.70)	(−2.43)	(−2.43)	(7.88)	(2.81)	(0.79)	(−1.87)
ΔGDP_P	1.0985***	1.0405***	0.9175***	0.5916***	0.418	0.446	1.011***
	(6.35)	(5.43)	(4.58)	(4.34)	(1.0)	(0.44)	(4.72)
ΔNIR_P	0.0509	0.0762	0.0943	−2.4785***	0.7584	1.7632**	0.1267
	(0.30)	(0.45)	(0.55)	(−3.56)	(0.43)	(2.33)	(0.72)
CRISIS_P	−0.0579***	−0.0588***	−0.0532***	0.0493***	0.0472	−0.0692	−0.0495***
	(−5.56)	(−5.42)	(−4.74)	(5.36)	(1.57)	(−1.22)	(−4.17)

SHARE_G		−0.1532					
		(−1.17)					
ROE_G		0.0226**					
		(2.45)					
DISTANCE		−0,0001*					
		(−1.69)					
SHARE_M			0.1361*	0.0273	0.1542	−0.4398	0.1059
			(1.94)	(0.6)	(0.68)	(−1.48)	(1.48)
ROE_M			0.0235**	0.0198***	0.0262	0.0701**	0.029***
			(2.51)	(2.81)	(1.18)	(2.11)	(2.84)
Constant	1.3246***	1.344	1.3329***	0.7335***	0.9335***	0.7516*	1.3161***
	(29.17)	(27.78)	(29.63)	(13.45)	(5.7)	(1.66)	(28.5)
n	2205	2205	2205	701	247	522	1683

Notes: Based on the WB and IMF database, Bankscope, central bank websites, banks annual statements and hand-collected data

t statistics are in parentheses. $^{*}p < 0.1$, $^{**}p < 0.05$, $^{***}p < 0.01$

structure of the parent banks is analysed, we observe that all the parent banks improved their funding position with the use the interbank market, but still, this is a less stable form of financing. This fact is reflected, for example, in the net stable funding ratio (NSFR), introduced by Basel 3, with the intention to stabilize liquidity of banks.

We introduce three group-specific variables, which reflect the role of the subsidiary in the group and the geographical distance between home and host countries (2.1.2). In this setting, the impact of banks' and countries' specific variables is the same as in the baseline model. The subsidiary's share in the parent group total assets' significance has not been confirmed, while a positive impact of subsidiaries' superior ROE on the loan growth can be concluded. While we find the distance between the host and home countries have a negative impact, its relevance is limited given the very low value of the estimated coefficient. These results indicate an important role played by capital allocation and its management. If subsidiaries' ROE is higher than ROE for the group in total, it may be considered as a convincing reason for lending expansion, but the size of the subsidiary and its share in the total group assets do not play such a role.

In further settings, we introduce market-specific variables that reflect the market position of a subsidiary in a given country (market share in terms of assets) and its outperforming ROE (2.1.3–2.1.7). For the group of all foreign banks in the region (2.1.3), both factors are found to have a positive significant influence on the loan growth, which means that outperforming ROE and a high market share convinced managers to strengthen the market position through further credit expansion. In the models which are estimated on the sample of the VI parent banks (2.1.4), only the stimulating role of outperforming ROE is confirmed, with no market share significance. In the case of some of the variables used throughout all the specifications, the impact of the parent banks that participate in the VI on subsidiaries is other than in the baseline model. An increase of the interest rates in the host and home countries is found to have destimulated credit growth, while in all the models based on the sample of foreign-owned banks, it is not statistically significant. The VI parent banks seem to pay more attention to the central bank policies in home and host countries than other parent banks. We find contrasting evidence for the impact of crisis dummies. The crisis in the host country had a negative impact on lending in the case of the subsidiaries of the VI parents, while the influence of the home country crisis is found to be positive. This confirms that the VI parent banks' policy differs from that of other parent banks. Also, two parent-specific variables are found to have a different nature of impact (positive in the case of size, negative in the case of Z-Score and not statistically significant in the case of funding). The VI parents are thus found to be more concerned about their financial strength while the impact of size may confirm their "too big to fail" position on the home market and therefore easier access to the lender of last resort or public aid. As a matter of fact, the VI parent banks are the biggest banks in their home countries, except for Bayerische Landesbank, Hypo Alpe-Adria and Volksbank.

In order to explore the determinants of loan growth in the subsidiaries embraced by the VI, we estimate a model based only on the sample of subsidiaries of the VI parent banks, who themselves are located in the VI countries (2.1.5). The set of determinants which are significant for the credit growth in this setting is quite different from the results in previous cases, which emphasizes their different situation. The only parent-specific variable whose statistical significance is confirmed is the size, which, again, highlights their role in the home market. The number of subsidiaries and host country-specific variables with statistically significant impact is also lower. In comparison with the baseline model, we find no confirmation of the significant impact of the Z-Score and GDP growth and find a negative impact of growth of interest rates. Moreover, two crisis dummies (home and host) and market-specific variables show no statistically significant impact (however, their signs are positive). Therefore, we claim that the behaviour of subsidiaries of the VI parent banks in the VI countries is much different from the patterns of other subsidiaries. This confirms country-specific features and the role the VI played in those countries.

Except for special interest in the VI parent banks, we also investigated whether G-SIBs parents (model 2.1.6) have different policies than other international banks (model 2.1.7). Both groups of the parent banks show remarkable differences. This is in line with the previous studies by Bonin and Louie (2017) and Iwanicz-Drozdowska and Witkowski (2016) confirming that a foreign-owned bank should not be treated as a monolith. The model estimated for other parents confirmed the findings of all foreign-owned banks model (2.1.3), except for the market share, while the model for G-SIBs confirmed statistical significance only of several parent bank and home country traits (change in nominal interest rates with a positive impact and ROE dummy, having the value of 1 if the subsidiaries' ROE is higher than the host market ROE). The model, however, confirmed the significance of the traits of G-SIBs' subsidiaries, with the exception of their size.

This fact may be interpreted as a sign of the subsidiaries' greater independence from their parent banks, but subsidiaries' ROE still plays an important role for the G-SIBs group-wide management. A tentative explanation of this phenomenon may be linked to very sophisticated organizational structures of G-SIBs and the necessity to delegate the responsibility to the local management. The subsidiaries of other international banks seem to be more dependent on the parents' overall policy.

4.2 Are Foreign-Owned Banks More or Less Procyclical than Domestic-Owned Banks?[2]

Another important aspect, relevant from both the theoretical and policy perspectives, is the procyclicality of credit provided by foreign-owned banks versus domestic banks in the CESEEs, especially during the GFC. The literature comprises empirical evidence for both the procyclical and stabilizing role of lending by foreign-owned banks, yet some studies, as well as our estimations in the previous section, point to heterogeneity of foreign banks' impact depending, for instance, on the host/home country conditions or parent bank characteristics.

4.2.1 Cyclicality of Foreign-Owned Banks' Lending

One stream of literature concludes that foreign-owned banks reduced lending to a greater extent than domestic banks in the host countries in response to the GFC. As mentioned above, Temesvary and Banai (2017) on a CEE sample show that the onset of the crisis reduced the lending growth of subsidiaries across the board, yet this effect depended on the parent banking group traits. Further, De Haas and van Lelyveld (2014) find that the slowdown in credit growth of foreign banks' subsidiaries during 2008–2009 (especially of those whose parent banks were relaying on wholesale funding) was almost three times larger than for domestic banks, a conclusion supported by Claessens and van Horen (2012) and Cull and Martínez-Pería (2013) in the CESEEs. Similarly, Ehlers and McGuire (2017) argue that the higher foreign-owned bank participation rate in emerging economies tended to include greater increases in their credit-to-GDP ratios in the pre-crisis period and decreases in busts thereafter, thus exacerbating the credit cycle. In line with this view, as already stated, also Bonin and Louie (2017) pointed to the foreign-owned banks (other than the Big 6 banks active in the CEE region) which decreased their lending aggressively during the crisis periods and exacerbated the business cycle in the host countries.

However, another stream of studies points to contrasting evidence arguing that foreign-owned subsidiaries tended to behave in a less procyclical manner than host countries' domestic banks during the times of crises. De Haas and van Lelyveld (2006) find that subsidiaries of financially strong parent banks did not reduce lending during the crisis and that foreign-owned banks had a stabilizing impact on credit growth, that is, reduced lending less than domestic banks in the CESEEs (Claessens and van Horen 2012), which was probably due to their business model in CESEE—the "second home market" hypothesis (Epstein 2014). Nevertheless, those effects depend on the stability and health of the banking systems in foreign banks' home countries (Claessens and van Horen 2012; Allen et al. 2017), so not all foreign banks' policies are alike. Moreover, Wu et al. (2011) find evidence that foreign-owned banks are less sensitive to contractionary monetary policy shocks in the host countries, as they adjust their loans and loan interest rates more gradually than domestic private banks, thus provide less procyclical lending.

4.2.2 *Measuring Bank Credit Procyclicality in the CESEEs*

Procyclicality, as a cyclical dimension of the systemic risk, might be regarded as self-reinforcing cyclical fluctuations in risk and leverage and their distribution within the financial system (Smaga 2014). It strengthens interconnectedness within the financial sector and between its functioning, and the real economy may negatively affect economic growth (Olszak and Pipień 2016). Procyclicality is especially pronounced in the banking sector, and it is mainly due to both exogenous and endogenous factors (Athanasoglou et al. 2014). As the bank credit is of the highest importance in the CESEEs' financial systems, in the analysis we focus on the credit cycle.

From the theoretical perspective, financial (credit) cycles can be regarded as periodical fluctuations in credit conditions (their demand, supply and price) in the economy, or self-reinforcing interactions between perceptions of value and risk, and attitudes towards risk and financing constraints, which translate into booms followed by busts (Borio 2014). Such an approach to understanding the credit cycle incorporates the hitherto main theoretical advances in this field, for example, Fisher (1933),

Schumpeter (1939), Minsky (1978), concluding that the impact of credit is not monotonic, and credit cycles might be regarded as a double-edged sword, that is, on one hand, they can bolster the economic upswing with credit expansion, but, on the other, they can aggravate the downturn with credit rationing and deleveraging.

Empirical evidence has largely confirmed these theoretical assumptions. Numerous studies have shown that financial cycles are considerably distinct from business cycles; they are longer and deeper, with much greater amplitude than business cycles, as credit cycles have lower frequency and medium- to long-term character, for example, Claessens et al. (2011), Hiebert et al. (2014), Galati et al. (2016). Both the duration and amplitude of the financial cycles have increased since the mid-1980s with an average duration of around 16 years (Borio 2014). Although distinct, business and financial cycles are closely interlinked, as recessions associated with financial crises tend to be longer and deeper than other recessions (Claessens et al. 2011; Stremmel 2015). According to Calderón and Fuentes (2014), during crisis-related downturns, real credit and asset prices tend to be more volatile in emerging economies than during regular recessions. Moreover, financial cycle peaks tend to precede peaks in the business cycle during crises in emerging economies. Both Kollintzas et al. (2011), as well as Apostoaie et al. (2014), being among the few studies on a sample of the CESEE countries, proved that there is a significant cyclical co-movement between credit and GDP.

The key issue in the empirical estimation of the credit cycle is the equilibrium level of credit growth, that is, determining at what level credit growth is excessive and might endanger financial stability as a credit boom (see Annex 1 with IMF proposals for technical definitions of credit booms in Dell'Ariccia et al. 2012). Quantifying credit cycles is more challenging in the CESEEs in particular, as rapid credit expansion in the CESEEs may simply mean convergence to values typical of the advanced nations, and not excessive borrowing (Geršl and Seidler 2011). In general, most studies use different filtering techniques to derive cyclical component from variables representing credit developments. The increase in the cyclical component can be regarded as an indicator of the upswing phase of the credit cycle, while its decrease as a sign of contraction phase of the cycle.

A financial cycle is usually measured with the credit-to-GDP gap. The most promising leading indicators of financial crises are gaps of the ratio of (private sector) credit-to-GDP and asset prices, especially property prices, as combining them appears to capture the link among the financial cycle, business cycle and crises, for example, Borio and Drehmann (2009), Borio et al. (2012), Giese et al. (2014a, b). European Systemic Risk Board (ESRB 2014) finds that the credit-to-GDP gap is the best single leading indicator for systemic banking crises associated with excessive credit growth for both the EU as a whole and for the majority of EU countries, including for the CESEE countries (Geršl and Seidler 2015). Similarly, the ratio is found to be a meaningful early warning indicator of growing financial imbalances (Alessi and Detken 2011) or banking crises (Aikman et al. 2015). The drawback[3] of using the credit-to-GDP ratio for credit boom identification is that it might erroneously indicate an increase in cyclical credit provision not because of a rise in credit but because of a decrease in GDP.

Therefore, we measured the credit cycle not only using gaps of the bank credit-to-GDP ratio, but also applying credit *growth* gaps, which does not have such drawback. Such a measure might allow capturing the volatility of the bank credit supply better than the credit-to-GDP ratio. Given the relatively higher volatility in GDP growth in the CESEE countries, this ratio might have provided mixed signals on the very credit dynamics we wished to analyse. Credit growth was also used by Jakubik and Moinescu (2015) to identify sustainable growth of the supply of loans in Romania. A similar approach to calculating credit gaps with the use of loan growth was proposed by Mendoza and Terrones (2012), as well as by Kick et al. (2015).

The stock of credit was the basis for the calculation of the trend value of credit growth. First, we calculated natural logarithms of the stock of (gross) loans granted by the banking sector (aggregated from bank-level data) in a given country collected from BankScope. The data sample covered banking sectors in 20 CESEE countries in the 1995–2015 period. This was preceded with a verification of the stationarity of the series. Next, we applied a frequency-based filter method to extract the trend, that is, the Christiano-Fitzgerald (CF) filter. Such an approach is in line with the methodology established in the literature for measuring credit cycles, as reviewed and used by Samarina et al. (2017). Credit gaps were extracted using a full-length asymmetric band-pass CF filter, and the credit cycle length for the CESEE countries was assumed to be between 8 and 20 years (Borio et al. 2010).

The calculation of the credit gap basing on the credit-to-GDP data followed a similar approach in the literature. Using annual data for credit-to-GDP for the CESEE countries 1995–2016[4] on the country level, we applied the popular Hodrick-Prescott (HP) filter in EViews with lambda 1560, being equivalent to 400,000 for quarterly data as recommended by Basel Committee on Banking Supervision (BCBS 2010).

In summary, we calculated two credit cycle measures using:

- stock of loans with CF and HP filters, including separately for banks with different type of ownership;
- credit-to-GDP ratio with HP filter.

The development of credit cycles for the CESEEs, including for banks with different types of ownership (see Figs. 4.1 and 4.2), brings valuable insight into their credit activities. The high amplitude of loan cycles shows the significant cyclicality of bank credit in the CESEEs. This confirms the build-up of cyclical imbalances and the credit boom-bust cycles in CESEEs, with the HP-filtered gaps in the credit-to-GDP ratio showing the cyclical swings in a more timely manner. As concerns the credit cycles of banks with different types of ownership, we uncover only partial evidence about the higher procyclicality of foreign-owned banks compared to domestic banks.

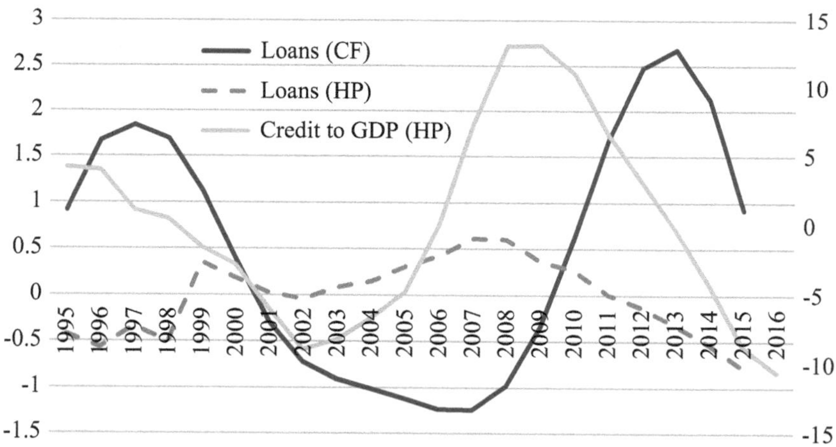

Fig. 4.1 Development of average credit gaps in the CESEEs for total banking sector. (Note: Loans (CF)—average credit gaps calculated using natural logarithms of the annual data for stock of (gross) loans with a full-length asymmetric band-pass CF filter with cycle length 8–20; LHS. Loans (HP)—average credit gaps calculated using natural logarithms of the annual data for stock of (gross) loans with an HP filter lambda 1600; LHS. Credit-to-GDP (HP)—average credit gaps calculated using annual data for credit-to-GDP ratios with an HP filter lambda 1560; RHS; Source: Own work)

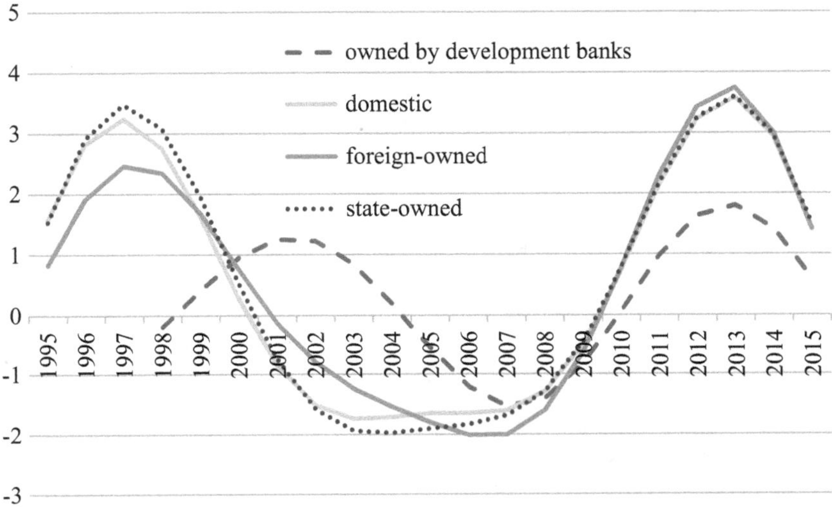

Fig. 4.2 Development of average credit gaps in the CESEEs for banks with different type of ownership (CF). (Note: Average credit gaps calculated using natural logarithms of the annual data for stock of (gross) loans with a full-length asymmetric band-pass CF filter with cycle length 8–20; Source: Own work)

The development of credit cycles suggests that before the GFC foreign-owned banks run at first somewhat less and then slightly more procyclical credit policy than domestic banks. However, the differences in the development of credit cycles for those two types of banks are not very high. Post-GFC, the cyclicality of credit provision is similar in both groups of banks. Additionally, we find that the credit cycles of state-owned banks follow similar patterns as for domestic banks, which is in line with Cull and Martínez-Pería (2013), who did not find evidence that government-owned banks in EE stepped up their lending compared to privately-owned banks. We also unveil mixed evidence for the credit cycles of banks owned by development banks, that is, their CF-filtered credit cycle points to lower procyclicality (even with some degree of countercyclicality compared to banks with other types of ownership). Yet, the results for cyclicality of lending by banks owned by developing banks have to be interpreted with caution due to the very small number of such banks included in the sample. Another caveat is that our sample comprises only 20 annual observations, which may be regarded as a relatively short period to capture the development of the whole financial cycle from the international perspective.

Altogether, while analysing bank credit growth and its procyclicality in the CESEEs, we find that it is predominantly driven by economic growth, thus confirming the link between the financial intermediation and economic conditions. The high amplitude of bank credit cycles underlines the significance of cyclicality of bank credit in the CESEEs. However, we argue that foreign-owned banks should not be treated as monoliths, as their impact on credit is heterogeneous and depends on various home and host country characteristics, as well as on traits of parent banks. Still, differences in the cyclicality of credit provided by domestic and foreign-owned banks are not very high, especially after the global financial crisis.

Notes

1. The list provided in De Haas et al. (2015). Almost all of them were rescued during the GFC with the use of public aid (so called bailout), except for DnB Nord, SEB and Swedbank.
2. This chapter develops on earlier work published by Kurowski and Smaga (2018) and Bongini et al. (2018).
3. According to the IMF (Dell'Ariccia et al. 2012) another potential drawback is that the aggregate measure of credit used in credit-to-GDP ratio captures only bank credit to the private sector and not the credit provided by non-bank financial institutions. However, as banking systems dominate in CESEEs, this is not a material issue in our case.
4. Data collected for credit-to-GDP ratio from World Bank (Domestic credit to private sector as % of GDP) for most CESEEs and from Federal Reserve Economic Data (Private Credit by Deposit Money Banks and Other Financial Institutions to GDP) for Estonia, Lithuania, Latvia, Slovakia, and Slovenia.

Bibliography

Aikman D, Haldane A, Nelson B (2015) Curbing the Credit Cycle. Econ J 125(585):1072–1109. doi:https://doi.org/10.1111/ecoj.12113

Alessi L, Detken C (2011) Quasi real time early warning indicators for costly asset price boom/bust cycles: A role for global liquidity. Eur J Polit Econ 27(3):520–533. https://doi.org/10.1016/j.ejpoleco.2011.01.003.

Allen F, Jackowicz K, Kowalewski O, Kozłowski Ł (2017) Bank lending, crises, and changing ownership structure in Central and Eastern European countries. J Corp Financ 42:494–515. https://doi.org/10.1016/j.jcorpfin.2015.05.001

Apostoaie CM, Percic S, Cocriş V, Chirleşan D (2014) Research on the Credit Cycle and Business Cycle with a Focus on Ten States from Central, Eastern, and Southeastern Europe. Emerg Mark Financ Tr 50(sup4):63–77. DOI: https://doi.org/10.2753/REE1540-496X5004S404

Athanasoglou PP, Daniilidis I, Delis MD (2014) Bank procyclicality and output: Issues and policies. J Econ Bus 72:58–83. DOI: https://doi.org/10.1016/j.jeconbus.2013.10.003

BCBS (2010) Guidance for national authorities operating the countercyclical capital buffer. BIS

Bertay A, Demirgüç-Kunt A, Huizinga H (2015) Bank ownership and credit over the business cycle: Is lending by state banks less procyclical? J Bank Financ 50(1):326–339. https://doi.org/10.1016/j.jbankfin.2014.03.012

Bongini P, Iwanicz-Drozdowska M, Smaga P, Witkowski B (2018) The Role of Credit Cycle in CESEE Countries: Exploring Non-standard Determinants of Economic Growth. Post-Communist Econ, in print

Bonin JP, Louie D (2017) Did foreign banks stay committed to emerging Europe during recent financial crises? J Comp Econ 45(4):793–808. https://doi.org/10.1016/j.jce.2016.08.003

Borio C (2014) The financial cycle and macroeconomics: What have we learnt? J Bank Financ 45(C):182–198. DOI: https://doi.org/10.1016/j.jbankfin.2013.07.031

Borio C, Drehmann M (2009) Assessing the risk of banking crises – revisited. Quarterly Review (March), Bank for International Settlements

Borio C, Drehmann M, Gambacorta L, Jiménez G, Trucharte C (2010) Countercyclical capital buffers: exploring options. BIS Working Paper, No. 317

Borio C, Drehmann M, Tsatsaronis K (2012) Characterising the financial cycle: don't lose sight of the medium term! BIS Working Papers, No. 380

Calderón, C., Fuentes, J. R. (2014). Have business cycles changed over the last two decades? An empirical investigation. J Dev Econ 109:98–123. DOI: https://doi.org/10.1016/j.jdeveco.2014.03.001

Claessens S, Kose MA, Terrones ME (2011) How do business and financial cycles interact? IMF Working Paper, No. 11/88

Claessens S, van Horen N (2012) Foreign Banks: Trends, Impact and Financial Stability. IMF Working Paper, No. 12/10

Costa Navajas M, Thegeya A (2013) Financial Soundness Indicators and Banking Crises. IMF Working Paper, No. 13/263

Cull R, Martínez-Pería M (2013) Bank ownership and lending patterns during the 2008–2009 financial crisis: evidence from Latin America and Eastern Europe. J Bank Financ 37(12):4861–4878. https://doi.org/10.1016/j.jbankfin.2013.08.017

De Haas R, Korniyenko Y, Pivovarsky A, Tsankova T (2015) Taming the herd? Foreign banks, the Vienna Initiative and crisis transmission. J Financ Intermed 24(3):325–355. https://doi.org/10.1016/j.jfi.2014.05.003

De Haas R, Naaborg I (2006) Foreign banks in transition countries: to whom do they lend and how are they financed? Financ Mark Instit Instrum 15(4):159–199. doi:https://doi.org/10.1111/j.1468-0416.2006.00116.x

De Haas R, Van Horen N (2013) Running for the exit? International bank lending during a financial crisis. Rev Financ Stud 26(1):244–285. https://doi.org/10.1093/rfs/hhs113

De Haas R, Van Lelyveld I (2006) Foreign banks and credit stability in Central and Eastern Europe. A panel data analysis. J Bank Financ 30(7):1927–1952. https://doi.org/10.1016/j.jbankfin.2005.07.007

De Haas R, van Lelyveld I (2014) Multinational banks and the global financial crisis: Weathering the perfect storm? Journal Money Credit Bank 46(1):333–364. https://doi.org/10.1111/jmcb.12094

Dekle R, Lee M (2015) Do foreign bank affiliates cut their lending more than the domestic banks in a financial crisis? J Int Money Financ 50:16–32. https://doi.org/10.1016/j.jimonfin.2014.08.00

Dell'Ariccia G, Igan D, Laeven L, Tong H, Bakker B, Vandenbussche J (2012) Policies for Macrofinancial Stability: How to Deal with Credit Booms. Staff Discussion Note, SDN/12/06, IMF

Ehlers T, McGuire P (2017) Foreign banks and credit conditions in EMEs. BIS Papers, No 91

Epstein RA (2014) When do foreign banks 'cut and run'? Evidence from west European bailouts and east European markets. Rev Int Polit Econ 21(4):847–877. https://doi.org/10.1080/09692290.2013.824913

ESRB (2014) Operationalising the countercyclical capital buffer: indicator selection, threshold identification and calibration options. ESRB Occasional Paper Series, No. 5

Festić M (2015) The Stability of the Credit Supply in the Globalized Banking Sector Environment: The Case of the EU New Member States-10. Prague Econ Pap 24(4): 386–398. https://doi.org/10.18267/j.pep.543

Fisher I (1933) The Debt Deflation Explanation of the Great Depression. Econometrica 1(4):337–357

Frey R, Kerl C (2015) Multinational banks in the crisis: Foreign affiliate lending as a mirror of funding pressure and competition on the internal capital market. J Bank Financ 50:52–68. https://doi.org/10.1016/j.jbankfin.2014.06.005

Galati G, Hindrayanto I, Koopman SJ, Marente V (2016) Measuring financial cycles in a model-based analysis: Empirical evidence for the United States and the euro area. Econ Lett 145(C):83–87. https://doi.org/10.1016/j.econlet.2016.05.034

Geršl A, Seidler J (2011) Excessive Credit Growth as an Indicator of Financial (In) Stability and its Use in Macroprudential Policy. CNB Financial Stability Report 2010/2011, Czech National Bank, p 112–122

Geršl A, Seidler J (2015) Countercyclical Capital Buffers and Credit-to-GDP Gaps: Simulation for Central, Eastern, and Southeastern Europe, Eastern Eur Econ 53(6):439–465. doi:https://doi.org/10.1080/00128775.2015.1102602

Giese J, Andersen H, Bush O, Castro C, Farag M, Kapadia S (2014a) The credit-to-GDP gap and complementary indicators for macroprudential policy:

Evidence from the UK. Int J Financ Econ 19(1):25–47. DOI: https://doi.org/10.1002/ijfe.1489

Giese J, Jahn N, Kakes J, Klaus B, Lang JH, Puzanova N, Welz, P (2014b) Operationalizing the Countercyclical Capital Buffer. ESRB Occasional Paper, No. 5

Hiebert P, Klaus B, Peltonen T, Schüler YS, Welz P (2014) Capturing the financial cycle in euro area countries. Financial Stability Review, European Central Bank, November

Houston J, James C (1998) Do bank internal capital markets promote lending? J Bank Financ 22(6–8):899–918

Houston J, James C, Marcus D (1997) Capital market frictions and the role of internal capital markets in banking. J Finan Econ 46(2):135–164. https://doi.org/10.1016/S0304-405X(97)81511-5

Ivashina V, Scharfstein D (2010) Bank lending during the financial crisis of 2008. J Finan Econ 97(3):319–338. https://doi.org/10.1016/j.jfineco.2009.12.001

Iwanicz-Drozdowska M, Smaga P, Witkowski B (2016) Bank restructuring in the EU. Which way to go? J Policy Model 38(3):572–586. https://doi.org/10.1016/j.jpolmod.2016.03.001

Iwanicz-Drozdowska M, Witkowski B (2016) Credit growth in Central, Eastern, and South-Eastern Europe: The case of foreign bank subsidiaries. Int Rev Finan Anal 43:146–158. https://doi.org/10.1016/j.irfa.2015.11.010

Jakubik P, Moinescu B (2015) Assessing optimal credit growth for an emerging banking system. Econ Syst 39(4):577–591. https://doi.org/10.1016/j.ecosys.2015.01.004

Jeon B, Olivero M, Wu J (2013) Multinational banking and the international transmission of financial shocks: Evidence from foreign bank subsidiaries. J Bank Financ 37(3):952–972. https://doi.org/10.1016/j.jbankfin.2012.10.020

Kick T, Pausch T, Ruprecht B (2015) The winner's curse: Evidence on the danger of aggressive credit growth in banking. Deutsche Bundesbank Discussion Papers, No. 32/2015

Kollintzas T, Konstantakopoulou I, Tsionas E (2011) Stylized facts of money and credit over the business cycles. Applied Financial Economics 21(23):1735–1755. DOI: https://doi.org/10.1080/09603107.2011.583215

Kurowski Ł, Smaga P (2018) Monetary Policy and Cyclical Systemic Risk – Friends or Foes? Prague Econ Pap, 27(5):522–540. https://doi.org/10.18267/j.pep.667

Laeven L, Valencia F (2008) Systemic banking crises: A new database, IMF Working Paper, No. 08/224

Mendoza EG, Terrones ME (2012) An anatomy of credit booms and their demise. NBER Working Paper, No. 18379

Micco A, Panizza U (2004) Bank ownership and lending behaviour. IDB Working Paper, No. 431

Minsky H (1978) The Financial Instability Hypothesis: A restatement. Thames Papers on Political Economy

Olszak M, Pipień M (2016) Cross Country Linkages as Determinants of Procyclicality of Loan Loss Provisions. Eur J Financ 22(11):965–984. DOI: https://doi.org/10.1080/1351847X.2014.983138

Peek J, Rosengren E (1997) The International Transmission of Financial Shocks: The Case of Japan. Am Econ Rev 87(4):495–505

Peek J, Rosengren E (2000) Collateral Damage: Effects of the Japanese Bank Crisis on Real Activity in the United States. Am Econ Rev 90(1):30–45. DOI: https://doi.org/10.1257/aer.90.1.30

Samarina A, Zhang L, Bezemer D (2017) Credit Cycle Coherence in the Eurozone: Was There a Euro Effect? J Int Money Financ 77:77–98. doi: https://doi.org/10.1016/j.jimonfin.2017.07.002.

Schumpeter J (1939) Business Cycles: A theoretical, historical and statistical analysis of the Capitalist process

Smaga P (2014) The Concept of Systemic Risk. Systemic Risk Centre Special Paper No 5, The London School of Economics and Political Science

Stremmel H (2015) Capturing the financial cycle in Europe. ECB Working Paper, No. 1811

Temesvary J, Banai A (2017) The drivers of foreign bank lending in Central and Eastern Europe: The roles of parent, subsidiary and host market traits. J Int Money Financ 79:157–173. https://doi.org/10.1016/j.jimonfin.2017.08.005

Wu J, Luca AC, Jeon B (2011) Foreign Bank Penetration and the Lending Channel in Emerging Economies: Evidence from Bank-Level Panel Data. J Int Money Financ 30(6):1128–1156. https://doi.org/10.1016/j.jimonfin.2011.05.011

CHAPTER 5

Impact of Foreign-Owned Banks on Financial Stability

Małgorzata Iwanicz-Drozdowska, Paweł Smaga, and Bartosz Witkowski

5.1 Global Financial Crisis in the Context of CESEE

5.1.1 *"State of Play" in CESEE Before the Crisis*

The banking sector dominates in financial systems in the CESEEs, while insurance and stock market sectors remain underdeveloped, with a limited potential impact on the stability of the whole system. The stock and debt markets' capitalization in the CESEEs is much lower than in advanced economies, and companies are still predominantly financed by internal sources (equity and retained profits) or bank loans with relatively low demand for funding from capital markets. Thus, the banking sector (as well as individual banks) and bank lending activity are the most likely primary sources of emerging risks, with a potentially systemic impact on the economy in the CESEEs and constitute the focus of this analysis. The banking sectors in the CESEEs had undergone a major restructuring process during the transition in the 1990s, from centrally planned economy to market economies. This was done to build efficient and stable banking systems as prerequisites for the economic growth and faster convergence. Moreover, a healthy banking

M. Iwanicz-Drozdowska et al.,
Foreign-Owned Banks, Studies in Economic Transition,
https://doi.org/10.1007/978-3-030-01111-6_5

sector ensures an efficient transmission of monetary policy impulses to the real economy, thus contributing to the effectiveness of central banks' policies. Yet, the level and depth of the development of banking sectors in the CESEEs are still relatively nascent as compared to the banking systems of Western Europe. Nevertheless, banking systems in both "Western" and "Eastern" parts of Europe are linked through financial integration into the global financial system. The unique feature of CESEE banking sectors is the high level of foreign bank penetration from advanced, mostly European, countries. On one hand, this was beneficial for boosting the economic growth and for the development of financial systems in the CESEEs before the GFC (see Fig. 5.1), but at the same time, left the CESEEs exposed to external shocks and contagion from the parent banks during the GFC.

The CESEEs are at a similar stage of financial system development and share a number of common characteristics as small open economies. The size of the financial system can be measured with assets of monetary financial institutions to GDP. On average, the pre-crisis period saw a significant increase in the size of financial systems in the CESEEs, which doubled, from around 50% of GDP at the beginning of the twenty-first century to nearly 100% of GDP in 2007–2008 (see Figs. 5.2 and 5.3). The financial system

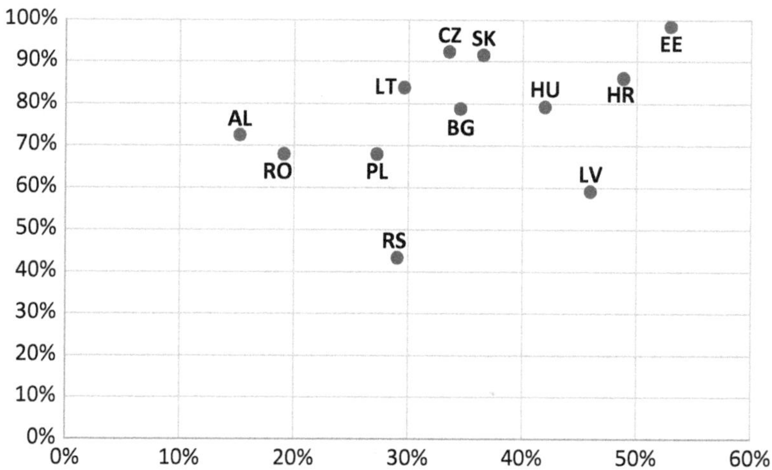

Fig. 5.1 Development of banking systems and the share of foreign-owned banks pre-GFC in selected CESEEs. (Note: Average credit-to-GDP ratio (2000–2008)—horizontal; average market share of foreign-owned banks to total assets (2000–2008)—vertical; Source: Own work based on data from World Bank, Federal Reserve Economic Data, Helgi Library, and national central banks)

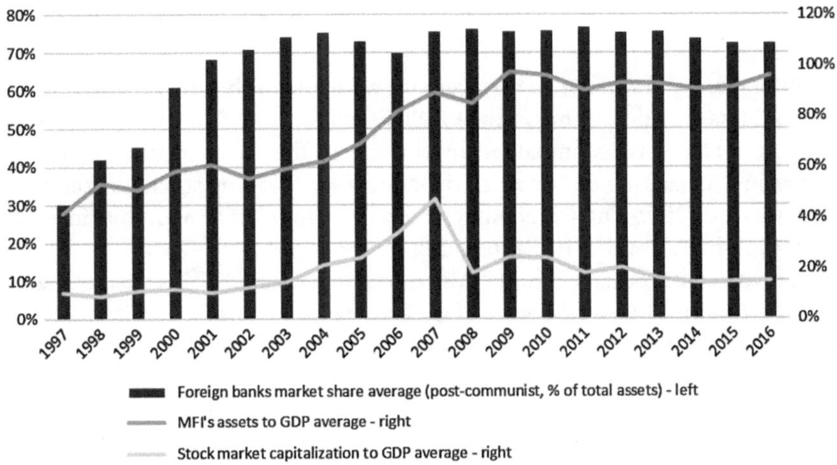

Fig. 5.2 Assets of Monetary Financial Institutions, stock market capitalization, and the role of foreign-owned banks (1997–2016). (Note: Arithmetic averages in both groups of countries. Based on data from ECB, World Bank, Helgi Library, RBI Research, and national central banks)

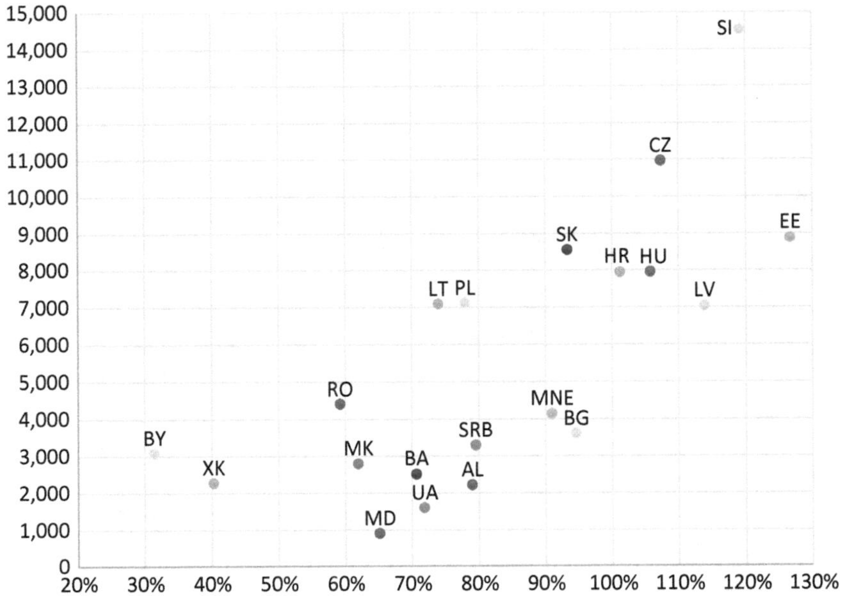

Fig. 5.3 MFI's assets to GDP and GDP per capita (in EUR) in the CESEE countries. (Note: Arithmetic averages for each country for the period of 1995–2016 of countries. Based on data from the ECB and World Bank)

growth rates (in nominal terms) were very volatile in the pre-GFC CESEEs. A rapid financial deepening in the CESEEs led to a build-up of high financial leverage. This was accompanied by the rise in the share of foreign-owned banks in the banking sector and a dynamic growth of the stock market capitalization to GDP. The wider entry of foreign banks led to a gradual increase in competition in the CESEE banking sectors.

The capital adequacy ratio (CAR) of banks in the CESEEs was strengthening from mid-90s to the start of the twenty-first century, and it ever since started to decrease until the GFC (see Fig. 5.4). Although the CARs were still above the regulatory minimum, this left the CESEE banks with insufficient resilience to shocks, as experienced during the GFC. At the same time profitability in the CESEEs, although changeable, was relatively higher than in Western banking sectors. Concurrently, on average, both the deposits to credits ratio and the liquidity ratio were significantly decreasing from the turn of the twenty-first century until the GFC in the CESEEs (see Fig. 5.5), hitting the bottom at below 100% and 0.3 respectively at the onset of the GFC. Such developments left banks in the CESEE exposed to risks of liquidity fluctuations and limited potential for credit supply. This in

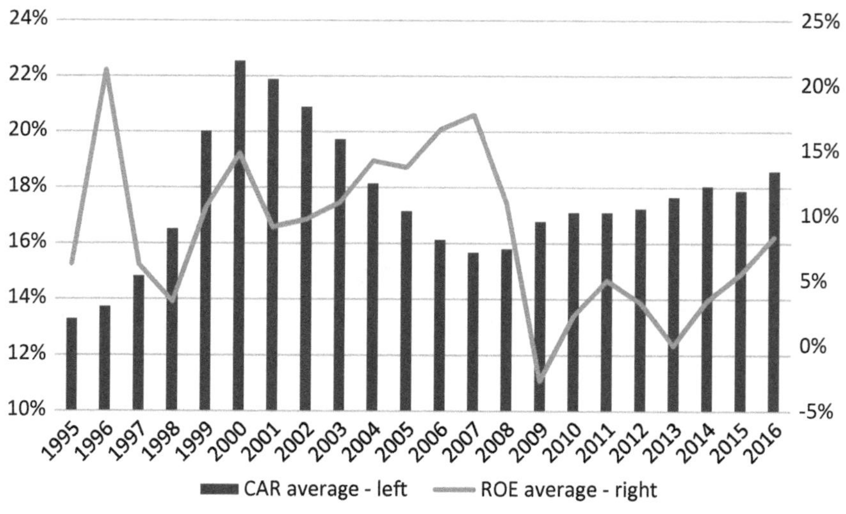

Fig. 5.4 Profitability and capital adequacy during the 1995–2016 period in CESEEs. (Note: Arithmetic averages; Source: Own work based on data from ECB, World Bank, IMF, and national central banks)

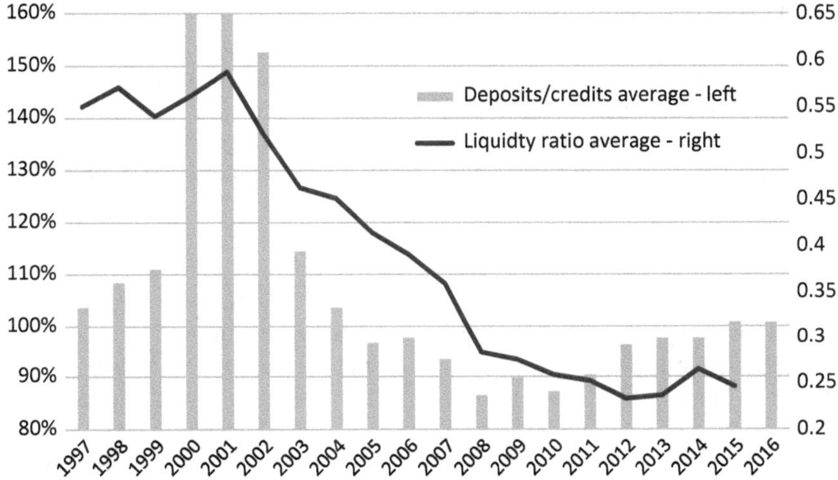

Fig. 5.5 Liquidity ratios and deposits/credits ratio during the 1997–2016 period. (Note: Arithmetic averages; liquidity ratio equals liquid assets to deposits and short-term funding; D/C ratio is 455% for 2000 and 323% for 2001; Source: Own work based on data from ECB and World Bank)

sum exposed banks in CESEE to shocks from abroad and spillovers from international financial markets.

Pre-GFC the CESEEs experienced a robust credit boom, which was partly due to the focus of the CESEE banks on the traditional business model of credit-deposit activities. Gardó and Martin (2010), by looking at banking sector vulnerabilities, note that the rising loan-to-deposit ratio signalled that the deposit growth could not keep up with the credit growth. Thus, banks had to increasingly rely on other refinancing sources, mainly foreign funding provided by parent banks. The growth of deposits was insufficient to fund the booming credit growth. The credit boom and lower deposits to credits ratios imparted higher reliance of subsidiaries in CESEE on relatively inexpensive foreign funding channelled through parent banks and intragroup liquidity pools (Barba Navaretti et al. 2010). This translated into a rising ratio of foreign liabilities over foreign assets in many CESEEs. Non-performing loan ratio decreased also over time, following transition-related banking reforms and the recent expansion of bank balance sheets due to strong credit growth. The latter was, to a large extent, driven by mortgage lending growth, which in turn was related to rapid growth in house prices resulting in overvaluation of house prices in some CESEE countries. Lower provisioning requirements, booming credit growth, rising bank efficiency, and better bank governance also led to increased bank profitability until 2008. Moreover, the liberalization of access to financial systems in CESEE as part of transformation had also opened a window for excessive capital flows. Financial openness ultimately increased their vulnerability to external shocks.

5.1.2 *The Perils of FX Lending*

The dominant presence of foreign-owned banks in the region's financial systems also indicates a high level of financial euroization.[1] Foreign-owned banks in the CESEEs were granting FX loans often at lower interest rates than domestic borrowing costs, as they acquired funding from parent banks. There are many drivers of FX loans in the CESEEs (see Fig. 5.6). The demand for FX loans in CESEEs was primarily driven by the interest rate differentials (lower interest on credit in foreign than in the national

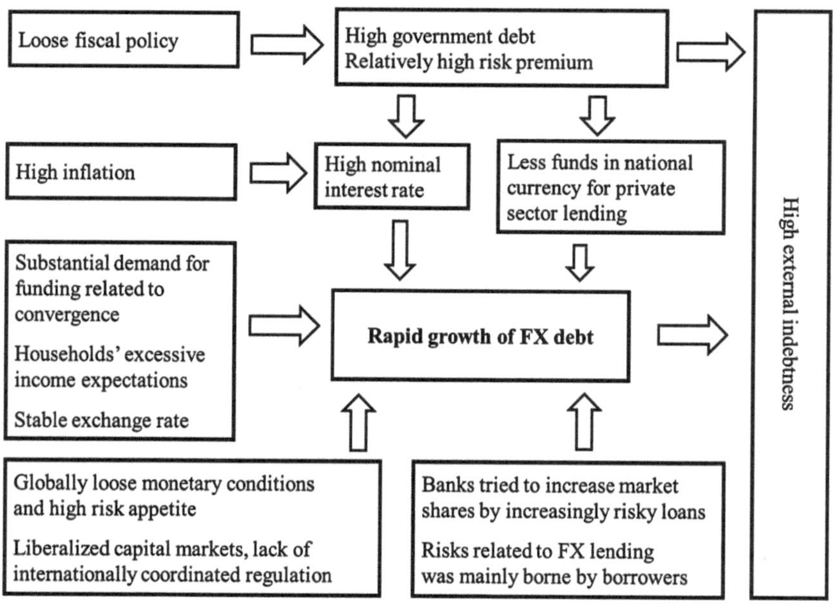

Fig. 5.6 Demand- and supply-side drivers of FX lending in the CESEEs. (Source: Adapted from Simor 2011)

currency) and by households' lack of adequate assessment of risks of exchange rate fluctuations. Lax global conditions and the drive to increase market share by banks drove the supply of FX loans. This fuelled the fast build-up of high stock of foreign-currency-denominated debt in the private sector and price bubbles on real estate markets. Although such a business practice was profitable on the micro level, it led to the accumulation of severe imbalances on a systemic scale.

The high share of FX loans left banks in CESEE exposed to the risk of maturity mismatch and the currency risk. The CESEEs most exposed to FX loans were, for example, LV, RS, HR, LT, AL, RO, BG, HU, and PL. According to Dell'Ariccia et al. (2012), Swiss franc borrowing, with its very low interest rates, became increasingly popular in some countries with floating exchange rates (Croatia, Hungary, Poland, and, to a lesser extent, Romania), while euro-denominated loans became more prevalent in countries with a currency pegged to the euro. Consequently, in the case of domestic currency depreciation, the debt-servicing cost for the debt expressed in the domestic currency is increased for local borrowers, as most of FX borrowing was unhedged. Unlike corporations, which might have income in a foreign currency from exports, households were usually not hedged against foreign exchange risk. Subsidiaries also faced the concentration risk (household mortgage loans). The need to maintain adequate matching in the form of FX liabilities caused liquidity and funding risks as borrowing short-term on the wholesale market and lending to borrowers long-term increased banks' exposure to market liquidity. Furthermore, with FX mismatches, volatility of exchange rates amplifies the volatility of capital adequacy. Josifidis et al. (2014) argue that the CEE countries with high currency mismatch ratios suffer from both fear of floating and fear of losing international reserves. The sharp depreciations of currencies in the CESEEs in the GFC (see Fig. 5.7) compounded with the worsening of the financial situation of households increased the risk of FX loans becoming a threat to the CESEEs' both financial and macroeconomic stability.

5.1.3 Unsustainable Credit Cycles in CESEEs: From Boom to Bust

The rapid credit expansion was a double-edge sword for the CESEEs—on the one hand, it was the key driver of their economic growth, but also the main factor contributing to the build-up of vulnerabilities. Internal reasons for the increased inflow of capital to the CESEEs (pull factors) include not only better macroeconomic perspectives, structural reforms and rapid

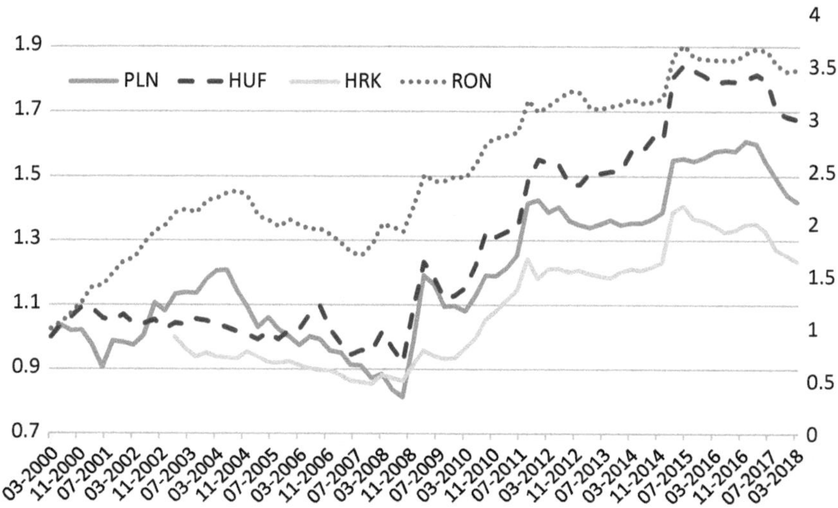

Fig. 5.7 Exchange rates of selected currencies in CESEEs. (Note: 2000 Q1 = 100; LHS: CHF/PLN, CHF/HUF, CHF/HRK; RHS: CHF/RON; Source: Own calculations using data from Bloomberg)

financial deepening, relatively higher interest rates, exchange rate and inflation stabilization, but also overall banking system (regulatory and supervisory) reforms, and privatization of the financial sector, as well as initial comparatively low level of household indebtedness. As concerns external (push) factors, relatively lower yield opportunities in Western countries and optimistic perception associated with advances with integration of the region with the EU fuelled precipitation of foreign capital inflow to CESEEs.

Already in 2005, Hilbers et al. (2005) elaborated that rapid financial (credit) deepening, from both macroeconomic and microeconomic perspectives, entailed two interrelated risks. First, in a situation of continued macro instability (inflation and/or external imbalances), financial stability would come under pressure and second, financial instability (a weak and vulnerable financial system) would contribute to macroeconomic imbalances. From the post-GFC perspective, it is clear that addressing these risks generally called for a comprehensive policy response, supplementing monetary and fiscal policies with prudential and supervisory measures.

A significant part of the credit boom in the CESEEs has been funded from abroad in the form of large capital inflows. This fostered strong credit growth in the pre-GFC period, which was in general seen as a positive development, as the CESEEs started from a relatively lower degree of financial deepening. The excessive credit expansion was mainly fuelled by growth of domestic banking systems along with increasing presence of foreign-owned banks. The large inflows of foreign capital fuelled borrowing by both firms and households, concurrently intensifying the currency mismatch in the CESEE banks, increasing their vulnerability to external shocks. Additionally, along with a gradually growing share of foreign investors in CESEE, foreign-owned banks were increasing their lending activities in profitable CESEE markets; which resulted in downwards pressure on lending rates and further stimulated credit demand, thus fuelling the credit boom. This was evidenced by excessive credit growth in many CESEEs, fuelled among others by foreign capital inflows and loans denominated in foreign currencies, thus the credit boom was accompanied with equally strong widening deficits of current account balance to GDP and dramatically decreasing net savings. As a result, the ratio of external debt to GDP in most CESEEs (e.g. Montenegro, Bulgaria, Croatia, and Slovenia) went up and overexposed them to the currency risk and an increase in the cost of debt refinancing.

Hilbers et al. (2005) further elaborate on the key features of credit booms in the CESEEs:

- Credit booms are accompanied by a sharp deterioration in the trade balance and current account balance.
- Credit booms coincide with a decline in inflation in most of the countries. Inflation at the start of the credit boom is much higher in the crisis countries and declines sharply during the credit boom episode.
- In the non-crisis countries, growth accelerates prior to the start of the credit boom episode and the cyclical upturn continues until the peak. Although growth decelerates in the end phase, unlike in the case of the crisis countries, a sharp downturn is not experienced.
- In most CEE countries, the fiscal position has been improving during the course of the credit expansion period, mainly due to cyclical factors.
- The initial lending-deposit rate spreads are much wider in the crisis countries and the CEE countries. The spreads have contracted in the CEE countries during the build-up phase.
- For most of the CESEEs, loans are also being financed increasingly with liabilities other than local deposits (increase in net foreign assets[2]).

The credit booms (see Table 5.1) could be identified in almost all the CESEEs in the years directly preceding the GFC and for some also following the EU accession. Although there is no universal methodology for identifying credit booms, usually it is done by analysing the credit growth and development of credit-to-GDP ratio. The most difficult issue is setting the threshold values that allow differentiating credit growth in line with fundamentals (equilibrium level) from unsustainable accumulation of cyclical systemic risks (Geršl and Seidler 2015). The thresholds used for the estimations in Table 5.1 were inspired by expert guidance of the IMF (Dell'Ariccia et al. 2012).

Table 5.1 Credit booms in CESEEs in the twenty-first century

Country	*Share of foreign-owned banks in banking sector assets (avg. 1995–2007)*	*Credit-to-GDP gap (increasing and > 0)*[a]	*Credit-to-GDP gap (> 2 STD)*[b]	*Credit-to-GDP growth rate (> 20 pp. y/y)*
Albania	64%	2006–2008	2007–2011	2004–2007
Bulgaria	94%	2007–2008		2002–2004 and 2007
Bosnia and Herzegovina	69%	2007–2008		
Czech Republic	85%	2008–2013		
Estonia	96%	2006–2009	2008–2010	2006
Croatia	66%	2005–2009	2006–2011	
Hungary	74%	2005–2008	2007–2011	
Lithuania	90%	2005–2008	2007–2010	2003–2006
Latvia	63%	2005–2008	2006–2011	2001–2006
Moldova	67%	2006–2007	2007–2009	2007
Macedonia	42%	2007–2008	2008–2010	2006–2008
Montenegro	85%	2007–2008	2007–2009	2003–2007
Poland	57%	2007–2008	2008–2011	2008
Romania	53%	2006–2009	2007–2011	2005–2007
Russia	n/a	2007–2009	2009	2009
Serbia	35%	2008–2010		2007
Slovakia	75%			
Slovenia	35%	2006–2010	2009–2011	
Ukraine	33%	2007–2008	2008–2009	2005–2008

Note: [a]Estimated for annual credit-to-GDP data for the CESEE countries 1995–2016 using HP filter in EViews with lambda 1560 (equivalent to 400,000 for quarterly data as recommended by BCBS (2010) and Drehmann et al. (2010)). Data collected for credit-to-GDP from World Bank (Domestic credit to private sector as % of GDP) and Federal Reserve Economic Data (Private Credit by Deposit Money Banks and Other Financial Institutions to GDP) for Estonia, Lithuania, Latvia, Russia, Slovakia, and Slovenia

[b]Estimated as in [a]and STD calculated only of positive gaps

Source: Own work

Among most CESEEs, the concerns that the credit growth was becoming unsustainable were downplayed on the notion of rapid income convergence (natural catching-up), lack of political popularity of any restrictive policies, belief in the robustness of regulatory frameworks or the belief that parent banks will guarantee safety and soundness of their subsidiaries, thus the cyclical systemic risks were underestimated. Further, as banking groups were increasingly headed from the headquarters in home countries, subsidiaries in host CESEEs were less affected by moral suasion by the host supervisors in their strategic decisions. Also, monetary policy pre-GFC has reacted rather weakly to the inflating positive output gaps in the CESEEs, keeping interest rates in general lower than the rates implied by the Taylor rules. The ECB (2010) underlines that owing to strong capital inflows and credit growththe latter fuelled by very low and in some cases even negative real interest rates—several CEE countries experienced strong rises in asset prices, in particular house prices. Yet, the ECB argues that in countries pursuing inflation targeting strategies, namely the Czech Republic, Hungary, Poland and Romania, the build-up of imbalances and the dependence on foreign financing was generally lower in the pre-crisis period, thereby limiting the susceptibility of the economies to a drying-up of external financing and increasing their ability to implement cuts in policy rates in reaction to the GFC. Moreover, just prior to the GFC, inflation in many CESEEs was going up, thus putting pressure on restrictive monetary policy actions. Banks in a booming environment were accumulating bigger risks and underestimated the borrowers' creditworthiness, thus raising their vulnerability to credit risk in a cyclical downturn.

5.1.4 Macrofinancial Impact of the Global Financial Crisis

The banking sector in the CESEEs were not directly exposed to the subprime market and "toxic" assets, as their banks have remained small, followed a traditional model of banking intermediation, with limited interconnectedness resulting from negligible exposure to financial instruments and derivatives like asset-backed securities or collateralized debt obligations. Gardo and Martin (2010) note that the CESEE financial sectors exhibited a low degree of sophistication: market penetration by complex financial products was low and the number of specialized financial intermediaries was small. Further, capitalizing on the profitable and booming local lending business in unsaturated markets seemed more promising for the CESEE banks than engaging in foreign structured products, for which the demand was low or non-existent. Moreover, the financial system exposures in the CESEEs are much more transparent with limited off-balance sheet claims, as compared with the Western countries. Thus the systemic risks pre-GFC in CESEE were primarily cyclical (credit booms) and not structural.

The collapse of Lehman Brothers in mid-September 2008 triggered the spread of the global risk aversion and capital inflows to the CESEEs came to a sudden stop. The CESEEs were particularly vulnerable to the financial contagion channel, as majority of them had accumulated large and sustained external (current account) deficits, which made them dependent on capital inflows to cover those deficits (see Fig. 5.8). The composition of the net capital inflows in the CESEEs shows that a significant part was composed of volatile private financial flows (stemming from the expansion of foreign-owned banks due to cross-border transactions in the CESEEs) targeted at the banking sector and real estate markets, with meagre greenfield FDI that would have been more stable during the GFC. Fortunately, most foreign-owned banks remained committed in the region and continued supporting their subsidiaries. According to Berglöf et al. (2009), the capital outflows were more limited in countries with a higher penetration of foreign-owned banks.

The initial and main trigger was shock (in the form of lower and more costly external financing) that hit the CESEEs in late 2008 and stemmed

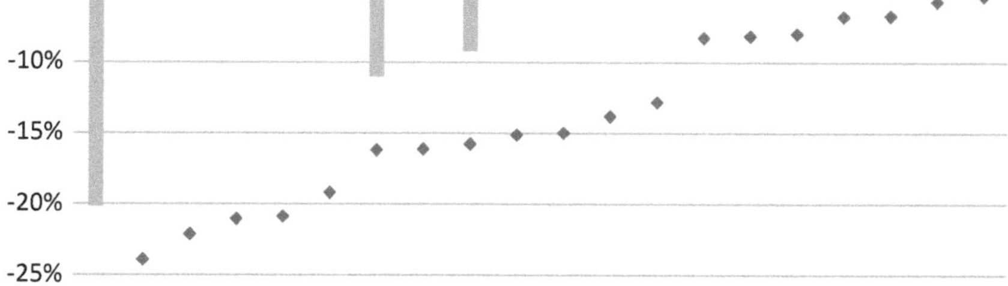

Fig. 5.8 Current account deficits in % of GDP in CESEEs. (Note: Bars—data for 2017; dots—pre-GFC minimum (−50% for ME); Source: Own calculations using World Economic Outlook data from IMF DataMapper)

from financial sectors of advanced, mainly Western, European countries. Additionally, the CESEEs experienced the reversal of the strong capital inflows that occurred during the credit boom, loss of external financing, tightened domestic credit conditions, and pressures on exchange rates, which in sum lead to the GDP decline. The direct macroeconomic impact of the GFC varied across the CESEE countries (see Table 5.2), as—to a large extent—it mirrored the degree of financial imbalances which had been accumulated during the credit boom (Llaudes et al. 2010), but also the degree of trade links, as the fall in foreign demand for the CESEEs' exports was one of the main reasons for the subsequent output drop via the trade channel. In general, the higher the external debt was in the CESEEs, the deeper the recession was.

However, the recessions in the CESEEs were overall relatively short-lasting. In the years directly after the GFC, GDP began to recover, as the adjustment process started in CESEE earlier than in the Western countries. Among the CESEEs, the Baltic States (Estonia, Latvia, and Lithuania) reported the highest economic growth rates before the GFC and consequently, faced very large (peak-to-trough) output contractions during the

Table 5.2 GDP growth rates (current prices, y/y) in CESEEs around the GFC

Country/Year	*2006 (%)*	*2007 (%)*	*2008 (%)*	*2009 (%)*	*2010 (%)*	*2011 (%)*
Albania	5.0	5.9	7.5	3.4	3.7	2.5
Bosnia and Herzegovina	6.2	6.8	5.4	−2.9	0.7	1.0
Bulgaria	6.5	6.9	5.8	−5.0	0.7	2.0
Croatia	4.8	5.2	2.1	−7.4	−1.7	−0.3
Czech Republic	6.9	5.5	2.7	−4.8	2.3	2.0
Estonia	9.5	10.4	7.9	−5.3	−14.7	2.5
Hungary	4.0	0.5	0.9	−6.6	0.8	1.8
Latvia	11.6	9.8	−3.2	−14.2	−2.9	5.0
Lithuania	7.4	11.1	2.6	−14.8	1.6	6.1
Moldova	4.8	3.1	7.8	−6.0	7.1	6.4
Montenegro	8.6	10.7	6.9	−5.7	2.5	3.2
Poland	6.2	7.2	3.9	2.6	3.7	4.8
Republic of Macedonia	5.1	6.5	5.5	−0.4	3.4	2.3
Romania	8.7	6.3	7.9	−6.8	−0.9	2.3
Russia	8.2	8.5	5.2	−7.8	4.5	4.3
Serbia	4.9	5.9	5.4	−3.1	0.6	1.4
Slovakia	8.3	10.7	5.4	−5.3	4.8	2.7
Slovenia	5.7	6.9	3.3	−7.8	1.2	0.6
Ukraine	7.3	7.9	2.3	−14.8	4.2	5.2

Source: World Bank

GFC (approx. 15–20%), with the average in the CESEEs being lower (5–10%). As the ECB (2010) points out, the countries that had grown particularly strong in the years before the crisis, namely Bulgaria, the Baltic States and Romania, subsequently saw the largest declines in output. On the other hand, countries like Poland, which entered the crisis with better fundamentals, were able to respond with more counter-cyclical policies, thus Poland experienced only slower, but still positive rate of growth. In general, the recession was steeper in the CESEEs with fixed exchange rate regimes than in those with floating exchange rates. Further, in general, the boom-bust cycles were costly more in terms of growth volatility rather than in terms of the average growth rate.

During market turmoil, banks in CESEE faced an unexpected deficit and increase in cost of access to liquidity from parent companies, which imparted their ability to extend credit during the GFC. Vujić (2015) provides evidence of the importance of group funding to financing the asset growth of the subsidiaries of foreign-owned banks in CESEE. The intergroup liquidity became limited when parent banks were less eager to support their subsidiaries in host CESEEs, for example, due to more stringent funding conditions in home countries and worsening of financial condition of the parent banks. Thus, increased solvency and liquidity risks in the parent banks were transferred to subsidiaries in CESEE host markets. Due to the importance of foreign-owned banks, this led to systemic liquidity problems in the CESEE banking systems, which had relatively low liquidity buffers directly prior to the GFC. Barjaktarović et al. (2013) note that the signs of the GFC in the CEE countries were present in the form of lower liquidity, higher funding costs, withdrawal of savings of private individuals, gradual stopping of bank lending to corporates and individuals, as well as an increase in the costs of foreign financing, a stronger pressure on the exchange rate, and an increase of the credit risk. In many cases, runs on bank deposits endangered the financial stability and aggravated tight domestic credit conditions caused mainly by drying-up of foreign savings.

Financial stability in the CESEEs was impaired by negative spillovers from abroad. The CESEEs were also hit by indirect contagion from financial markets, when the loss of confidence by investors led to local currency depreciation and impaired growth via reduced consumption and investment activity. The results of study by Josifidis et al. (2014) show that external financial shocks exerted a negative influence on domestic macroeconomic conditions in ten European emerging economies, as growing international financial integration increased their vulnerability to such shocks. The stock market contagion is confirmed by, for example, Egert and Kočenda (2007), who found short-term spillover effects in terms of both returns and volatility among the CESEE markets and from the Western markets to the CEE markets. Significant co-movements and international interdependencies between financial markets in the CESEE countries and advanced markets are also evidenced by Caporale and Spanolo (2011), Bubák et al. (2011), Barunik and Vacha (2013), Horvath and Petrovski (2013). The economic spillovers from the euro area to the CESEE region are additionally confirmed by Backé et al. (2013), due to significant intensification of interlinkages between the CESEE region and the euro area. They find that material spillovers transmitted via the trade channel and via the financial channel to CESEE. Also, Karkowska (2014) provides evidence for the liquidity contagion to subsidiaries market from the parent bank model, measured with credit default swap (CDS) spreads.

In the CESEEs, the financial market turmoil erupted, risk spreads widened, stock prices experienced severe declines, and local currencies faced depreciation pressures. Also, parent banks had difficulties in raising capital from market sources in their home countries (higher costs of market funding in crisis-affected home countries). In addition, the reduced possibility for fiscal stimulus constrained the possibilities of recapitalization, all of which contributed to deleveraging of foreign-owned banks and their reduced exposure in the CESEEs during the GFC. Although rational from the perspective of parent banks, it was done at the expense of stability of host banking sectors in CESEE. Banks in the CESEEs were forced to restrict credit availability and accumulate liquidity. As the ECB (2010) argues, following the tightening of financing conditions, including the rise in the costs of financing and significant deterioration in the economic outlook, the credit growth plummeted in particular in those countries which before the crisis had relied heavily on foreign capital to finance credit booms (i.e. Romania, the Baltics).

The deleveraging might proceed in general through capital increase, reduction of risk exposure, or shedding assets. While the first option is preferred from the perspective of systemic stability, it might be unfeasible and too costly in the times of crisis. Sale of assets of subsidiaries might induce changes in ownership but at the same time risks the reduction of credit activity in host countries and fire sale effects, leading to contagion between parent banks and subsidiaries (Tressel 2010). The retrenchment of lending by foreign-owned banks was driven by the need to support lending in home countries. Yet, empirical analyses point to the overall, rather limited effects of deleveraging. According to Raiffeisen Research (2014, 2017), since the GFC, overall cross-border banking exposures on a global level and in the CESEEs have been on a downtrend. The most deleveraging and de-risking at the Western European banks was achieved through substantial cuts to the intra-euro area and global exposures, while the reduction of cross-border exposures in the CESEEs turned out to be more modest than initially expected and not disorderly (except for Russia and Ukraine for geopolitical reasons), yet heterogeneous among the CESEE countries. The pace of deleveraging was diminished by, for example, the significance of presence and depth of regional ownership ties of the Western banks in CESEE, as well as the CESEEs still maintaining a substantial growth and earnings potential.

As the Roaf et al. (2014) notices, although the deleveraging process was concentrated on host countries which had seen the strongest inflows during the credit boom (including the Baltics, Bulgaria, Hungary and Slovenia), there were only limited divestments in transition countries, and foreign-owned banks continued to dominate the landscape. The retrenchment of foreign-owned banks in the CESEEs was driven by several factors, that is, strategic group decisions, the need to improve the parent bank's own equity and a form of downsizing, being one of many conditions for the parent banks to receive state aid during the GFC (Iwanicz-Drozdowska eds. 2016). Still, in case of (uncontrolled) default of a subsidiary with a high market share in a CESEE, with no adequate, cross-country resolution frameworks and burden-sharing arrangements, the consequences would have potentially been much worse. The absence of such agreements between home and host countries further exacerbated the risk of bank runs. Fortunately, the process of retrenchment of foreign-owned banks proved to be less damaging to the CESEEs' stability than originally anticipated. This was partially due to relatively strong financial integration/expansion of parent banks' activities into the CESEEs' banking systems, that is, second home market hypothesis (Epstein 2013) and effectiveness of the Vienna Initiative activities.

The credit boom in the CESEEs was followed by bust. The boom in the form of a strong domestic demand accelerated the GDP growth and large current account deficits, as well as mounting indebtedness, general overheating, rapid asset price increases and oversized non-tradable sectors. In general, the eruption of the GFC caused an episode of heightened uncertainty, which reduced lending volumes and credit activity in fear of not transparent enough exposures of banks to toxic debts. This sudden stop curtailed the inflow of credit to the CESEEs, to a large extent basing on external factors, and not macroeconomic fundamentals of a country. Nevertheless, this sudden stop was mitigated by information advantage at the disposal of the parent banks with regard to the solvency of their subsidiaries, as compared to external creditors. Limited access to new loans for business purposes and inability to roll over existing ones added to the economic downturn in the CESEEs. Additionally, decreases in housing prices occurred, especially in the Baltics, which in turn lowered collateral valuation of mortgaged flats and reduced consumption through wealth effect. There was a vicious circle between worsening of economic activity and deteriorating asset quality in the banking system.

After the GFC, starting from 2010, the CESEEs were not directly hit by the sovereign debt crisis in the in the euro area periphery countries, as CDS spreads and exports to euro area only initially remained stable. The CESEEs became vulnerable to the financial market contagion in 2011 and to the confidence crisis, when parent banks faced deepening of the sovereign debt crisis and consequently, also CDS spreads of banks in CESEE began to increase, while banks in CESEE suffered rating downgrades, usually as a result of declining ratings of their parent banks. This renewed the pressure on exchange rates and funding positions of banks in CESEE weighted heavily on the credit growth and renewed withdrawal of foreign-owned banks. Fortunately, the negative spillovers to the CESEEs started to recede owing to the successful crisis management measures by the ECB and ESM financial support to troubled euro area countries in the following years.

As a result, after the GFC, the size of the CESEEs' financial systems levelled-off and slightly declined (down below 100%), as did the share of foreign-owned banks in the banking sector assets. Also, credit cycles eased in most CESEEs, as the post-GFC busts lowered the credit-to-GDP ratios (see Fig. 5.9) and slowed down credit expansion. This was especially visible in the Baltics, although a similar cyclical pattern is observed also in CEE and SEE (see Figs. 5.10, 5.11 and 5.12). Banks in CESEE were characterized by lower profitability in the post-GFC environment, but also by gradual strengthening of their capital adequacy after the GFC (consisting largely of high loss-absorbing Tier 1 capital), reduction of trading assets and of excessive lending.

Consequently, due to cyclical economic deceleration, the quality of the banks' credit portfolio, proxied by NPL ratio, worsened and ultimately hit the profitability (via increased provisions) in the few years following the GFC. Nevertheless, since then the profitability started to recover, yet its heterogeneity among the banking sectors in CESEE went up. Still, the NPLs in the CESEEs remained elevated in the post-GFC period and reduced the potential for credit supply. This was an additional credit-constraining factor for subsidiaries highly reliant on foreign funding from parent companies.

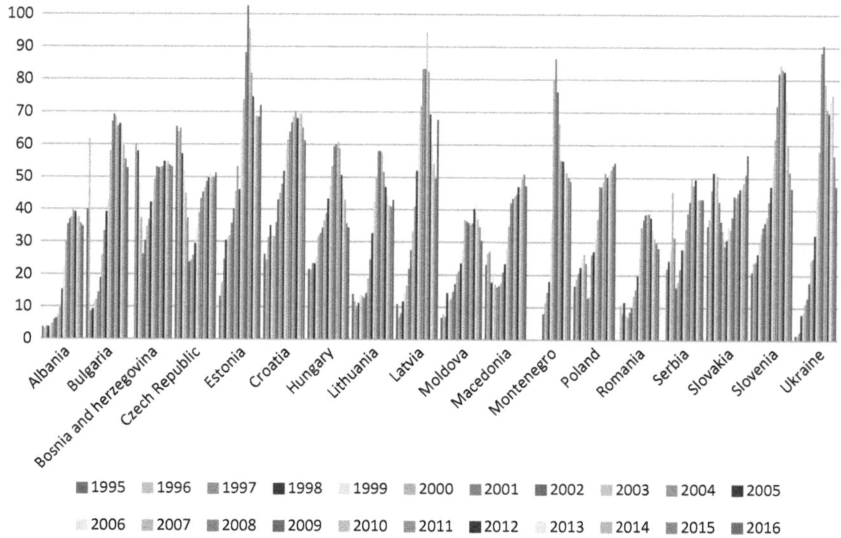

Fig. 5.9 Credit-to-GDP ratios in CESEEs 1995–2016 (in %). (Source: World Bank and Federal Reserve Economic Data)

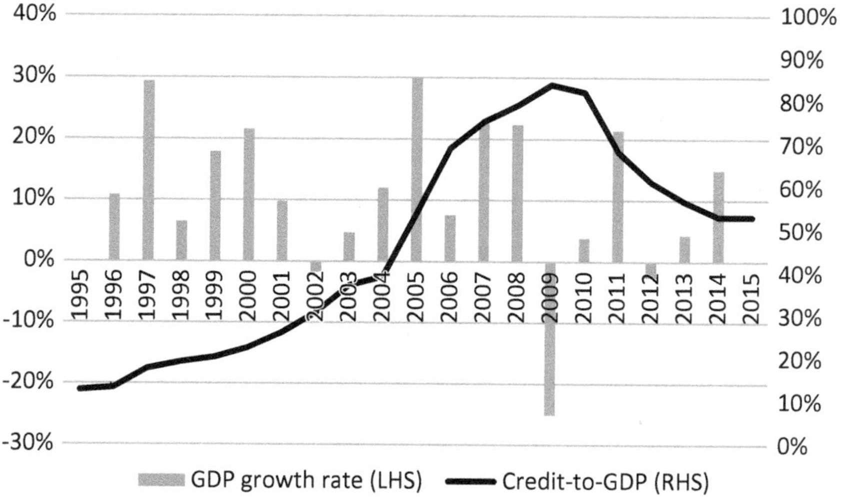

Fig. 5.10 GDP growth rate and credit-to-GDP in the Baltics. (Note: Average GDP growth rate is weighted with GDP of countries in the sample. Baltics include EE, LT, LV; Source: Own work using data from World Bank and Federal Reserve Economic Data)

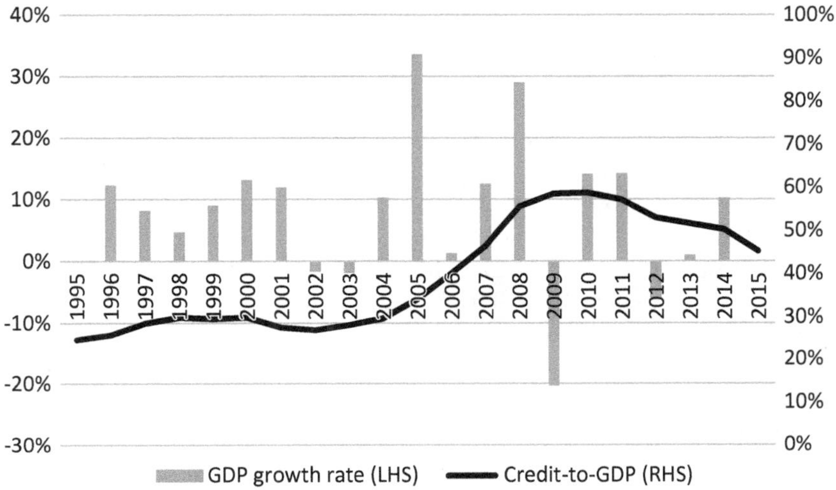

Fig. 5.11 GDP growth rate and credit-to-GDP in the CEE. (Note: Average GDP growth rate is weighted with GDP of countries in the sample. CEE includes BY, CZ, HU, PL, SK, SI, UA; Source: Own work using data from World Bank and Federal Reserve Economic Data)

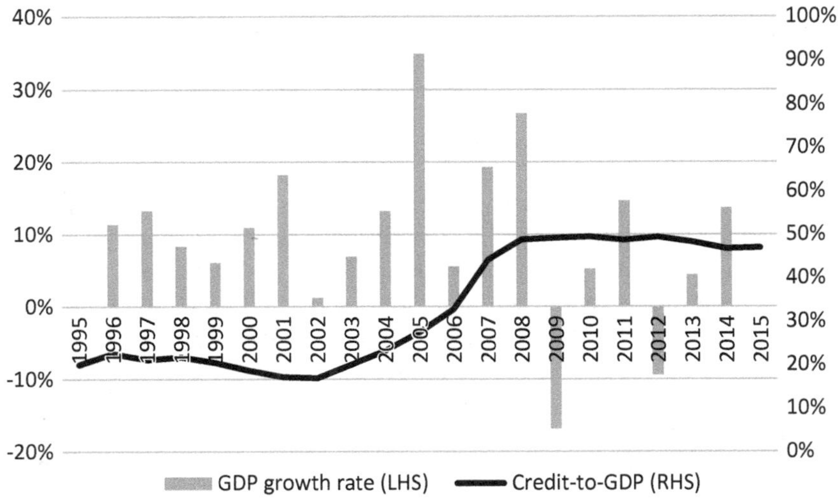

Fig. 5.12 GDP growth rate and credit-to-GDP in the SEE. (Note: Average GDP growth rate is weighted with GDP of countries in the sample. SEE includes AL, BA, BG, HR, KV, ME, MD, MK, RO, RS; Source: Own work using data from World Bank and Federal Reserve Economic Data)

CESEEs with more dynamic rates of credit growth before the crisis (such as Albania, Moldova and Ukraine) experienced relatively higher levels of NPLs during and after the GFC. Despite generally high capital buffers, unresolved stock of NPLs put a considerable strain on the banking system, especially if economic growth remains feeble or economies experience future recessions.

As a result of the GFC, an average public debt-to-GDP ratio in the CESEEs virtually doubled and budget deficits widened. This was driven by the cyclical GDP decline, lower tax revenues (drop in domestic demand), and increased public sector expenditures/stimulus packages aimed at containing the economic fallout. The fiscal tightening that would be necessary to offset the inflows of capital was too huge to be politically feasible. In the following years, this resulted in fiscal consolidations and austerity measures in many CESEEs to stabilize the mounting public debt. Although the public debt levels in the CESEEs are below those in the Western EU countries, the debt burden and financing needs are still relatively high in some of the CESEE countries, creating pockets of vulnerability to a renewed sharp increase of global risk aversion or interest rate hikes. At the same time, the current account deficits moderated and have much improved since their peaks around the GFC, even moving to surpluses in some CESEEs. This points to overall lower dependence of the region on large continuous inflows of external financing as opposed to the pre-GFC situation and an adjustment process towards more sustainable external positions.

5.1.5 Reponses to the Crisis

The ability of the CESEEs to face financial crises depended on pre-crisis vulnerabilities and any buffers which they built up. The CESEEs are small and open economies, and thus usually have fewer domestic resources to withstand crises and might be more sensitive to changes in investors' sentiment on global markets. As explained above, the resilience of banking sectors in the CESEEs was only satisfactory in the run-up to the GFC, yet it shielded the CESEEs to some extent from a devastating combination of a currency and banking crisis as was the case in the Asian crisis. The fiscal position in many CESEEs was benign at the onset of the GFC, which left material fiscal space for any government interventions during the GFC. Additionally, progress in improving regulatory and supervisory frameworks, as well as prior-GFC macroprudential measures, acted to some extent as the first line of defence against financial instability and allowed mitigating systemic meltdown of financial systems in CESEEs. As indicated by Cocozza et al. (2011), a proactive supervisory attitude on the part of national central banks and their risk awareness have significantly contributed to the resilience of the CESEEs' banking systems. According to Cocozza et al. (2011), the CESEE countries entered the GFC with varying degrees of policy space, which was reflected in their different abilities to mitigate the fallout from the GFC. Overall, the counter-cyclical policy responses to the GFC had to be balanced between supporting growth, containing external imbalances and financing needs. The responses were also shaped to a great extent by the type of exchange rate regime in place.

In the pre-GFC period, faced with rising inflation risks caused by rapid credit growth, most CESEE countries embarked on monetary tightening policies. According to Dell'Ariccia et al. (2012), the CESEEs that were the most proactive in trying to tame the credit boom were either non-EU members (e.g. Croatia and Serbia) or those that entered the EU only in 2007, that is, Bulgaria and Romania. Further, some countries, but not all, took macroprudential measures, at times specifically targeted at foreign currency lending (Croatia, Poland, Romania, and Serbia, in particular). The CESEEs that had fixed exchange rate regimes encountered substantial difficulties in responding to massive capital inflows before the global financial crisis, as such regimes constrain the ability of the central bank to raise policy rates insofar as it may attract more capital flows and, in turn, induce pressure on the exchange rate (Allegret and Sallenave 2015). There were also signs of the financial stability paradox, when in a booming environment, bank prudential indicators improved, bank profitability was increasing (and NPLs were dropping), as did collateral valuations as asset prices in the CESEEs. Macroprudential measures to control the growth of bank lending to the private sector included limits on the FX loans' growth, maximum ratios of FX loans to banks' capital and were introduced to increase the cost of borrowing in FX loans. Imposed tighter requirements included (Becker et al. 2010; Kolev and Zwart 2013) special reserve requirements and lower interest rates paid on those reserves, tighter provisioning and asset-qualification rules, stricter non-price requirements (e.g. higher down payments, additional collateral), higher capital requirements or other measures applied to FX borrowings. The implementation of macroprudential measures intensified in line with the speeding-up credit supply. Faced with mounting imbalances, in many CESEEs, central banks and prudential supervisors were also using moral suasion and communication to point to the risks of unsustainable credit spree to raise bank risk awareness.

Yet, the effectiveness of macroprudential measures was mixed. The analysis of Geršl and Jašova (2014) shows that in 11 CESEE countries thee were as much as 82 measures aimed at stemming the credit booms (see Table 5.3). The overall results indicate that tighter asset classification and provisioning

Table 5.3 List of policy measures to limit credit growth in CEE (2003–2007)

Monetary measures

Measures	*Interest rate response*	*Reserve requirements*				
			Changes in the required level	*Differentiated by currency*	*Differentiated by type of deposit*	*Broaden the reserve base*
CZ						
SK						
LT						
LV	X	X	X		X	X
EE		X	X			
HU						
PL	X					
RO	X	X	X	X		X
BU		X	X			
HR		X	X			
SI						

Macroprudential and Supervisory measures

Measures	*Capital requirements or higher risk weights*	*Liquid asset requirements*	*Tighter asset classification rules*	*Tighter provisioning rules*	*Tighter eligibility criteria for certain loans*	*Limit on Loan-to-Value*		*Measures targeting FX borrowing*		*Soft measures: non-binding guidelines for banks*	*Tighter supervision*
						Limit on Loan-to-Income / Payment-to-Income	*Tighter rules on valuation criteria*	*Targeting unhedged borrowers*	*Tighter net open position limits*		
CZ											
SK		X								X	

LT	X							X	X	X	
LV	X			X	X	X		X X	X	X	X
EE	X									X	
HU	X				X					X	X
PL	X	X						X X		X	
RO	X		X	X	X	X X		X X			X
BU	X		X	X						X	X
HR	X	X						X X		X	
SI							X			X	

Administrative and other measures

Measures	*Capital controls*	*Credit ceilings*	*Change in taxes on real estate transactions*
CZ			
SK			
LT	X		
LV			X
EE			
HU			
PL			
RO		X	
BU		X	
HR		X	
SI			

Source: Based on Geršl and Jašova (2014)

rules and stricter loan eligibility criteria (like LtV[3]/DtI[4] limits) might have been effective in taming bank credit growth. They point out that concerns regarding excessive credit growth were predominantly observed in the CESEE countries with fixed exchange rate regimes and that in general, the policy measures employed in the region (predominantly 2005–2006) were reactive rather than proactive or counter-cyclical. Unless confronted with a serious issue, most policy responses were "late risers", and the inaction bias might have been partially caused by the lack of macroprudential frameworks at that time. The monetary policy measures served as the first line of defence, but once they reached their limits, specific prudential and supervisory tools were applied afterwards, apart from the widespread soft measures, that is, moral suasion. Evidence is also provided using a unique quarterly database of 29 types of macroprudential measures for 16 CESEEs during the 1997–2011 period by Vandenbussche et al. (2015), who showed that in the CESEEs changes in the minimum capital adequacy ratio and non-standard liquidity measures were effective in slowing down the growth of real estate prices and, to some extent, also household credit and foreign funding. Surprisingly, changes in other types of instruments (including provisioning rules, average reserve requirements, and credit eligibility criteria) did not appear to have had significant effects (possibly reflecting data limitations in the estimations, as some of these policies were used only in a few instances), especially as reserve requirements were frequently used in CESEEs. Further, the in-depth study by Vandenbussche et al. (2018) on 4 CESEEs argue that only strong, broad-based macroprudential measures which address circumvention had a chance to truly contain credit booms. Specifically, binding marginal reserve requirements related to credit growth ("credit growth ceilings") helped contain domestic credit growth; strong sectoral capital measures and the introduction of meaningful LtV and DtI ceilings also helped limit household credit growth. Similarly, targeted capital measures and strong, targeted reserve requirements measures contributed to the curbing of the share of foreign-currency-denominated loans provided by the domestic banking systems; as well as heavy reserve requirements measures on banks' foreign borrowing helped slow it down. Measures taken during the bust had, according to Vandenbussche et al. (2018), no discernible impact. Effectiveness of macroprudential measures in 11 CESEEs in 2000–2003 is partially confirmed also by Dumičić (2017). The main finding is that in the run-up to the GFC, macroprudential policies were more successful in slowing down credit growth to households than to the non-financial corporate sector. The reason is that household credit growth was significantly affected by a larger number of macroprudential measures than the growth of credit to non-financial corporations. The latter could also get funding from sources that were not subject to macroprudential measures, such as non-bank financial institutions and direct cross-border credit.

The effectiveness of the discussed measures was hindered by increased competition among banks, as well as the lack of international coordination between host authorities. Moreover, subsidiaries were directing customers to the Western parent banks granting direct cross-border lending from abroad or from non-bank sources, thereby circumventing subsidiaries and local regulations, which undermined prudential policies and left domestic-owned banks in host countries with poorer quality borrowers. Further, Dumičić (2017) observes that the substitution among credit sources can be indirectly confirmed by the correlation between the highest share of cross-border bank loans in total loans to the private sector generally observed in the CESEEs characterized by an intensive use of macroprudential policies. Nevertheless, even though the effectiveness of the applied macroprudential measures might be debated and there are numerous non-linearities in their impact, they undoubtedly strengthened the resilience of the banking sectors (capital and liquidity buffers) in the CESEEs and increased their ability to withstand subsequent downturns.

To cope at the onset of the GFC with the risks to which the banking sectors in CESEE were exposed, several policies might have been considered, incl. capital flow measures, monetary policy, flexible exchange rates, as well as counter-cyclical fiscal and macroprudential policies. According to Gardo and Martin (2010), during the first two months after the crisis unfolded, central banks in the CESEEs faced challenging choices. On the one hand, they needed to stimulate the demand by lowering the interest rates. On the other hand, they needed to prevent excessive currency depreciation—which may have reignited inflation—by retaining a positive interest rate differential vis-à-vis other countries. Therefore, the monetary policy remained very cautious in most CESEE countries until the end of 2008. In the final quarter of 2008 most CESEE countries with flexible exchange rates started the process of monetary easing, intervened verbally and/or through market operations. Some CESEE countries tightened up their prudential policies, for example, by raising liquidity and capital requirements, but this was not enough to reduce the appetite for lending.

The policy response in the CESEEs consisted of standard and non-standard central bank policy actions as well as fiscal policy measures. In an attempt to manage the fallout of the GFC in the CESEEs and restore the confidence in financial markets, safety net authorities adopted a series of extraordinary measures aiming at stabilizing the banking system and providing liquidity support (see Table 5.4). Most CESEE central banks

Table 5.4 Measures adopted by national authorities in CESEEs as a response to the GFC

		Albania	*Bosnia and Herzegovina*	*Bulgaria*	*Croatia*	*Czech Republic*	*Estonia*	*Hungary*	*Latvia*
Banking system liquidity policy measures	Relaxation of reserve requirements		Oct. 08, Dec. 08, May 09	Oct. 08, Dec. 08, Jan. 09	Oct. 08, Dec. 08, Jan. 09	Oct. 08		Nov. 08	Oct. 08, Nov. 08, Dec. 08
	Domestic currency liquidity injections	Nov. 2008 onwards				Oct. 08 onwards			
	Foreign exchange liquidity injections							Oct. 08 onwards, Mar. 09	
	Increase in deposit insurance coverage	Mar. 09	Dec. 08	Nov. 08	Oct. 08	Oct. 08	Oct. 08	Oct. 08	Oct. 08
	Interventions in individual institutions—liquidity injection								Nov. 08, Feb. 09
Policy measures to protect bank solvency	Recapitalization fund							Feb. 09	
	Relaxation of capital/provisioning requirements			Mar. 09					
	Interventions in individual institutions—capital injection								Nov. 08
Monetary policy rate changes	Policy interest rate cuts	Jan. 09				Aug. 08 onwards		Nov. 08 onwards	Mar. 09, May 09

		Lithuania	*Macedonia*	*Montenegro*	*Poland*	*Romania*	*Serbia*	*Ukraine*	*No countries*
Banking system liquidity policy measures	Relaxation of reserve requirements	Nov. 08		Oct. 08, Feb. 09, Jan. 09	Jun. 09	Nov. 08, May. 09	Oct. 08	Oct. 08, Dec. 08, Feb. 09	12
	Domestic currency liquidity injections				Oct.08 onwards	Oct. 08 onwards	Apr. 09	Oct. 08 onwards	6
	Foreign exchange liquidity injections				Oct. 08 onwards		Apr. 09		3
	Increase in deposit insurance coverage	Oct. 08			Oct. 08	Oct. 08	Dec. 08	Oct. 08	13
	Interventions in individual institutions—liquidity injection								1
Policy measures to protect bank solvency	Recapitalization fund								1
	Relaxation of capital/ provisioning requirements			Aug. 09					2
	Interventions in individual institutions—capital injection							Apr. 09	2
Monetary policy rate changes	Policy interest rate cuts		Sep. 08 onwards		Nov. 08 onwards	Feb. 09 onwards	Jan. 09, Apr. 09, Jun. 09	Jan. 09, Jun. 09	9

Source: Based on Bakker and Klingen (2012)

took liquidity-easing measures (e.g. reducing domestic reserve requirements, broadening eligible collateral and increasing the frequency of auctions), while some also used measures to support foreign exchange markets. The Roaf et al. (2014) note that the measures aimed at safeguarding financial stability and maintaining the confidence of depositors and debt holders in the CESEEs included—being the most common and often gradual—relaxation of reserve requirements (e.g. Croatia, Bosnia-Herzegovina, Serbia) to pump liquidity into the financial sector.[5] Additionally, domestic and foreign currency liquidity supply operations were introduced by central banks, which were often possible through swap and repo arrangements with Western European central banks.[6]

The CESEE central banks did not, however, undertake credit or quantitative easing measures. In most CESEEs there were few big-scale capital injections or liquidity support programmes. Dietz et al. (2009), by analysing 4 CESEE countries argue that rather than going for comprehensive rescue packages, the governments have implemented ad hoc measures for single institutions, including the possibility of already established state capital injections. Yet, if implemented, the rescue packages resembled most of the measures taken in Western Europe, for example, Poland; the rescue package comprised of state guarantees and public recapitalization. Further, the most effective tools for containing the crisis were the support measures from the IMF, World Bank, the EBRD, and the EU.[7] Despite having agreed on ex ante cooperation mechanism/memoranda among home and host supervisors, the information-sharing was insufficient and when faced with a systemic crisis, the perspective of stability of national banking systems prevailed. This left the host supervisors in the CESEEs partially handicapped when dealing with the GFC.

The potential effectiveness of monetary policy was constrained in many CESEEs during the GFC, a result of the increased risk and liquidity premia on the interbank markets. Further, high stock of FX loans impaired the monetary policy transmission mechanism, as the impact of local central banks in the CESEEs on interest rates of assets denominated in euro- or Swiss francs and liabilities in host banking systems was limited. The policymakers in CESEE faced several dilemmas. Naturally, an expansionary policy was deployed by lowering interest rates in most CESEEs, but it was feared that this might have intensified capital outflows and add to the deprecation of the local currency. Further, had central banks in the

CESEEs defended the exchange rate by increasing the interest rates, it would likely have led to the reduction of the loan portfolio quality, given the dominant role of loans with variable interest rates in the CESEEs. The CESEE countries with floating currency regimes were not forced to use a restrictive policy to additionally defend the fixed exchange rate regime. According to Cocozza et al. (2011), continued financial market instability and the accompanying uncertainty further impaired the already weak (because of high euroization) interest rate and credit channels of the monetary policy transmission mechanism in the CESEEs. Further, the scope of available policies concerning the use of capital flows measures was constrained by the depth of financial integration prior to the GFC and additionally, in some CESEEs in the EU as they are not allowed to use capital controls because the single market provisions and free movement of capital principle prohibits the use of such measures.

The possibility to implement a counter-cyclical policy response was generally limited also by the fixed or quasi-fixed exchange rate regime in the CESEEs, for example, monetary policy easing using interest rates was not available in Bosnia-Herzegovina and Montenegro. In the CESEEs with a relatively high stock of FX- denominated financial assets and liabilities (a high level of financial euroization) and a fixed exchange rate regime, monetary policy had limited capacity to contain rapid credit growth. On the other hand, the CESEEs with exchange rate flexibility[8] were able to insulate their economies and banking systems more successfully against real and external shocks with more space for effective expansionary monetary policy. Flexible exchange rates proved to be shock absorbers acting as a stabilizing factor against external shocks, for example, in Poland. The CESEE countries with floating exchange rate regimes, owing to currency depreciation, experienced lower output decline in the aftermath of the GFC shocks. In the "floating" countries, local currency depreciation led to the tightening of monetary conditions, which led to lesser build-up of imbalances, lower current deficits, and less pronounced booms. On the other hand, CESEE countries with currency pegs[9] have been very constrained to use their monetary policy (Cocozza et al. 2011; Allegret and Sallenave 2015) as raising interest rates would only attract more inflows.

Andrieș et al. (2016) assessed the effectiveness of intervention measures adopted by central authorities during 2005–2012 in 12 CEE countries. Their empirical findings suggest that interest rates cuts, as well as foreign and domestic liquidity injections had a significant impact on bank stability (as measured using Z-Score and NPLs), although it depended on bank characteristics. They found that those measures decreased the stability of domestic-owned banks but increased it for those less capitalized. Yet, the effectiveness of the central banks' liquidity measures was limited due to domestic interbank markets not being a significant source of bank funding. Therefore, it was important to strengthen deposit insurance schemes instead to maintain confidence in banks in the CESEEs. In addition, to stabilize the banking system and avoid bank panic, numerous countries increased the level of deposit insurance and government deposit guarantee schemes up to certain limits were (temporary) introduced, for example, in Lithuania to €100,000.

Few CESEEs implemented regulatory measures before the GFC to reduce the pace of credit growth and limit FX loans, especially risky practices like loans that pass foreign exchange risk to unhedged retail customers. In general, most countries exposed to risks from FX loans focused pre-GFC only on monitoring and prudential measures were introduced after the crisis erupted (see Table 5.5). Steiner (2011) states that the measures taken in the CESEEs in order to contain FX loans on the supply side included: (i) tightening the requirements on foreign currency liquidity and on capital adequacy; (ii) using higher risk weights according to the cur-

Table 5.5 Policy measures to curb FX lending in the CESEEs

Measure/country	*Latvia*	*Hungary*	*Poland*	*Romania*	*Croatia*
Higher risk weights, provisioning or reserve requirements in relation to banks FX exposure	● X	●	●	● X	● X
Narrowing interest rate differentials			X		
Increase of flexibility of exchange rate			X	X	
Cross-border supervisory intervention	X				
Active monitoring of FX risk	X	X	X	X	X
Disclosing FX risks to customers		● X	● X		
Tightening eligibility criteria for FX borrowing (LTV, LTI)	X	● X	● X		
FX position limits	X				●
Restrictions on FX lending	●		●		
Codes of conduct discouraging use of FX lending		●	●		
Ban on FX lending		●			

Note: Pre-crisis X mark, post-crisis dot

Source: Based on European Commission (2017) and Brown and Lane (2011)

rency denomination of loans, and (iii) tightening the rules on loan concentration. The demand-side measures included, for example, credit eligibility requirements, limits on loan-to-value, and debt-to-income ratios. There were also more "hard" measures as forced conversion to loans denominated in local currency or recommendations on outright ban on FX loans, for example, in Hungary. The prudential and supervisory measures directly targeting the supply of foreign currency loans have been implemented to a significant extent mainly in Hungary, but also to a lesser degree, mostly in a preventive manner, in Poland, Romania, and Croatia. In general, those measures can be assessed as affective in stemming the flow of FX loans in the CESEEs, but still the issue of outstanding stock of FX loans to households remains one of key vulnerabilities in the post-GFC landscape. One of the reasons is that, according to OeNB Euro Survey in CESEEs by Beckmann et al. (2011), both the supply and demand factors continued to drive foreign currency loans and still high (despite being dampened by the GFC) attractiveness of FX loans suggested that foreign currency borrowing was unlikely to have vanished without a policy intervention that followed. It was argued that gains from lower real interest on FX loans outweighed the costs associated with a possible and maybe temporary depreciation of local currencies.

Apart from "hard" prudential measures, also cooperation in the form of the VI have proven instrumental in mitigating retrenchment of foreign-owned banks from the region and management of cross-border spillovers. The VI " (VI) was established in January 2009 as a multilateral agreement (a public-private platform) that was not formally binding, but successfully served as a forum for voluntary cooperation and coordination of actions between commercial banks on one side and regulators/supervisors from both home and host countries on the other. It covered such countries as Bosnia and Herzegovina (non-EU), Hungary, Latvia, Romania (EU member since 2007), and Serbia (non-EU). The parent bank participating in the VI were as follows: parent banks participating in the VI (Alpha Bank, Bayerische Landesbank, Erste, Intesa Sanpaolo, KBC, Raiffeisen, Unicredit, Eurobank EFG, National Bank of Greece, Societe Generale, Volksbank, Piraeus, Hypo Alpe-Adria, NLB Group, DnB Nord, Nordea, Swedbank, SEB).[10]

In particular, public institutions participating in the VI comprised central banks, ministries of finance, supervisory authorities as well as international financial institutions like IMF, World Bank, European Bank for Reconstruction and Development, European Investment Bank, and

European Commission. VI's main aims included making home and host countries to continue providing support to subsidiaries in the CESEEs, as well as encouraging EU-based parent banks (large cross-border banking groups) to stay committed to the local markets. The VI was primarily created as an emergency response to prevent foreign-owned banks from retrenching from the region and ensuring they remain committed to refinance loans to subsidiaries and keep them adequately capitalized during the GFC to reduce the potential for contagion and systemic spillovers in the CESEE region. The work of the VI is led by the Steering Committee and is organized along work streams/groups, with annual meetings (Full Forum) taking place every year.

After the GFC, the VI in early 2012 was reinstated as "Vienna Initiative 2.0" motivated by concerns of the euro area sovereign debt crisis and Basel III impact. The VI was gradually transformed into a platform for cooperation rather than for crisis management and focuses more on coordination and information-exchange between supervisors to foster cross-border financial integration in Europe. The VI started to concentrate on providing solutions to structural challenges for financial institutions in the CESEEs. Areas of focus of the VI work include: monitoring of credit developments (deleveraging) in the CESEE region, monitoring of NPLs and discussion on NPL reduction strategies, credit guarantee schemes, implementation of Banking Union and Capital Market Union, resolution frameworks, minimum requirement for own funds and eligible liabilities (MREL), as well as cross-border impact of the EU banking regulations on the CESEEs.

In hindsight, the VI was unique in its design and functions. The VI activities significantly contributed to stabilizing the banking systems in the CESEEs during the GFC and filled the void of lacking effective dialogue and cross-border cooperation frameworks for crisis management between home and host authorities in the CESEEs for the benefit of financial stability of both sides. Owing to the VI the feared financial meltdown from the GFC did not materialize in the CESEEs. The VI continues to foster regulatory cooperation within and between EU and non-EU SEE countries, by promoting the best practices concerning banking regulations and supervisory actions, and strengthening financial stability in potential EU accession countries in SEE. At the same time, the VI remains crucial in mitigating negative cross-border spillovers of prudential measures taken by home countries on host countries conditions. Empirical studies confirm the key role of the VI. As indicated in Chap. 4, the empirical analysis of De Haas et al. (2015) also confirms the stabilizing effect of lending by foreign-owned banks taking part in the Vienna Initiative. Moreover, the VI banks did not retrench from non-VI countries in order to maintain exposures to countries where they signed commitment letters. Further, Temesvary and Banai (2017) argue that a subsidiary's participation in the VI significantly mitigated the negative across-the-board shock that the crisis imposed on lending growth. Lastly, the VI's positive impact is supported by empirical studies of Cetorelli and Goldberg (2011), who studied transmission of cross-border lending and liquidity shocks.

5.2 Measures of Financial Stability in CESEE Countries[11]

Financial stability is an elusive concept. There is no consensus regarding the concept of financial stability and systemic risk. A wide range of different definitions of financial stability are used as it is determined by a myriad of macrofinancial factors. The absence of a single, universally accepted definition may result from a different and often evolving nature of financial crises, diverse roles played by both characteristics of national financial systems, as well as global factors. The lack of consensus on its definition and its complex nature implies the need for various measures and principles to measure financial stability. It is difficult to determine unequivocally whether the system is stable or not in current conditions, thus financial stability is hardly observable. While an ex post assessment of financial stability is usually clear, it is the ex ante accumulation of vulnerabilities potentially endangering financial stability that should become the focus of the analysis. Yet, defining financial stability is the first and key step in measuring it.

Financial stability can be defined in a broad or narrow manner. The first approach bases on presenting the characteristics of the condition of the financial system and economy, which may be considered stable. The disadvantage of the first approach includes describing financial stability in too broad terms, while using mostly theoretical concepts, which are hard to measure. This may adversely affect the clarity and transparency of the financial stability as a policy objective and hinder construction of an operational version of the definition, that is, a measure which could be used in practice by policymakers. The second approach takes a more simplified view and defines financial stability *a contrario* by determining what financial *instability* is. It focuses on the occurrence of a financial crisis and thus is not a solely theoretical concept. This makes it easier for policymakers to understand the concept of financial instability as a tangible example is given. While the first approach tries to include the multidimensional nature of financial stability, the second approach often limits the perception of financial stability strictly to the lack of a financial crisis. This might not always be true, since asset and credit bubbles can build up and systemic risk can accumulate in the absence of visible signs of the crisis and be accompanied by robust bank financial condition ratios, which was evidenced in the CESEEs before the GFC. Therefore, it is more prudent, yet more challenging, too, to adopt the wider approach.

Further, financial stability cannot be regarded as being a single, unique state of equilibrium, as the perception of financial stability depends on the assessment method used and the degree of risk tolerance of the policymakers, which is not universal. This is in line with the approach by Schinasi (2005), who proposes a *continuum* approach. Since the financial system is in a perpetual state of flux, the concept of financial stability does not refer to a single, sustainable position or time path to which the financial system returns after a shock, but rather the current financial conditions are within a range or a continuum. This continuum is multidimensional: it occurs across a multitude of observable, measurable variables which can be used to quantify (albeit imperfectly) how well the financial system is performing its facilitative functions.

According to Smaga (2013), who surveyed financial stability frameworks in national central banks in the EU, most of them have adopted such a definition. Central banks in the EU focused on providing definitions of financial (in)stability rather than definitions of a financial crisis and/or systemic risk (see also Oosterloo and de Haan 2003). Most of the time definitions take the broad approach and their definitions are of own design. Financial stability definitions are often placed in the first (and sometimes also in subsequent) editions of the Financial Stability Reports or central bank's webpages which can be considered a "best practice" in terms of fostering transparency of the central bank's financial stability policy. For central banks in the EU, financial stability is usually associated with the financial system that properly fulfils its functions, even in case of adverse shocks.

A review of financial stability frameworks of national central banks in the CESEEs and their Financial Stability Reports brings similar conclusions. Virtually all national central banks in the CESEEs have adopted the financial stability definition in a broad sense, focusing on the financial system's efficient functioning and resilience to shocks. Additionally, having established macroprudential policies after the GFC, half of the central banks also introduced the concept of the systemic risk as a risk of disruption of the financial system with negative consequences to the economy, usually distinguishing between its cross-section and time dimensions. This is in line with the most common understating of such a concept in the literature and EU national central bank practice (Bisias et al. 2012; Galati and Moessner 2013; Smaga 2014).

Measuring financial stability and systemic risk in the CESEEs is determined (limited) by several features. First, as banking sectors dominate their financial systems, it is usually the banking sector's stability in focus of financial stability measures. The credit risk is the most important driver of bank performance and risk in these countries. Second, financial markets are not well developed and not efficient enough to provide reliable indicators of financial market conditions from market data. Third, supervisory data reporting systems are not as sophisticated (especially in non-EU CESEEs) as in the EU countries, thus the choice of variables and the length of time series is rather limited. Therefore, this chapter will focus on the available and most widespread approach to measuring financial stability in the CESEEs, which is creating financial (banking sector) stability indicators using balance sheet data. This is one of the simpler approaches to measuring financial stability, as more advanced methods (but also more demanding in terms of data and analytical potential) include stress tests and network analysis.

The purposes of the financial stability analyses carried out by the central bank usually include assessing the risk taken by individual institutions, the existing and expected systemic risk (potential for contagion), and the driving forces for such a situation. Such an analysis comprises, apart from banking sector variables in the strict sense, also macrofinancial factors (e.g. interest rates, inflation, GDP, asset prices, market liquidity, exchange rate, sectoral indebtedness) and qualitative aspects (e.g. regulations, financial safety net, behavioural factors). All those factors affect the condition of the banking sector and its resilience to shocks but are difficult to quantify in a comparable manner. Further, an effective analysis of financial stability requires systematic monitoring of all its determinants, their variability over time and non-linear relationships between them. This is undoubtedly a strenuous task, as the scope of the analysis is open-ended.

The initial step in banking stability measurement is calculating and publishing indicators of the condition of the banking sector (*financial stability indicators, financial soundness indicators* (FSIs) like CAR,[12] ROA,[13] NPL,[14] or liquidity ratios. In a wider sense, FSIs might be computed also for the real economy, corporate and household sectors, external sector, financial sector, financial markets (Gadanecz and Jayaram 2009). Preparation of FSIs proves higher awareness of the central bank's role in analysing financial stability. Indicators allow conducing structured analyses, serve as a valuable source of data for further research, modelling and stress testing. Often only the central bank, being a microprudential supervisor, has direct access to supervisory reporting data. Computing FSIs improves the process of the financial stability analysis and enhances the contents of the Financial Stability Report, while making it easier for others (institutions, researchers, etc.) to analyse the financial sector. A failure to calculate and publish FSIs could lead to imprecise assessment of the financial system stability and consequently, to an improper calibration of measures used for financial stability purposes.

The construction of FSIs often bases on the so-called CAMELS methodology, which has been one of the most popular approaches to assessing the financial strength of individual banks. In its basic form, this methodology requires knowledge of the bank's capital adequacy (C), asset quality (A), management (M), liquidity (L), earnings (E), and sensitivity to market risk (S). The CAMELS approach is used to assess the bank risk and vulnerability, basing on accounting values (Sinkey 1979). Financial and accounting ratio proxies for capital adequacy, asset quality, managerial capability, earnings, liquidity, and, more recently, sensitivity to the market risk are considered relevant signals of imbalances at the individual-bank level. Indeed, the empirical literature on individual-bank distress has widely confirmed the ability of CAMELS ratings to assess bank vulnerability and predict bank distress (for a review, see Poghosyan and Cihak 2011). Simple indicators, despite strong simplifications in the assumptions, have the advantage of being able to be constructed using basic sectoral data, and thus allow comparability between countries. The use of CAMELS and CAMELS-like systems by banking supervisors to assess individual banks is popular in the CESEE countries (Green and Petrick 2002), due to its simple numerical approach.

Usually, the financial stability indices can be calculated according to the methodology of the IMF, European System of Central Banks (ESCB), or the European Systemic Risk Board (ESRB). The IMF (2006) proposed two lists of FSIs, that is, the core set (12 indicators) and the encouraged set (27 indicators), which should be regularly monitored by institutions in charge of the stability of individual institutions as well as the financial stability (see Table 5.6). As the most important indicators the IMF consid-

Table 5.6 Financial soundness indicators: the core and encouraged sets according to the IMF

Core set	
Deposit takers (CAMELS approach)	
Capital adequacy	Regulatory capital to risk-weighted assets
	Regulatory Tier 1 capital to risk-weighted assets
	NPLs net of provisions to capital
Asset quality	NPLs to total gross loans
	Sectoral distribution of loans to total loans
Earnings and profitability	ROA
	ROE
	Interest margin to gross income
	Non-interest expenses to gross income
Liquidity	Liquid assets to total assets (liquid asset ratio)
	Liquid assets to short-term liabilities
Sensitivity to market risk	Net open position in foreign exchange to capital
Encouraged set	
Deposit takers	Capital to assets
	Large exposures to capital
	Geographical distribution of loans to total loans
	Gross asset position in financial derivatives to capital
	Gross liability position in financial derivatives to capital
	Trading income to total income
	Personnel expenses to non-interest expenses
	Spread between reference lending and deposit rates
	Spread between highest and lowest interbank rate
	Customer deposits to total (non-interbank) loans
	Foreign-currency-denominated loans to total loans
	Foreign-currency-denominated liabilities to total liabilities
	Net open position in equities to capital
Other financial corporations	Assets to total financial system assets
	Assets to GDP
Non-financial corporations sector	Total debt to equity
	ROE
	Earnings to interest and principal expenses
	Net foreign exchange exposure to equity
	Number of applications for protection from creditors
Households	Household debt to GDP
	Household debt service and principal payments to income
Market liquidity	Average bid-ask spread in the securities market[2]
	Average daily turnover ratio in the securities market[2]
Real estate markets	Real estate prices
	Residential real estate loans to total loans
	Commercial real estate loans to total loans

Source: Based on IMF (2006)

ers capital adequacy, asset quality, earnings and profitability, liquidity, and sensitivity to market risk. The core set focuses on the indicators used to analyse the condition of individual (banking) institutions, while the encouraged set includes the ratios of the condition of non-banking financial institutions, non-financial enterprises, households and the real estate market, allowing a more complete assessment of stability from the macro-financial perspective. Such measures of health of a country's financial sector are the key and integral part of the macroprudential toolkit (Sundararajan et al. 2002; Costa Navajas and Thegeya 2013). The IMF FSI methodology has gained wide acclaim among central banks, although usually only FSIs from the core set are calculated.

As regards the ESCB methodology (Mörttinen et al. 2005), it proposes macroprudential indicators, the list of which is wider and calculated on the basis of consolidated data on an annual basis. The "youngest" set of FSIs is put forward by the ESRB (2018) as indicators to identify and measure the systemic risk through a "risk dashboard", which is published on a quarterly basis and contains eight groups of variables measuring: interlinkages and composite measures of systemic risk, macro risk, credit risk, funding and liquidity, market risk, profitability and solvency, structural risk, and risk related to central counterparties.

Calculating and using FSIs includes numerous challenges. The advantage of this approach is its objectivity and a relatively simple method of calculation, comparability, as well as possibility in determining the trend of a given value development over time. However, the gaps and delays in data availability might prove troublesome, especially when faced with changes in reporting/accountancy standards. The selection of an appropriate set of indicators which could best assess the condition of the financial system might be problematic. Another challenge is the construction of the so-called leading or early-warning indicators, which would inform about the incoming crisis, while being based on historical data. Another difficulty, after calculating the indicators, is setting their reference values, which, once exceeded, would signal instability intolerable by policymakers. Further, negative changes in the values of FSIs result not only from the accumulation of systemic risk but might be a sign of fundamental factors or structural changes in the financial system, so the set of FSIs must be constantly developed and updated as well. The interpretation of FSIs bases mostly on expert knowledge, especially as they rarely reflect contagious interconnectedness between financial system sectors and institutions or institutional and regulatory changes. Further discussion on the financial stability indicators may be found in Sundararajan et al. (2002), Moorhouse (2004), Mörttinen et al. (2005). As Smaga (2013) notes, national central banks in the EU do report, though not always regularly publish financial stability indicators (e.g. according to the IMF's or similar methodology) and present them on their websites or in Financial Stability Reports and subsequently use them in financial stability analyses. This is also characteristic of several national central banks in the CESEEs (e.g. in AL, BY, RS).

Apart from FSIs, several central banks in CESEE additionally use a colour-coded map of risks in the form of a cobweb chart (see Fig. 5.13) as a method to measure, visualize and communicate financial stability/systemic risks, frequently basing on FSIs and inspired by the Global Financial Stability Map used by the IMF. For example, the Bank of Albania (2017)

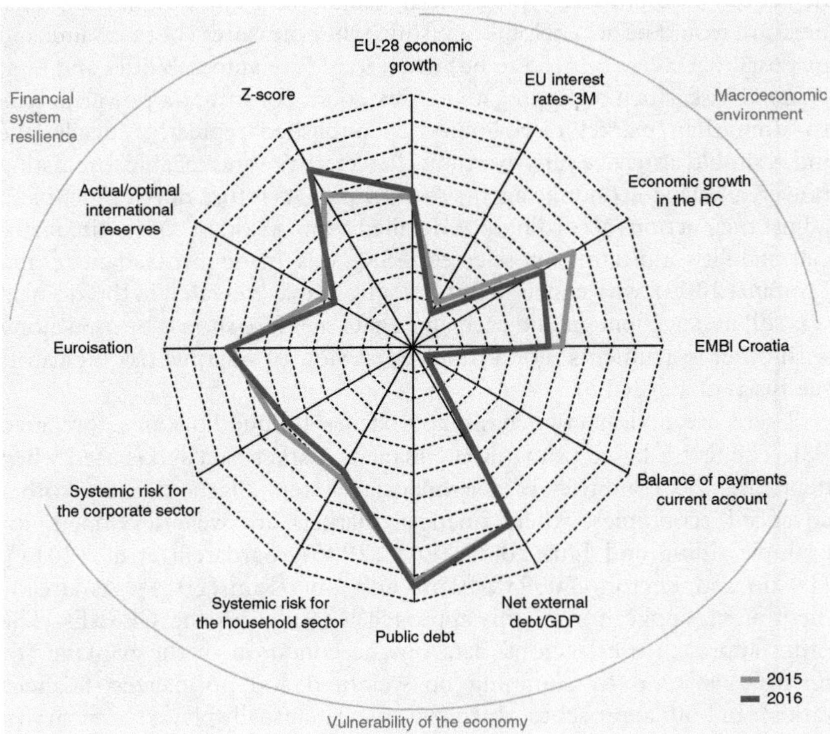

Fig. 5.13 Example of a cobweb financial stability map—Croatia. (Source: Croatian National Bank 2016)

uses the Financial Stability Map to show the allocation of risk in the banking sector, external and internal environment, and the real economy agents. A similarly constructed risk diagram is also used by the Bank of Latvia (Sinenko and Lielkalne 2015; Bank of Latvia 2017) and by the Central Bank of the Republic of Kosovo (Maloku Bakija and Mustafa 2016; Central Bank of the Republic of Kosovo 2017) graphically representing the measures of risk across eight dimensions. Lastly, cobweb representation of key FSIs for banking sector and macroeconomic risks is employed by the Croatian National Bank (2016), the National Bank of Ukraine (2017) and the National Bank of Serbia (2018).

The next logical step in measuring financial stability is the aggregation of selected FSIs into a financial stability index. This is an attempt to make financial stability definition operational and develop an index which would depict the "current state" of financial stability in a single variable. Such a measure would be also helpful to justify policy measures (both ex ante and ex post) that were (or need to be) taken to reduce vulnerabilities and limit systemic risk. Such an aggregated index could constitute a powerful tool to strengthen market discipline when published regularly. Ideally, the index should also have early-warning characteristics and reliable forecasting power, allowing economic agents to anticipate its future development and adjust their actions accordingly. A detailed comparison of composite financial stability indicators in selected FSRs was made by Gadanecz and Jayaram (2009), who concluded that central banks' research in this domain was still in development and each aggregate measure should be used along with other instruments. For a thorough review of systemic risk indicators see Bisias et al. (2012).

There are at least two basic approaches to building an aggregated FSI. The first is based primarily on financial market data and is used when depicting the condition of the financial system in the US and other advanced economies, where financial markets are well developed, for example, Illing and Liu (2006), End (2006), Cardarelli et al. (2011), Hakkio and Keeton (2009a), Islami and Kurz-Kim (2014). As already mentioned, application of this approach is limited in the CESEEs. The other approach uses sectoral data on the condition of the banking (or financial) system (by summing up weighted and normalized financial ratios). In both approaches, real economic data usually play a secondary (if any) role in the index. Yet, different FSIs in the literature are often correlated, mainly due to the use of overlapping or very similar data (Kliesen et al. 2012). The majority of the abovementioned studies are single-country studies.

However, the CAMELS variables have also been complemented with another accounting-based indicator, the Z-Score, mainly because the latter is less data-demanding, can be computed for both unlisted and listed banks, while it delivers similar results (Chiaramonte et al. 2015). Indeed, the Z-Score has become a widely used proxy for the bank risk, for example, Laeven and Levine (2009), Foos et al. (2010), Altunbas et al. (2011), Bertay et al. (2013), De Nicolò and Loukoianova (2007), despite being a relatively simple and unsophisticated measure. The Z-Score ratio requires a limited number of bank-specific variables: the ratio of equity to total assets (ETA), the ROA, and the standard deviation of the ROA. The Z-Score is usually computed as follows:

$$Z-\text{Score} = \frac{\text{ROA}+\text{ETA}}{\sigma_{\text{ROA}}} \tag{5.1}$$

Given the three basic ingredients, the final estimate depends on how each variable is measured. The literature describes a plethora of approaches, mixing current and average values of the variables used for the numerator and rolling windows or sample period observations for the denominator.

The financial stability indices according to the CAMELS approach are constructed primarily by national central banks, for example, Hanschel and Monnin (2005), Swiss National Bank (2006), Bank of Finland (2007), Jahn and Kick (2012), including those in the CESEEs. Few national central banks in CESEE officially use the Z-Score for financial stability analysis including, for example, the Croatian National Bank and the National Bank of the Republic of Macedonia. The CAMELS-based index for the banking sector is compiled by the Czech National Bank (Geršl and Heřmánek 2006), being a weighted average of indicators of bank's capital adequacy, asset quality, profitability, liquidity, interest rate risk, foreign exchange risk, which allows for analysing the evolution of banking stability over time and elaborating the driving forces behind it. Similarly, the National Bank of Serbia (2014) calculates the banking sector stability index using normalized and weighted CAMELS-like indicators.

There are very few cross-country studies with FSIs, for example, Cardarelli et al. (2011), Slingenberg and de Haan (2011), Vermeulen et al. (2015), ECB (2018), but they do not explicitly cover the CESEE countries. Among those few which do, Jakubík and Slačík (2013) use a broad range of indicators from money, bond, equity and foreign exchange markets, to develop a comprehensive financial instability index that gauges the level of financial market stress in nine CESEE countries, as a comprehensive "market thermometer" measure. They argue that credit growth, combined with the level of credit to the private sector, the public debt combined with the budget deficit and the risk attitude towards emerging markets, the risk appetite prevailing in advanced economies, and the credit risk are key determinants of the financial instability index. Cevik et al. (2013) propose the financial stress index for Bulgaria, the Czech Republic, Hungary, Poland, and Russia incorporating banking sector fragility, time-varying stock market return volatility, sovereign debt spreads, an exchange market pressure index, and trade credit. The index captures key aspects of financial stress in those countries and impulse response functions based on bivariate VARs show some significant relationships between financial stress and most measures of economic activity. Similarly, Karanovic and Karanovic (2015) develop the financial stability index for nine CESEEs (Balkan countries) over 1995–2011, covering 16 variables of financial development, vulnerability and soundness, as well as the world economic climate. The analysis finds that overall financial stability of the Balkan region is at relatively low levels and some support for instability spillovers from global economic activity. An interesting Multi-Level Performance Score using weighted variables of the banking sector condition data and the Z-Score is proposed by Miklaszewska and Kil (2015), who calculated it for 11 CESEEs for 2004–2014. The index allows tracking evolution of the banking sector condition and has proven useful in differentiating countries with the strongest and the weakest bank performance. Lastly, among rare single-country indices for the CESEE countries, Manolescu and Manolescu (2017) construed the Financial Stability Index using the Vector Autoregression model (VAR) for Romania on the basis of 12 indices of macroeconomic, financial market and banking data to find that during the economic crises periods there is a close correlation between the index and GDP.

After the GFC, the policy discussion and subsequent analyses, as well as financial stability measures, focused on how to identify system-wide problems. The GFC underlined the need to develop early-warning systems (EWI) for detecting not only individual problem banks but also signalling build-up of system-wide risks. This intensified the construction of systemic risk measures. More recently, studies have begun to employ micro data in creating system-wide indicators of financial soundness to measure the health of a country's financial system and test their efficiency as EWIs in predicting banking crises (Čihák and Schaeck 2010; Costa Navajas and Thegeya 2013). The authors suggested different statistical methodologies, depending on whether a global or country-specific crisis was under investigation. They also underlined the need to carefully consider setting thresholds, as there is a sharp trade-off between correctly identifying crises and false alarms. Apart from EWIs, an important question is how to measure systemic risk, with academics proposing a variety of market-based measures like Composite Indicator of Systemic Stress (CISS) by Holló et al. (2012) using market data (further developed by, for example, Kurowski and Rogowicz (2017)) and supervisors relying on accounting and confidential supervisory data (for a review, see Bongini and Nieri 2014). Further, a corresponding issue is how to assess the contribution to the systemic risk "made" by institutions deemed to be systemically important, for example, CoVar by Adrian and Brunnermeier (2016). The single financial stability measure is not a simple sum of the condition of the institutions/sectors of the financial system, because it would not capture the structural dimensions of the systemic risk, that is, the direct and indirect connections among them. Hence, another question involves measuring contagion and interconnectedness among financial institutions, linking the risk of individual institutions with the systemic risk. In this regard, a promising strand of the literature has studied the structure and dynamics of financial networks and how they respond to shocks, for example, Minoiu and Reyes (2013), Castrèn and Rancan (2014), Cimini et al. (2015), Smaga et al. (2018).

After the GFC national central banks in the CESEEs have also started to develop measures not only of the banking sector's condition, but rather indicators of the systemic risk and credit cycles and use them regularly in the financial stability analysis (presented in Financial Stability Reports). While the initially constructed financial stability indices used mainly bank balance sheet data, the post-GFC growing number of systemic risk measures in the CESEEs often adopt a mixed approach, that is, combine both accounting- and market-based data, as well as data from the banking system, macroeconomy and financial markets, to capture the systemic risk to a wider extent. Developing reliable systemic risk measures is the key challenge of measuring financial stability in the CESEEs going forward.

The Bank of Albania proposes the Financial System Stress Index (Kota and Saqe 2013), which aggregates into a single composite indicator the developments of different markets of the financial system (banking sector, money market, FX market, housing market). Such a composite indicator methodology is based on the portfolio theory and allows assessment of the interlinkages (time-varying cross-correlation) of various market segments through evaluation of their impact on economic growth.

Using similar input data categories, the Croatian National Bank (Dumičić 2016) composed two complementing systemic risk indices using Principal Component Analysis. The systemic risk accumulation index and the systemic risk materialization index use balance sheet, macroeconomic and financial market data. An analysis of constructed composite indicators suggests that the process of risk accumulation in Croatia was to the greatest extent related to strong lending activity, while the materialization of systemic risks was foremost manifested in banks' balance sheets as an increase in the NPL ratio, which also reflected negative developments in the real sector.

Simple financial stress index was additionally presented by the Bank of Latvia in, for example, Bank of Latvia (2009) and Siņenko et al. (2014). The stress index of Latvia's banking sector, by using Principal Components Analysis and empirical cumulative distribution functions, takes into account information from various sources (market price indicators, balance sheet indicators of banks, macroeconomic indicators), characterizing the potential stress symptoms in the banking sector. The dynamics of the index mirror stress level changes in Latvia's financial system, enabling identification of episodes of heightened stress, as well as episodes of excessively rapid and imbalanced development of the financial system. The stress index is useful as a measure summarizing the trends of many factors into a single easy-to-interpret and comparable measure, which allows clearly decomposing the elements that contribute to the index level.

Additionally, the National Bank of Ukraine (Tyshchenko and Csajbok 2017) developed a daily Financial Stress Index for the comprehensive quantitative measurement of the degree of stress in Ukraine's financial system. The index uses 14 individual indicators grouped into four sub-indices—the banking sector, the corporate debt, the government debt, and the foreign exchange market. The normalized variables were aggregated using a weighting approach based on the size/relative importance of the various segments in Ukraine's financial system. Retrospectively, the index seems to have captured all the major external or domestic shocks that were transmitted to the financial system and has potential to signal the start of a financial crisis in the future.

The National Bank of the Republic of Macedonia (2016) and Muceva-Mihajlovska and Petreski (2016) have introduced seven financial stability indices covering banking, as well as financial market and macroeconomic data. The indices were constructed using mainly various modified portfolio methods. The seven index values were averaged to a single index, as it proved to be more reliable than using individual indices for identification of the state of the financial system. The high degree of risk diversification reduces the mistakes from different research methods and the averaged index has the smallest standard deviation and the smallest error in prediction, which means it can be used for early detection of financial crises. Specifically, it is shown that credit and deposit activity of banks are the main drivers of financial stability.

Moreover, the National Bank of Slovakia (2011) has proposed a stress indicator for Slovakia's economy and financial system as a tool which can draw attention to the current problems. The data comprises macro variables, interest rates, price variables, as well as banking condition variables and lending. Both monthly and quarterly indicators capture the onset of the crisis period from late 2008 and show that the economy and financial system was under peak stress at the beginning of 2009.

Several national central banks in the CESEEs focused on the financial market data in the construction of stress indices. The Magyar Nemzeti Bank (Szendrei and Varga 2017) has developed a new measure providing information about the current level of tension in the financial system—the Factor based Index of Systemic Stress. The aim of the index is to capture common components of the data describing the financial system. The index is calculated with a dynamic Bayesian factor model methodology, which compresses a dataset of 19 financial market variables into a single index, the performance of which shows it is capable of capturing the core dynamics of financial instability on the Hungarian financial markets regardless of the source of the event. Similarly, the National Bank of Serbia (2012) provides the composite financial stress index composed of key financial market variables which are relevant to real economic activity, including the spread between the BEONIA interest rate and the NBS key policy rate, stock market volatility, volatility of the foreign exchange rate and the spread between the yield on government bonds and the NBS key policy rate. The financial stress index is the sum of standardized deviations of the said variables. As expected, GDP growth was inversely proportional to the financial stress index. Also, the Bank of Lithuania (2016) proposes three quantitative indicators of systemic risk. First, the purpose of the composite systemic stress indicator is to identify, in real time, the heightening vulnerability of the Lithuanian financial system on the basis of daily data reflecting developments in certain important segments of the financial market. Second, the indicator of banks' average contribution to the systemic risk reveals how much, on average, a bank operating in Lithuania would contribute to the sector's systemic risk (like CoVar). Third, the weighted indicator of banks' default probability is identified as an increase in stress in the Lithuanian banking sector on the basis of balance sheet data of the banks operating in the country and their foreign parent institutions, as well as financial market information.

Some national central banks have additionally developed indices used explicitly for macroprudential policy purposes. The National Bank of the Republic of Belarus (2017) makes use of the aggregated index of systemic risk (with a set safety threshold value), which accumulates such variables as the credit gap (the deviation of the current level of loans to the economy from a long-term equilibrium trend), the level of systemic liquidity (the ratio of the volume of interbank loans to customer deposits), the financial leverage, and the capital flows indicator (the ratio of funds attracted by banks from non-residents to current claims on non-residents). Likewise, Czech National Bank in Plašil et al. (2016) also developed a financial cycle indicator. The indicator expresses cyclical swings in financial risk perceptions in the financial and real sectors and is composed of: credit growth, property prices, lending conditions, debt sustainability in non-financial corporations and households, asset prices and the adjusted current account deficit-to-GDP ratio. The indicator aims at signalling the emergence of future problems in a timely fashion and takes into account the changing cross-correlation structure and applies its highest values at times of rising synchronization between the monitored variables characterizing various aspects of the financial cycle. The results show that the indicator is able to capture individual phases of the financial cycle and predict the size of the banking sector's future loan losses six quarters ahead. The National Bank of the Republic of Belarus (2017) has additionally created nine indicators[15] of financial cycles that combine into the composite indicator, which in turn allows assessing the current phase of the cycle and the financial system's exposure to cyclical risks. Lastly, the National Bank of Poland (2016) has estimated numerous early-warning models containing both international, as well as domestic data, including macroeconomic and financial data, for example, the credit gap, credit dynamics, GDP, financial system's contribution to GDP, debt service ratio, CBOE Volatility Index (VIX), Treasury-EuroDollar rate (TED) spread. The weighted average of signals from numerous models allow estimating the probability of a banking crisis in Poland, which is useful from the macroprudential perspective to set the level of a counter-cyclical buffer.

However, any aggregated index or the Z-Score must be used with caution. Bongini et al. (2018) show that the use of Z-Scores to measure the financial strength of the overall banking system, for example, as in Demirgüç-Kunt et al. (2008), Chiaramonte et al. (2015) in the CESEEs should be reconsidered, as they fail to signal periods of systemic distress. This confirms the conclusions of Cole and Gunther (1998) that the informational quality of CAMELS-based ratios in assessing bank strength is rather weak. While the CAMELS framework was not initially designed to handle systemic crises, it will require significant enhancements to be effectively used in systemic monitoring in the CESEE countries. Cihák and Schaeck (2010) also caution against using aggregate prudential indicators to identify banking crises, as they may disguise problems with individual banks or groups of banks and are typically based on backward-looking data. Given that accounting-based measures are widely used in academic research and as prudential policy tools, this calls for reduction of their deficiencies, for example, partially by increased reliability of accounting information.

The discussed financial stability measures are subject to several limitations. The evolving structural changes in the financial system and the unpredictable nature of the systemic risk make it difficult to design an aggregate measure. When constructing such a measure, it remains difficult to balance the ease of interpretation on the one hand, and a comprehensive approach encompassing the entire financial system, on the other. The measure should ideally be of a universal nature and at the same time allow taking into account country-specific risk factors. The limited or lacking complete and timely data for comparable calculations is a hurdle as well. Next, relying on historical data to pre-emptively signal a future increase in systemic risk might not be reliably achieved. Moreover, when constructing a composite measure, it is often unavoidable to face the choice of selection of indicators, which determines the frequency, thus usefulness, of its calculation. Constructing such a measure requires adopting certain, frequently strong assumptions which limit the application of the index. Another dilemma is assigning weights to the subcomponents of the index, which is often based on expert judgement, as is setting the (tolerated) threshold value for the index. All of this might limit the interpretation and information content provided by the index values. Therefore, a reasonable approach is to attempt to construct the indicator for a part of the financial system, for example, only the banking sector. In terms of the index policy use, there is a risk that the central bank by using a single measure would have reduced flexibility in response to index changes, for example, would be under pressure to act immediately after the index exceeds a certain level. Consequently, a sound financial stability analysis must be adaptable and take into account multiple indicators/sources of data and their heterogeneity. There is no perfect approach to financial stability measurement, so conclusions drawn on the basis of results obtained using one method should be cross-checked with results based on another one, as various approaches have their own advantages and disadvantages.

5.3 Do Foreign-Owned Banks Promote Financial Stability? Differences Between Foreign-Owned and Domestic-Owned Banks[16]

There is no simple, unequivocal answer to the question of whether foreign-owned banks are shock absorbers or shock transmitters. The assessment of foreign-owned banks' impact on financial stability is limited in CESEE by several factors. First, measuring financial stability is subject to debate and different proxies might provide various results. Second, financial stability and the systemic risk are determined by a myriad of factors, not only lending or activities of foreign-owned banks, so, for example, even a positive impact of foreign-owned banks on the sector's stability can be surpassed by a negative impact of macroeconomic conditions. Third, foreign-owned banks exert both positive and negative effects on financial stability and the "net effect" is not easily observable. Thus, the effect of foreign-owned bank presence on financial stability is ex ante unclear and may depend on: (i) the degree to which foreign-owned banks are active in a given market (the larger the market share, the greater the potential impact), (ii) their lending policies, (iii) their funding sources (a stable local deposit base vs more volatile interbank or parent bank funding), and (iv) their form of presence (subsidiaries controlled by local regulators are considered more stable than branches). Given the abovementioned caveats, in this chapter we review the relevant literature.

Few studies have analysed the impact of foreign-owned banks on the financial stability of host countries. In the majority of studies, the impact on financial stability was analysed in combination with many other factors (e.g. lending policy, performance) and not given priority, for example, Unite and Sullivan (2003), Choi and Hasan (2005), De Nicolò and Loukoianova (2007), Lee et al. (2012). Only a few studies have explicitly focused on modelling the impact of foreign-owned banks on bank risk and financial stability in host countries, for example, Barth et al. (2004), Yeyati and Micco (2007), Hsieh et al. (2013). Most of these studies either cover the impact of foreign-owned banks on particular countries (or regions) or use larger datasets to examine countries at different levels of economic development. Moreover, a great majority of studies analyse the period before the GFC, for example, Lee et al. (2012), Hassan et al. (2012), Ghosh (2012), Buch et al. (2013). Concurrently, only a few take into account the post-2007 data, for example, Hsieh et al. (2013), Bremus and Buch (2015), Stremmel and Zsámboki (2015). Claessens and van Horen (2012) elaborate that in the pre-GFC view it was generally considered that foreign-owned banks added to domestic competition, increased access to financial services, enhanced financial and economic performance of their borrowers, and brought greater financial stability, for example, Clarke et al. (2003), Claessens (2006), Chopra (2007), Cull and Martinez Peria (2013). The scarcity of studies on the post-crisis period creates a need to verify whether the pre-crisis view of the role of foreign-owned banks has changed, as in the literature there are two, not-mutually exclusive main explanations of the direction (positive or negative) of the financial stability impact of foreign-owned banks.

Cull et al. (2017) argue that foreign stabilizing influence on the host banking sector depends on the nature of the shocks which hit the host economy. If the shocks are domestic (idiosyncratic) in nature, then foreign-owned banks can play a stabilizing role, because the parent banks might provide (diversification of) liquidity and capital via support to their subsidiaries in the CESEEs in the case of risks materializing on the host country level through internal capital markets and intragroup credit, for example, Buch et al. (2003), De Haas and Van Lelyveld (2006, 2010), Barba Navaretti et al. (2010), Hameter et al. (2012). Cull et al. (2017) further note that by virtue of having international operations, foreign-owned banks are typically more diversified than domestic-owned banks and, hence, should be less affected by domestic shocks. This notion assumes that foreign-owned banks entering the market are international banks with diversified operations and that domestic-owned banks are exclusively local. Efthyvoulou and Yildirim (2014) show that the market power is higher for foreign-owned banks than for domestic-owned banks in CESEE and this is associated with higher levels of capitalization, thus higher resilience of foreign-owned banks. Foreign-owned bank entry also brings greater efficiency in the banking sector, for example, Drakos (2003), Bonin et al. (2005), Fries and Taci (2005), Poghosyan and Poghosyan (2010), Jeon et al. (2011), reduces the incidence of crisis (Demirgüç-Kunt et al. 1998) and lowers bank risk proxies (Choi and Hasan 2005).

These positive effects of foreign-owned banks are additionally exerted via their impact on asset quality, that is, by lowering NPLs as their presence improves risk management of domestic-owned banks (Ghosh 2012). Also, foreign-owned banks implement more rigorous provisioning standards, which results in higher loss-absorption capacities than in domestic-owned banks (Crystal et al. 2001) and less risky loan portfolios than those of domestic-owned banks (Detragiache et al. 2008).

At the same time, however, foreign-owned banks can import shocks from abroad, either from their home countries or from other countries in which they have significant operations. Financial, ownership and reputational links between parent banks and subsidiaries might serve as a contagion channel, especially during turbulent market conditions and ultimately even lead to draining—not providing—liquidity and capital from subsidiaries to parent banks, for example, Pawłowska et al. (2014), Frey and Kerl (2015). This, in turn, can destabilize the host banking sector. According to Demirgüç-Kunt et al. (1998), foreign-owned banks may—especially during periods of stress—stimulate capital outflows, support flight to quality, bust asset bubbles and retrench to home countries, ultimately depressing lending activity in host countries. Stremmel and Zsámboki (2015) provide evidence that higher foreign-owned banks presence magnifies the amplitude of the financial cycle in the EU countries, particularly during upswing phases. Both De Nicolò and Loukoianova (2007) and Yeyati and Micco (2007) showed that foreign-owned banks have significantly higher risk profiles than domestic and state-owned banks. Negative effects of foreign-owned bank presence might also occur through the NPL channel, as according to Unite and Sullivan (2003) and Hassan et al. (2012) increased activities of foreign-owned banks can be associated with higher loan loss provisions and lower credit portfolio quality, which might be explained by the fact that because domestic-owned banks are squeezed out of the credit market by foreign competitors, which forced them to grant credits to less creditworthy customers. Further, during the crisis, local banks may suffer increased costs of external funding and reduced access to international financial markets, while foreign-owned banks would have diversified funding bases, including access to liquidity from the parent banks, which may lower their funding costs (Claessens and van Horen 2012). In turn, local banks being subject to market discipline, might face a deposit rate premium requested from depositors as compensation for such a weakness. Additional spillover effects occur when deleveraging forces foreign-owned banks to withdraw from a host country, following unexpected losses in another country (Goldberg 2009).

5.3.1 *Financial Strength Index and Z-Score*

In this chapter, we explore which factors were driving financial stability in the CESEEs. For this purpose, we introduce FSI and Z-Scores as proxies for the banking sector stability and provide our empirical analysis on the role of foreign-owned banks, after taking stock of experiences of CESEEs' banking sectors during the GFC. As elaborated in the previous chapter, the credit risk is the most important driver of bank performance in these countries. Since the CESEE countries represent bank-based financial systems, we limit the aggregated indices to the banking sector, which is the key determinant of financial stability in the CESEE countries. We use both bank- and cross-country-level data for 20 CESEE countries between 1995 and 2015.[17]

We follow the methodology presented by, for example, Das et al. (2004), Geršl and Heřmánek (2006), and several national central banks in the CESEEs (e.g. National Bank of Serbia 2014), which combines IMF FSI-like indices or financial (accounting) ratios representing the CAMELS-based approach by applying different weighting systems. However, unlike most studies in the literature being single-country ones, we utilize a wide panel of the CESEE countries to construct comparable FSIs and Z-Scores. Our index reflects the most important elements of the CAMELS-based approach and includes fundamental factors impacting bank's financial standing (capital adequacy and profitability), as well as the main types of risks (credit and liquidity).

We use five bank-specific variables (see Table 5.7) to build an FSI. First, we cover banks' capital adequacy, which represents their resilience and ability to absorb losses, by using the capital ratio *ETA* ratio. Second, we use the typical profitability ratio *ROA*, which illustrates banks' ability to generate income and provide sources for the future build-up of equity capital. Third, we include a measure of liquidity (*LAF, liquid assets to total funding ratio*) to account for banks' ability to withstand short-term shocks (e.g. in the form of deposit outflows). Fourth, we include the structural liquidity ratio *LD (loans to customers to deposits from customers ratio)* to represent banks' funding stability and capacity to expand lending. Fifth, we cover banks' asset quality using *LITA (impairment charges to total assets ratio)*, which shows banks' levels of credit risk. High *LITA* may be the result of insufficient loan portfolio diversification and has the potential to reduce profitability and hamper credit growth. A higher index value reflects improved conditions in the banking system. Our choice of financial ratios is constrained (see Das et al. 2004) by the need to choose the same financial ratios available for the full sample of the CESEE countries over the period from 1995 to 2014. Due to significant data gaps, it was not possible to use, for example, the Basel CAR or the NPL ratio, so we choose a smaller set of variables but for a larger number of countries.

We calculate the minimum and maximum values for the abovementioned variables over the full period from 1995 to 2014, separately for each country. In the next step, we apply empirical normalization to each variable for each bank in each year using the following formula:

$$I_{it}^{n} = \frac{I_{it} - \min(I_i)}{\max(I_i) - \min(I_i)} \quad (5.2)$$

where I_{it} is the value of variable i in year t, and Max(I_i) and Min(I_i) are the maximum and minimum values of the given ratio during the 1995 to 2014 period for each respective country. As a result, we obtain normalized values between the interval of 0 and 1 for the 5 variables.

The FSI represents the weighted sum of the five normalized variables for banks and was calculated for banks of all types of ownership (the variable names are the same as in Table 5.7):

$$\text{FSI} = 0.2 \cdot \text{ETA} + 0.2 \cdot \text{ROA} + 0.2 \cdot \text{LAF} - 0.2 \cdot \text{LD} - 0.2 \cdot \text{LITA} \quad (5.3)$$

The theoretical values of FSI range from −0.4 to 0.6. We calculate the index for each bank in a CESEE country for each year from 1995 to 2015. Next, we aggregate the micro data to calculate the FSI on the country level by weighting the bank-level index with the total assets of each given bank.[18] The result is the asset-weighted average value of the FSI for each CESEE country from 1995 to 2015.

Table 5.7 Variables used to calculate the FSI

Category	*Variable*	*Calculation method*	*Weight*	*Impact*	*Data source*
Capital adequacy	ETA	Equity to total assets	0.2	Positive	Bankscope
Profitability	ROA	Return on assets	0.2	Positive	Bankscope
Liquidity	LAF	Liquid assets to total funding	0.2	Positive	Bankscope
Liquidity	LD	Loans to customers to deposits from customers	−0.2	Negative	Bankscope
Asset quality	LITA	Impairment charges to total assets	−0.2	Negative	Bankscope

Source: Own work

The weights assigned to each variable reflect their importance in the aggregated index. As there is no universal way of setting weights for each variable, using expert judgement we assign an equal weight to each of the five variables (0.2),[19] which is a solution most commonly used in the literature and by, for example, European Banking Authority (2015). As a robustness check, we introduce FSI with weights assigned on the basis of the principal components analysis (PCA)[20] (hereafter: FSI PCA), as used for a purpose similar to ours by, for example, Hakkio and Keeton (2009a), Klomp and de Haan (2012), and Cevik et al. (2013).

We additionally calculate the Z-Scores according to seven alternative formulas, for example, Boyd et al. (2006), Beck and Laeven (2006), Maecheler et al. (2007), Yeyati and Micco (2007), Lepetit and Strobel (2013, 2015), ECB (2016):

$$\text{Z-Score}_1 = \frac{\text{ETA}_t + \mu_{\text{ROA}}}{\sigma_{\text{ROA}}}, \tag{5.4}$$

$$\text{Z-Score}_2 = \frac{\text{ETA}_t + \text{ROA}_t}{\sigma_{\text{ROA}}}, \tag{5.5}$$

$$\text{Z-Score}_3 = \frac{\mu_{\text{ETA}} + \text{ROA}_t}{\sigma_{\text{ROA}}}, \tag{5.6}$$

$$\text{Z-Score}_4 = \frac{\text{ETA}_t + \text{ROA}_t}{\text{INST}\,\sigma_{\text{ROA}}}, \tag{5.7}$$

$$\text{Z-Score}_5 = \frac{\text{moving}\,\mu_{\text{ETA}} + \text{moving}\,\mu_{\text{ROA}}}{\text{moving}\,\sigma_{\text{ROA}}}, \tag{5.8}$$

$$\text{Z-Score}_6 = \frac{\text{ETA}_t + \text{ROA}_t}{\text{moving}\,\sigma_{\text{ROA}}}, \tag{5.9}$$

$$\text{Z-Score}_7 = \frac{\text{ETA} + \mu_{\text{ROA}}}{\text{moving}\,\sigma_{\text{ROA}}}. \tag{5.10}$$

where ETA_t is the value of ETA in period t, σ_{ROA} is the standard deviation of ROA for each bank for the whole sample, μ_{ROA} is the average value of ROA over the sample period and ROA_t is the value of ROA in period t. The Z-Score is calculated on a bank level for 1995–2015.

As concerns banking stability measures, subsidiaries of foreign-owned banks were, on average, as stable as domestic-owned banks before the GFC

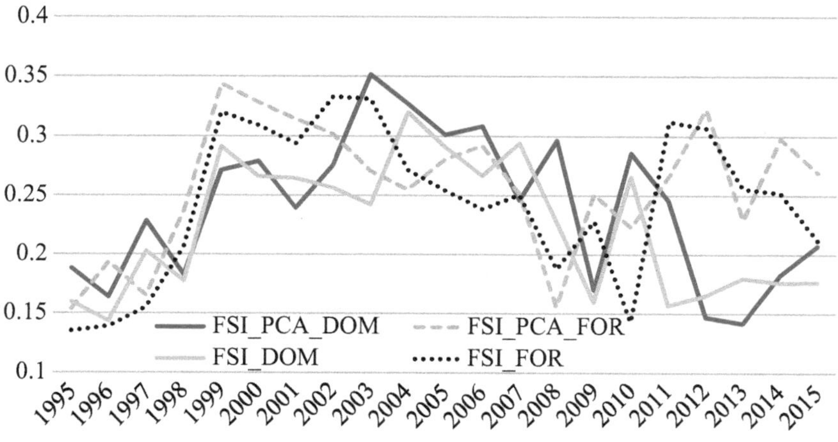

Fig. 5.14 Development of asset-weighted average FSI and FSI PCA for domestic and foreign-owned banks in CESEEs. (Source: Own work)

(see Fig. 5.14). Both the FSI and FSI PCA developed in a similar pattern for foreign-owned banks and for domestic-owned banks until 2011. From the beginning of the twenty-first century until the GFC there was a gradual decline in the FSIs in both groups of banks, signalling an increase in the vulnerability to shocks of the banking systems in the CESEEs. After the crisis, there is preliminary evidence that foreign-owned banks' condition started to somewhat improve (the FSI PCA), while condition of domestic-owned banks remains low, below pre-GFC peaks. Further, the changes of the FSI and FSI PCA (see Fig. 5.15) also reflect the cyclical conditions as those indicators are partially in line with the development of the credit gap, that is, decreasing credit gaps are associated with decreasing FSI and FSI PCA (which holds for both indicators calculated especially for foreign-owned banks). In contrast, development of the Z-Score measures for foreign-owned banks (see Fig. 5.16) do not change significantly over the analysed period, with a slight decrease before the GFC and an increase afterwards. Our findings are in line with Buch et al. (2013), who argues international banks are not riskier than domestically active banks. However, this contradicts De Nicolò and Loukoianova's (2007) findings; they claim that foreign-owned banks have significantly higher risk profiles than domestic and state-owned banks. At the same time, the country-level analysis (see Figs. 5.17 and 5.18) reveals there is no clear pattern between the share of foreign capital in the banking sector and its stability (as measured with FSI).

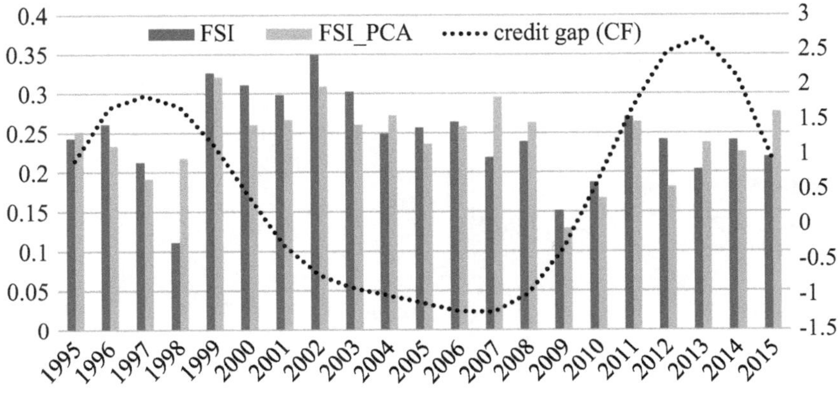

Fig. 5.15 Development of asset-weighted average FSI and FSI PCA and the average of credit gap for banks in the CESEEs. (Note: FSI and FSI PCA is LHS and credit gap (CF) is RHS; Source: Own work)

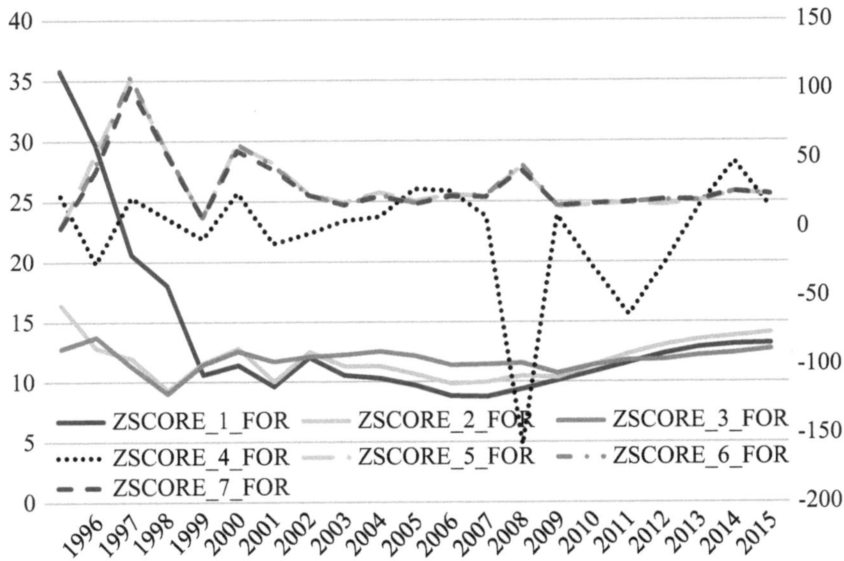

Fig. 5.16 Development of asset-weighted average Z-Scores for foreign-owned banks in the CESEEs. (Note: Z-Scores 1–3 is LHS and Z-Scores 4–7 is RHS; Source: Own work)

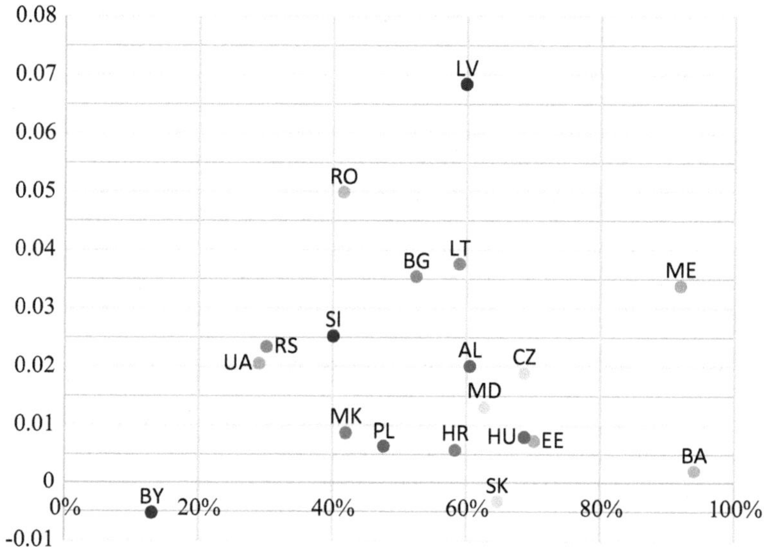

Fig. 5.17 Average level of FSI and share of foreign ownership in the banking sector pre-GFC (1995 to 2006). (Notes: Due to data gaps, the data for KV are not shown, horizontal line—average share of foreign ownership in banking sector assets, vertical line—average level of FSI)

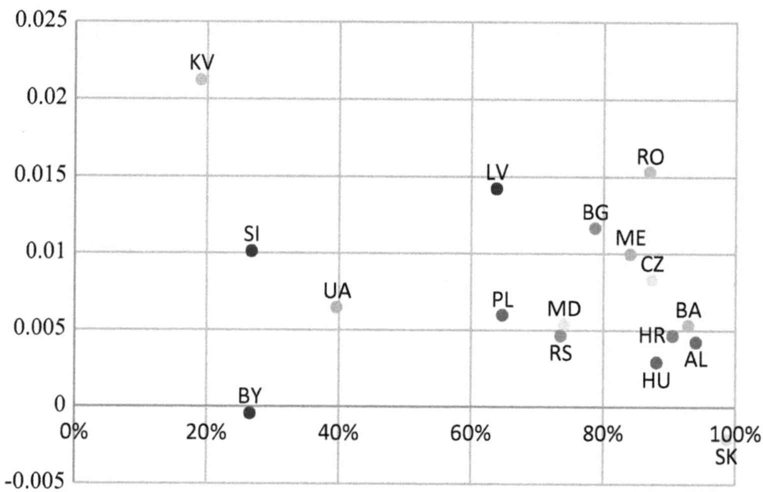

Fig. 5.18 Average level of FSI and share of foreign ownership in the banking sector post-GFC (2007 to 2014). (Notes: Horizontal line—average share of foreign ownership in banking sector assets, vertical line—average level of FSI)

5.4 What Drives Financial Stability in CESEE Banking Sectors?[21]

Next, we test the extent to which the stability of the CESEE banking sectors is dependent on macroeconomic situation, banking sector development, credit policies and safety net characteristics to determine what role foreign capital plays in the host country's financial stability. We raise the research question about the factors which determine the change of the Z-Score (increase and decrease). For this purpose, we have introduced a binary variable, which takes 0 in the case of a decrease or no change in the Z-Score or 1 if the index of strength is higher for the complete set of banks.

The results for the FSI and FSI PCA used as a dependent variable are available in Iwanicz-Drozdowska et al. (2017). Here, we have chosen the Z-Score (according to $Z\text{-}Score_3$ formula above) as a dependent variable to verify the consistency of the results. The independent variables are listed in Table 5.8.[22] The selection of variables is based on an in-depth review of the literature. Since banking systems in the CESEE countries are bank-based, credit activity is a driving force of their business, and excessive credit growth may overheat the economy and undermine the stability of the banking sector. Therefore, we focus on selecting variables on loans. This is reflected in the loan growth ratio (a proxy for a bank's credit policy), the credit-to-GDP ratio (a proxy for financial development, for example, Bremus and Buch 2015) and the share of loans granted by foreign-owned banks out of the total number of loans (a proxy for the role of foreign-owned banks). A typical measure used to reflect the role of foreign-owned banks is their share in total bank assets, for example, Yeyati and Micco (2007), Angkinand and Wihlborg (2010). Using the ratio of share of loans granted by foreign-owned banks in relation to total loans forms a more accurate picture of their credit activity and its potential role in (in)stability. We also control for the structure of banks' balance sheets (loans vs other assets) by including a ratio of other assets (e.g. debt securities issued by governments) to GDP. The macroeconomic country-level control variables include GDP growth in real terms, for example, De Nicolò and Loukoianova (2007), Angkinand and Wihlborg (2010), the change in real interest rates (e.g. Angkinand and Wihlborg 2010) and, for a robustness check in nominal interest rates, the change in real effective exchange rates (similar to De Nicolò and Loukoianova 2007). Additionally, we control for a financial safety net (measured by an FSN index).[23] This is motivated by the role of regulation and supervision, as shown by Anginer et al. (2017). We introduce an FSN index using an approach similar to La

Table 5.8 Independent variables included in the model of the direction of the Z-Score change (year over year)

Notation	*Definition*	*Expected impact*	*Source of data*
LOAN_growth	Loans growth in real terms (n/n−1)	−	Bankscope
Credit_to_GDP_growth	Credit-to-GDP (sum of loans to GDP) change (year over year)	−	Bankscope and WB database
OA_to_GDP_growth	Other assets (total assets less loans) to GDP—change (year over year)	−	Bankscope and WB database
GDP_growth	Change in GDP in real terms (year over year), $(GDP_t - GDP_{t-1}) / GDP_{t-1}$	+	WB database
NIR_growth	Nominal interest rate change (year over year)	−	WB database and central banks websites
RIR_growth	Real interest rate change (year over year)	−	WB database and central banks websites
RER_growth	Change in the real effective exchange rate of a country. As in Bruno and Shin (2015), it is logarithm of the nominal exchange rate times the ratio of US inflation and domestic inflation.	+/−	WB database and central banks websites
FSN	Compound index for financial safety net—change (year over year)	+	own
FOREIGN_SHARE_growth	Share of loans granted by foreign-owned banks in total loans—change in share (year over year)	+/−	Bankscope and own

Source: Own work

Porta et al. (1998) to measure anti-director rights. The FSN index is based on our own data and reflects changes in the FSN composition in the CESEE countries over the entire period, including supervision, deposit insurance, the central bank's role, and the resolution mechanism.

We consider a twofold outcome, that is, the increase or decrease of the Z-Score. As a consequence, we have to use binary regression approaches such as logit or probit models. We start with a random effects specification:

$$y_{it}^* = x_{it}'\beta + \alpha_i + \varepsilon_{it}$$
$$y_{it} = \begin{cases} 0 \; if \; y_{it}^* < 0 \\ 1 \; if \; y_{it}^* \geq 0 \end{cases} \tag{5.11}$$

where y_{it}^{*} is the latent (unobservable variable), $x_{it}^{\prime}$ is the vector of the regressors given in Table 5.8, α_i is the random effect of the individual country i, ε_{it} is the spherical error term and y_{it} is the observable dependent variable. In the first case, $y_{it} = 1$ in the case of an increase and 0 in the case of a decrease or no change in the Z-Score for the group of banks from the i-th country in year t. In the second case, $y_{it} = 1$ if the index of strength is higher for the complete set of banks from the i-th country in year t and 0 if the index of strength is higher for banks owned by foreign capital. Two natural approaches include probit and logit regressions, which are used in the first and the second case, respectively. This selection is made on the basis of the regressions' fit to the data (in the second case, there is a minor preference for the logit vs the probit model, whereas the opposite is true for the other case). The log-likelihood ratio test of the hypothesis of zero variance in the random effects rejects the null hypothesis in the first case ($p < 0.001$); it does not do so in the other case ($p = 0.54$). This suggests that the random effects probit should be used as the final model in the first case, but that the individual effects in the random effects logit should be dropped in the second case. These steps yield the pooled logit model with no individual effects. As a result, the final structures used are as follows:

$$y_{it}^{*} = x_{it}^{\prime}\beta + \alpha_i + \varepsilon_{it}$$
$$y_{it} = \begin{cases} 0 \; if \; y_{it}^{*} < 0 \\ 1 \; if \; y_{it}^{*} \geq 0 \end{cases} \tag{5.12}$$

where y_{it}^{*} is the latent (unobservable variable), $x_{it}^{\prime}$ is the vector of regressors given in Table 5.8, α_i is the individual normally distributed random effect of country i, ε_{it} is the spherical logistically distributed error term and $y_{it} = 1$ in the case of an increase and 0 in the case of a decrease or no change in the FSI for the group of banks from the i-th country in year t.

We present descriptive statistics in Table 5.9. In most cases, the credit growth is more volatile in the case of foreign-owned banks than it is in the sector as a whole, which translates into a material variability of average credit-to-GDP growth. Concurrently, the non-credit part of balance sheets is relatively more stable over time. The FSN proxy also varies significantly.

Altogether, we estimate five models with the Z-Score as a dependent variable: baseline Model 1, and four other models with an emphasis on robustness checks (Models 2–5). While the interest rates might be relevant

Table 5.9 Descriptive statistics

Notation	*Mean*	*Std. Dev.*	*Min*	*Max*
LOAN_growth	0.170	0.388	−1.197	2.702
Credit_to_GDP_growth	0.021	0.118	−0.953	0.860
OA_to_GDP_growth	0.009	0.067	−0.463	0.406
GDP_growth	0.035	0.062	−0.147	0.890
NIR_growth	−0.017	0.160	−1.127	2.117
RIR_growth	−0.135	0.659	−11.364	0.901
RER_growth	−6.292	682.653	−8809.233	7917.913
FSN	1.599	0.835	0	3.750
FOREIGN_SHARE_growth	0.0280	0.104	−0.415	0.989

Source: Based on the WB database, Bankscope, central bank websites, bank annual statements, the IMF and hand-collected data

factors of the financial situation, it is difficult to establish a single economically obvious type of rate; thus, we use the change in the nominal interest rate (NIR) in the baseline Model 1. However, in Models 2–5, we substitute the change in NIR with the change in real interest rates (RIR) as one of the regressors. Further, as FX loans are a key deadweight in the banking systems in the CESEEs, in Models 3 and 5 we try to verify whether the change in the real effective exchange has a meaningful impact on banks' condition via the market risk associated with FX loans. Finally, in Models 2 and 3 we include the FSN index in the set of regressors in order to check the stability of the results. In the discussion, wherever we use the concept of significance of a variable, we assume 10% level of significance for brevity.

The results of the estimation of the model given by the formula above are presented in Table 5.10. The number of factors that impact the change in the Z-Score is quite limited throughout all of the models and includes the loan growth (supply side) with a negative impact and both the growth of GDP (demand side), as well as other assets, with a positive impact.

As the GFC has proven, excessive credit activity in catching-up economies like the CESEEs may lead to unsustainable risk-taking, the accumulation of cyclical imbalances and ultimately to a credit boom undermining financial stability. The importance of credit growth for banks' financial strength is a result of their business profile, which is traditionally focused on deposits and loans. If the booming loan growth is accompanied by more liberal credit standards, this may lead to a higher credit risk and therefore higher impairment charges and lower profitability. Additionally, if credit growth exceeds deposit growth, this eventually exposes the bank

Table 5.10 Estimates of the direction of change in Z-Score logit model determinants on country-level data

Notation	*Model 1*	*Model 2*	*Model 3*	*Model 4*	*Model 5*
LOAN_growth	**−1.072***	**−1.075***	**−1.156***	**−1.145***	**−1.221***
	(−2.00)	**(−2.06)**	**(−2.15)**	**(−2.19)**	**(−2.27)**
Credit_to_GDP_growth	0.710	0.801	0.947 (	0.821	0.970
	(0.48)	(0.55)	0.64)	(0.56)	(0.66)
OA_to_GDP_growth	**5.341***	**5.401***	**5.451***	**5.407***	**5.487***
	(2.26)	**(2.29)**	**(2.24)**	**(2.29)**	**(2.25)**
GDP_growth	**6.531***	**7.144***	**7.160***	**6.729***	**6.874***
	(1.98)	**(2.14)**	**(2.10)**	**(2.04)**	**(2.02)**
NIR_growth	0.475				
	(0.52)				
RIR_growth		−0.090	−0.076	−0.069	−0.061
		(−0.44)	(−0.39)	(−0.36)	(−0.32)
RER_growth			0.001		0.001
			(1.22)		(1.21)
FSN		0.159	0.131		
		(1.03)	(0.84)		
FOREIGN_SHARE_growth	1.750	1.803	1.667	1.676	1.558
	(1.49)	(1.52)	(1.41)	(1.42)	(1.33)
Constant	−0.119	−0.441	−0.381	−0.132	−0.126
	(−0.79)	(−1.32)	(−1.11)	(−0.87)	(−0.81)

Notes: $N = 321$, t-statistics are in parentheses, *$p < 0.05$

Source: Based on the WB database, Bankscope, central bank websites, bank annual statements, the IMF and hand-collected data

to excessive funding and liquidity risks. Hence, our results confirm the negative link between credit exuberance and banks' stability in the CESEEs.

The model additionally suggests the GDP has a positive impact on the Z-Score change, as improvement in economic conditions leads to lower NPLs (better asset quality), thus a lower credit risk, which is the key risk factor that determines stability in the CESEE banking sectors. Additionally, a higher GDP increases the loan demand, enhancing profitability prospects for banks and ultimately leading to a stronger financial position. Improved profitability provides opportunity for retention of earnings to strengthen the capital base and banks' resilience to shocks.

The structure of the balance sheet (credits vs other assets) matters as well. If banks (including foreign-owned ones) instead of credits place more importance on other assets, such as T-bills, T-bonds, or deposits, in parent banks, this positively impacts the financial strength of the whole banking sector. This is consistent with the negative impact of loan growth, that is, the higher the growth of other assets, the potentially lower the growth of lending, thus the negative effects of excessive lending are reduced.

Surprisingly, the composition of the FSN is not statistically significant. This may be explained by the fact that the financial safety net in most CESEE countries is well developed, with the strong position of the central bank and the deposit guarantee scheme. It has been developing gradually since the beginning of the economic transformation, catching up with international trends and good practices as well as EU requirements. This is in contrast to Fang et al. (2014), who found that having an explicit deposit insurance policy reduces financial stability, while institutional and banking law reforms improve stability in transition economies.

Our results are highly robust throughout all of the models, which reinforces the conclusions drawn. In summary, we highlight that the factors that are important to the changes in banks' stability, as proxied by the Z-Score, are linked to credit growth (bank asset structure) and the overall macroeconomic situation. The results of our panel models suggest that foreign capital in the banking sector is not a decisive factor in determining the sector's stability. This is in line with the results of Haselmann and Wachtel (2007), who find that excessive risk-taking is not characteristic of a specific ownership type of banks in transition economies. This shows that it is not the type of owner that determines the bank's impact on financial stability, but rather other determinants are worth exploring. Overall, our results cannot unequivocally support either the studies showing the positive impact, for example, Demirgüç-Kunt et al. (1998) and Choi and Hasan (2005) or those arguing for the negative impact of foreign capital, for example, Unite and Sullivan (2003), Yeyati and Micco (2007), Angkinand and Wihlborg (2010), Hassan et al. (2012). Therefore, their impact might depend on the environment in which the foreign-owned banks operate. Further, in contrast to most studies, we did not analyse foreign-owned bank impact through NPL or loan loss provisions, but rather employed the Z-Score to proxy the financial strength of banks. Our findings show that it is the host country's conditions that affect the stability of foreign-owned banks, meaning that foreign-owned banks must react to local conditions and that foreign-owned banks' success is the same as the host country's success. We find that banks' stability is more dependent on country-specific conditions and banks' credit policies. It is more likely that foreign ownership indirectly affects financial stability via the credit policy channel reflected in the structure of foreign-owned banks' assets.

Robust economic growth in the CESEE countries incentivizes the expansion and aggressive credit policies of both domestic and foreign-owned banks, which contributes to credit boom and boom-bust cycles.

5.5 Financial Stability Outlook in the CESEEs

The GFC may be regarded as a structural break in the development of the CESEEs, which has verified many pre-GFC views and provides valuable policy lessons. According to the IMF (Cocozza et al. 2011), the impact of the GFC has left the CESEE countries with three main legacies: on the positive side, a substantial correction in the current account deficit, while on the negative side, tighter credit conditions and a significant deterioration in public finances, with both larger budget deficits and higher debt-to-GDP ratios. Moreover, external debt has increased significantly since 2009. Going forward, these challenges will weigh on the pace of growth in CESEEs.

After the GFC there are changes to the ownership structures in the CESEEs' banking sectors in general in the form of a modest downtrend of foreign ownership from its pre-GFC peak levels, which is particularly visible in Poland and Hungary. This mostly resulted from M&A activity, the Western parent banks selling their subsidiaries in the CESEEs[24] (e.g. as part of the parent restructuration processes), along with the increasing stake of state-owned banks in the banking sector assets. The evolution of the banking landscape in the CESEEs was driven simultaneously by an expansion of locally owned institutions, as well as the reduction of foreign-owned banks' operations after the GFC. On one hand, this reflects more selective market strategies (mainly by exits) of parent Western banks, and on the other, conscious national political and regulatory actions aimed at strengthening the role of the host banking systems. Nevertheless, such developments call for stronger monitoring of potential risks to the financial stability arising potentially from lower credit quality and profitability, typically associated with (either directly or indirectly controlled) state-owned banks.

Additionally, future challenges for banks in CESEE include the need to address legacy assets more decisively (NPLs) to continue lending activity on a sustainable level. The progress in reducing NPL levels remains slow. The CESEEs should not depend on "growing out of" the NPLs due to an economic upturn, but rather address structural impediments to NPLs, such as inadequate insolvency and weak debt enforcement regimes. The persistency of high level of NPLs might reflect structural or institutional challenges and weight on banks' profitability and future lending potential.

In most countries the role of FX mortgage loans is clearly on a declining path, usually as a result of a series of supervisory or legislative measures (e.g. Hungary). Further, although the flow of FX loans was largely halted in the CESEEs, the progress in de-euroization has been very gradual due to the still high stock of outstanding FX loans in many CESEEs (e.g. Serbia, Macedonia). This still poses a looming risk to financial stability in the event of significant national currency depreciation, which would increase the debt burden of households and corporates, consequently curtailing internal demand and putting pressure on the increase of NPLs. However, this risk is to some extent mitigated by the still ample FX deposits in some CESEEs (Gächter et al. 2017). Nevertheless, the GFC altered the funding structures of subsidiaries, which have become much more reliant on local deposit bases as more stable sources of funding (Gallego et al. 2010). Yet, subsidiaries in the host countries continue to rely on funding from their parent banks, even if to a smaller extent than pre-GFC. Thus, they still remain exposed to a sudden reduction of foreign bank funding and liquidity risk in foreign currency.

The GFC has underlined that the division of supervisory responsibilities between host and home countries in the EU and the lack of detailed burden-sharing provisions was a major hindrance for the resolution of the crisis and the functioning of the single market. This was a system of incompatible incentives, as the responsibility for the stability of subsidiaries belonged to the home country supervisor, while the responsibility for the stability of the financial system (in which those subsidiaries operated) was in the merit of the host supervisors in the CESEEs. An example of conflicting incentives was the drive of home supervisors to enable unconstrained flow of intragroup capital and liquidity on a cross-border basis, to geographically diversify the risk and ensure stability of transnational banking groups. At the same time, host supervisors were in favour of ring-fencing liquidity at the national level to insulate subsidiaries from liquidity contagion from the group. Moreover, the effectives of prudential policies applied in CESEEs to restrain the credit booms was limited by the international dimension of risks driven by global factors. This also calls for international coordination of policies to improve their efficiency and limit any negative spillovers to CESEEs.

Moreover, the need for the CESEEs to follow evolving regulatory and prudential landscape (e.g. implementation of Basel III), as well as national-induced reforms (e.g. new bank levies and conversion measures for FX loans) and the emergence of the FinTech sector will surely preoccupy the banking sectors in CESEE in the years to come and most probably put a downwards pressure on their profitability. This is especially relevant as the CESEEs tend to be rule-takers rather than rule-makers. The centralization and harmonization of prudential frameworks in the banking union—the home of the parent banks of majority of banks in the CESEEs—will likely result in the need to adjust policies in the CESEE to the banking union standards. There is a risk that such harmonization will reduce flexibility of national supervisors in reacting to risk specific only for the CESEEs or that the rules will be tailored for Western banks with different business models. For the CESEEs in the EU, also potential participation in the euro area[25] and opting-in to the banking union pose key policy dilemmas going forward (Belke et al. 2016). Thus, national regulatory, supervisory and resolution policies in CESEE should become more cyclically sensitive and coordinated, given the challenges to limit any "collateral damage" to the CESEE banking sector resulting from adjustment to the Western regulatory standards. The IMF (Impavido et al. 2013) elaborates on potentially possible unintended consequences of the adoption of the new capital framework for banks in the CESEEs. The decline in cross-border funding could be excessive and concentrated, thus hampering economic growth by reducing credit provision, especially in the case of growth-enhancing infrastructure finance and trade finance booked by the subsidiary. Moreover, the cost of financing could increase in the region due to inconsistencies in the application of capital rules at the solo and consolidated levels.

The effective and prudent capital and liquidity management in subsidiaries in the CESEEs might be additionally hindered by waivers granted by home country supervisors (e.g. ECB in the banking union) allowing capital and liquidity management on the group level. Therefore, the CESEEs should embark on strengthening both their micro- and macroprudential frameworks in order to increase their financial systems' resilience, as well as to improve their capacity to timely react counter-cyclically to signals of macrofinancial imbalance build-ups (e.g. credit booms). Should preemptive measures fail, it is necessary for the CESEEs to maintain appropriate crisis management and resolution framework for cross-border banking institutions. Additionally, as indicated by Iwanicz-Drozdowska (2011), the deposit insurance funds in the CESEEs must improve their payout capability in order to provide actual protection to depositors and prepare for the next economic downturn. It will be challenging for policymakers to balance increasing the resilience of banking sectors while minimizing short-term negative impact of prudential measures on bank financial intermediation.

According to the CESEE report by Raiffeisen Research (2017), the general outlook in the long term for the CESEEs is positive, with a fair chance for another round of financial deepening, yet with much fewer imbalances at the micro- and macro-level (e.g. more local refinancing, less aggressive growth, less dispersion among individual markets, less FX exposure, lower macroeconomic imbalances). The transition to the new post-GFC reality requires foreign-owned banks in the CESEEs to adopt a more sustainable and balanced business model with strengthened liquidity and capital ratios, while abandoning the most aggressive (FX) lending policies, having stronger control over costs and credit risk management, in order to provide lending supporting economic development with risk-adequately priced products, as well as higher reliance on funding from local sources. Nevertheless, the CESEEs remain exposed to several risks in a post-crisis environment. In line with the IMF (2016), the downside risks to financial stability include—due to the economic and financial links—lower economic growth in the euro area and in the US, tighter and more volatile global financial conditions, and continued weakness in multiple emerging economies. Moreover, geopolitical factors (e.g. Russia-Ukraine crisis) add to uncertainty and instability risks across the region. Still, the risk of re-emergence of unstable capital outflows and spillovers of policies from Western countries in the CESEEs in the future cannot be disregarded.

Summing up, our research cannot clearly support neither positive nor negative impact of foreign-owned banks. The banking sector stability in the CESEEs is determined by banks' conditions, their business models, the procyclicality of their lending policies, rather than just the ownership type. While the broad-based unsustainable credit boom is unlikely to reoccur, a number of new post-GFC challenges emerged and will continue to shape the banking landscape in the CESEEs. Still, it seems that, despite the turmoil of the GFC, the foundations for financial stability in the CESEEs have been strengthened along with establishment of national macroprudential frameworks and improvement of banking regulatory standards, all of which will most likely be put to the test in the years to come.

Notes

1. Impavido et al. (2013) also notes that excessive euroization of the economy may impair the conduct of monetary policy and emergency liquidity assistance function of the central bank, so it needs to be accompanied by a large volume of foreign reserves to prevent balance of payment crises.
2. Net foreign assets are the sum of foreign assets held by monetary authorities and deposit money banks, less their foreign liabilities.
3. Loan-to-Value—the ratio of the amount of the loan to the value of the collateral.
4. Debt-to-Income—the ratio of the amount of debt arising from loans to disposable income (e.g. expressed in monthly terms).
5. For example, Belarus, Bosnia and Herzegovina, Hungary, Latvia, Romania, Serbia, and Ukraine.
6. In Hungary and Poland, Latvia and Estonia.
7. The IMF and European Commission in 2008–2009 offered stabilization programmes to countries that were worst-hit by the financial crisis, that is, Latvia, Romania, Serbia, Bosnia and Herzegovina, Hungary, Belarus, Ukraine. The main aim was to enable those countries to continue servicing external debt when faced with increasingly unbalanced external position and significant current account deficits. The rollover of their external debt during the GFC came under pressure, as a major part of this debt was held by multinational parent banks. Some of the parent banks agreed—via commitment letters—to maintain their exposures and capitalize the subsidiaries over the programmes' effective periods.
8. CESEEs with floating, managed float or crawling peg include, for example, AL, PL, CZ, MD, RO, SR, HU, and HR.
9. CESEEs with pegs or currency boards include, that is, LT, BG, EE, LV, Bosnia-Herzegovina and Montenegro, Macedonia. LV and LT joined the euro zone in 2014 and 2015, respectively.
10. The list provided in De Haas et al. (2015).
11. This chapter develops earlier work published in Smaga (2013, 2014), Iwanicz-Drozdowska et al. (2017), Bongini et al. (2018).
12. CAR (capital adequacy ratio)—ratio of bank's capital to risk-weighted assets.
13. ROA (return on assets)—ratio of banks net profit to total assets.
14. NPL (non-performing loans)—ratio of NPL to total loans.
15. Those include the ratio of banks' claims on the economy to GDP; the ratio of average price of a square metre of residential real estate in the city of Minsk to average wages; the ratio of ruble money supply M2 to gold and foreign exchange reserves; the ratio of foreign trade turnover to domestic foreign exchange market turnover; terms of lending (the indicator calculated as the ratio of the average term of lending to average interest rate); bank leverage; the ratio of value of shares issued by organizations to

the revenues from sale of products produced thereby; the ratio of value of government securities circulating in the domestic market to the consolidated budget revenues; and the ratio of banks' interest revenues under transactions with natural persons to households' monetary incomes.

16. This chapter develops on earlier work published as Iwanicz-Drozdowska et al. (2017).
17. We collected the bank-level data from the Bankscope database. For the panel modelling, we use country-level data collected from the World Bank database, central bank websites, the IMF database and hand-collected data.
18. We do not calculate the indices for banks or banking groups operating in several CESEE countries because we are not able to grasp intragroup transactions, especially with the parent company; therefore, each bank is included separately.
19. An attempt to assign different weights (ranging from 0.1 to 0.25) to the five financial ratios yields comparable results.
20. We use country-level groups of variables which we assume are linearly correlated, while we assume that the proportion of variance described by each extracted factor is time-constant. We differentiate each group by the type of bank ownership. Following Kaiser-Guttman's rule, we retain only those characteristics with eigenvalues greater than 1. The authors would like to thank Karol Rogowicz for his valuable assistance.
21. This chapter bases on earlier work published as Iwanicz-Drozdowska et al. (2017), Bongini et al. (2018).
22. In additional estimations we also included a crisis dummy. Its impact on both dependent variables was not statistically significant. Those results are available from the authors on request.
23. The FSN index methodology is available as attachment to Iwanicz-Drozdowska et al. (2017).
24. Subsidiaries often sold were the ones which accounted for significant shares in their groups' profits. Examples include the sales of (or sale of stakes in): JSC Swedbank (UA) by Swedbank in 2013; BZ WBK (PL) by KBC/Santander in 2013; KBC Serbia (RS) by KBC and Societe Generale in 2013; NLB (SI) by KBC in 2013; Erste Bank Ukraine (UA) by Erste in 2013; Santander Consumer Bank (PL) by Santander in 2014; Nordea Bank Polska S.A. (PL) by Nordea in 2014; Sberbank Slovensko (SK) by Sberbank Europe AG in 2015; CitiBank HU (HU) by CitiBank in 2015; Volksbank Romania S.A. (RO) by Österreichische Volksbanken-AG in 2015; Raiffeisen Banka (SK) by Raiffeisen Bank International AG in 2016; Splitska banka (HR) by Societe Generale in 2017; Bank Pekao (PL) by UniCredit in 2017; VS Bank (UA) by Sberbank Europe AG in 2017; Bancpost S.A.(RO) by Eurobank Group in 2018.
25. Among the CESEEs, Estonia, Latvia, Lithuania, Slovakia and Slovenia are members of the euro area, while Kosovo and Montenegro have officially adopted the euro as their sole currency through euroization (in 2002).

Bibliography

Adrian T, Brunnermeier MK (2016) CoVaR. Am Econ Rev 106(7):1705–1741. DOI: https://doi.org/10.1257/aer.20120555

Allegret JP, Sallenave A (2015) Capital flow bonanzas and monetary policy in emerging Europe: responses to the global financial crisis, Post-Communist Econ 27(4):429–447. DOI: https://doi.org/10.1080/14631377.2015.1084709

Altunbas Y, Manganelli S, Marques-Ibanez D (2011) Bank risk during the financial crisis do business models matter? ECB Working Paper Series, No. 1394

Andrieş AM, Ieşan-Muntean F, Simona N (2016) The effectiveness of policy interventions in CEE countries. Eastern Journal of European Studies 7(1):93–124

Anginer D, Cerutti E, Martínez-Pería MS (2017) Foreign Bank Subsidiaries' Default Risk during the Global Crisis: What Factors Help Insulate Affiliates from their Parents? J Financ Intermed 29:19–31. https://doi.org/10.1016/j.jfi.2016.05.004

Angkinand A, Wihlborg C (2010) Deposit insurance coverage, ownership, and banks' risk-taking in emerging markets. J Int Money Financ 29(2):252–274. https://doi.org/10.1016/j.jimonfin.2009.08.001

Backé P, Feldkircher M, Slačík T (2013) Economic Spillovers from the Euro Area to the CESEE Region via the Financial Channel: A GVAR Approach. Focus on European Economic Integration Q4/13, OENB

Bakker B, Klingen C (2012) How Emerging Europe Came Through the 2008/09 Crisis. An Account by the Staff of the IMF's European Department. IMF

Bank of Albania (2017) Financial Stability Report, 2017 H1

Bank of Finland (2007) Bulletin Financial Stability. Special Issue 2006

Bank of Latvia (2009) Financial Stability Report

Bank of Latvia (2017) Financial Stability Report

Bank of Lithuania (2016) Financial Stability Review/2016

Barba-Navaretti G, Calzolari G, Pozzolo AF, Levi M (2010) Multinational Banking in Europe: Financial Stability and Regulatory Implications Lessons from the Financial Crisis. Econ Policy 25(64):703–753. https://doi.org/10.1111/j.1468-0327.2010.00254.x

Barjaktarović L, Paunović M, Ječmenica D (2013) Development of the Banking Sector in CEE Countries – Comparative Analysis. Journal of Central Banking Theory and Practice 2(2): 93–114

Barth JR, Caprio G, Levine R (2004) Bank regulation and supervision: what works best? J Financ Intermed 13(2):205–248. https://doi.org/10.1016/j.jfi.2003.06.002

Baruník J, Vácha L (2013) Contagion among Central and Eastern European Stock Markets during the Financial Crisis. Financ Uver 63(5):443–453

Beck T, Laeven L (2006) Resolution of failed banks by deposit insurers: Cross-country evidence. World Bank policy paper, No. 3920

Becker T, Daianu D, Darvas Z, Gligorov V, Landesmann M, Petrovic P, Pisani-Ferry J, Rosati D, Sapir A, Weder Di Mauro B (2010) Whither growth in central and eastern Europe? Policy lessons for an integrated Europe. Volume XI, Bruegel Blueprint Series

Beckmann E, Scheiber T, Stix H (2011) How the Crisis Affected Foreign Currency Borrowing in CESEE: Microeconomic Evidence and Policy Implications. Focus on European Economic Integration Q1/11, OENB

Belke A, Dobrzańska A, Gros D, Smaga P (2016) (When) should a non-euro country join the banking union? The Journal of Economic Asymmetries 14(A):4–19. https://doi.org/10.1016/j.jeca.2016.07.008

Berglöf E, Korniyenko Y, Plekhanov A, Zettelmeyer J (2009) Understanding the crisis in emerging Europe. Working Paper, No. 109, EBRD

Bertay AC, Demirguc-Kunt A, Huizinga H (2013) Do we need big banks? Evidence on performance, strategy and market discipline. J Financ Intermed 22(4):532–558

Bisias D, Flood M, Lo A, Valavanis S (2012) A Survey of Systemic Risk Analytics. Annu Rev Financ 4(1):255–296. https://doi.org/10.1146/annurev-financial-110311-101754

Bongini P, Iwanicz-Drozdowska M, Smaga P, Witkowski B (2018) In Search of a Measure of Banking Sector Distress: Empirical Study of CESEE Banking Sectors. Risk Manag 20(3):242–257. https://doi.org/10.1057/s41283-017-0031-y

Bongini P, Nieri L (2014) Identifying and Regulating Systemically Important Financial Institutions. Economic Notes 43:39–62. doi:https://doi.org/10.1111/ecno.12013

Bonin JP, Hasan I, Wachtel P (2005) Bank Performance, Efficiency and Ownership in Transition Countries. J Bank Financ 29(1):31–53. https://doi.org/10.1016/j.jbankfin.2004.06.015

Boyd J, De Nicoló G, Jalal A (2006) Bank risk-taking and competition revisited: New theory and new evidence. IMF Working Paper, No 06/297

Bremus F, Buch CM (2015) Banking market structure and macroeconomic stability: are low-income countries special? Pac Econ Rev 20(1):73–100. doi: https://doi.org/10.1111/1468-0106.12095

Brown M, Lane P (2011) Debt overhang in emerging Europe. The World Bank Policy Research Working Paper, No. 5784

Bruno V, Shin HS (2015) Capital Flows and the Risk-Taking Channel of Monetary Policy. J Mon Econ 71(C):119–132. https://doi.org/10.1016/j.jmoneco.2014.11.011

BCBS (2010) Guidance for national authorities operating the countercyclical capital buffer. BIS

Bubák V, Kočenda E, Žikeš F (2011) Volatility transmission in emerging European foreign exchange markets. J Bank Financ 35(11):2829–2841. https://doi.org/10.1016/j.jbankfin.2011.03.012

Buch CM, Kleinert J, Zajc P (2003) Foreign Bank Ownership: A Bonus or Threat for Financial Stability? Securing Financial Stability: Problems and Prospects for New EU Members. SUERF Studies, No. 2003/4, SUERF

Buch CM, Koch CT, Koetter M (2013) Do Banks Benefit from Internationalization? Revisiting the Market Power–Risk Nexus. Rev Financ 17:1401–1435 doi:https://doi.org/10.1093/rof/rfs033

Caporale GM, Spagnolo N (2011) Stock Market Integration between Three CEECs, Russia, and the UK. Rev Int Econ 19(1):158–169. doi:https://doi.org/10.1111/j.1467-9396.2010.00938.x

Cardarelli R, Elekdag S, Lall S (2011) Financial stress and economic contractions. J Financ Stabil 7:78–97. https://doi.org/10.1016/j.jfs.2010.01.005

Castrèn O, Rancan M (2014) Macro networks: an application to euro area financial accounts. J Bank Financ 46:43–58. https://doi.org/10.1016/j.jbankfin.2014.04.027

Central Bank Of The Republic Of Kosovo (2017) Financial Stability Report, Number 12, December

Cetorelli N, Goldberg LS (2011) Global Banks and International Shock Transmission: Evidence from the Crisis. IMF Econ Rev 59(41):41–76. https://doi.org/10.1057/imfer.2010.9

Cevik EI, Dibooglu S, Kutan AM (2013) Measuring financial stress in transition economies. J Financ Stabil 9(4):597–611. https://doi.org/10.1016/j.jfs.2012.10.001

Chiaramonte L, Croci E, Polk F (2015) Should we trust the Z-score? Evidence from the European banking industry. Global Finance J 28:111–131. https://doi.org/10.1016/j.gfj.2015.02.002

Choi S, Hasan I (2005) Ownership, Governance, and Bank Performance: Korean Experience. Financial Markets, Inst. & Inst. 14:215–242. doi: https://doi.org/10.1111/j.0963-8008.2005.00104.x

Chopra A (2007) Opening up to Foreign Banks: Harnessing the Benefits and Avoiding the Pitfalls. Mimeo, International Monetary Fund

Čihák M, Schaeck K (2010) How well do aggregate prudential ratios identify banking system problems? J Financ Stabil 6(3):130–144. https://doi.org/10.1016/j.jfs.2010.03.001

Cimini G, Squartini T, Garlaschelli D, Gabrielli A (2015) Systemic Risk Analysis on Reconstructed Economic and Financial Networks. Sci Rep 5:15758. doi: https://doi.org/10.1038/srep15758 (2015)

Claessens S (2006) Competitive Implications of Cross-Border Banking. Policy Research Working Paper Series 3854, The World Bank

Claessens S, van Horen N (2012) Foreign Banks: Trends, Impact and Financial Stability. IMF Working Paper, No. 12/10

Clarke G, Cull R, Peria MSM, and Sanchez SM (2003) Foreign Bank Entry: Experience, Implications for Developing Economies, and Agenda for Further Research. World Bank Res Obs 18(1):25–59

Cocozza E, Colabella A, Spadafora F (2011) The Impact of the Global Crisis on South-Eastern Europe. IMF Working Paper, No. 11/300

Cole RA, Gunther JW (1998) Predicting Bank Failures: A Comparison of On- and Off-Site Monitoring Systems. J Financ Serv Res (13):103. https://doi.org/10.1023/A:1007954718966

Costa Navajas M, Thegeya A (2013) Financial soundness indicators and banking crises. IMF Working Paper, No. 13/263, IMF

Croatian National Bank (2016) Financial Stability. No. 17, July

Crystal JS, Dages BG, Goldberg LS (2001) Does foreign ownership contribute to sounder banks in emerging markets? The Latin American experience. Staff Reports 137, Federal Reserve Bank of New York

Cull R, Martínez-Pería MS (2013) Bank Ownership and Lending Patterns During the 2008–2009 Financial Crisis: Evidence from Latin America and Eastern Europe. J Bank Financ 37(12):4861–4878. https://doi.org/10.1016/j.jbankfin.2013.08.017

Cull R, Martínez-Pería MS, Verrier J (2017) Bank Ownership: Trends and Implications. IMF Working Paper No. 17/60

Das SU, Quintyn M, Chenard K (2004) Does Regulatory Governance Matter for Financial System Stability? An Empirical Analysis. IMF Working Paper No. 04/89

De Haas R, Korniyenko Y, Pivovarsky A, Tsankova T (2015) Taming the herd? Foreign banks, the Vienna Initiative and crisis transmission. J Financ Intermed 24(3):325–355. https://doi.org/10.1016/j.jfi.2014.05.003

De Haas R, Van Lelyveld I (2006) Foreign banks and credit stability in Central and Eastern Europe. A panel data analysis. J Bank Financ 30(7):1927–1952. https://doi.org/10.1016/j.jbankfin.2005.07.007

De Haas R, Van Lelyveld I (2010) Internal Capital Markets and Lending by Multinational Bank Subsidiaries. J Financ Intermed 19(1):689–721. https://doi.org/10.1016/j.jfi.2009.02.001

De Nicolò G, Loukoianova E (2007) Bank Ownership, Market Structure and Risk. IMF Working Paper, No. 07/215

Dell'Ariccia G, Igan D, Laeven L, Tong H, Bakker B, Vandenbussche J (2012) Policies for Macrofinancial Stability: How to Deal with Credit Booms. Staff Discussion Note, SDN/12/06, IMF

Demirgüç-Kunt A, Detragiache E, Tressel T (2008) Banking on the principles: Compliance with Basel Core Principles and bank soundness. J Financ Intermed 17(4):511–542. https://doi.org/10.1016/j.jfi.2007.10.003

Demirgüç-Kunt A, Levine R, Min G-H (1998) Opening to Foreign Banks: Issues of Stability. In: Lee S (ed) Efficiency, and Growth, The Implications of the Globalization of World Financial Markets, Bank of Korea, Seoul, p 83–115

Detragiache E, Tressel T, Gupta P (2008) Foreign Banks in Poor Countries: Theory and Evidence. The Journal of Finance 63(5):2123–2160. doi:https://doi.org/10.1111/j.1540-6261.2008.01392.x

Dietz T, Protsyk T, Keller E (2009) Similar but different? The financial crisis in matured Western and emerging Eastern European countries. Banks and Bank Systems 4(3)

Drakos K (2003) Assessing the Success of Reform in Transition Banking 10 Years Later: An Interest Margins Analysis. J Policy Model 25(3):309–317. https://doi.org/10.1016/S0161-8938(03)00027-9

Drehmann M, Borio C, Gambacorta L, Jiménez G, Trucharte C (2010) Countercyclical capital buffers: exploring options, Bank for International Settlements Working Paper, No. 317

Dumičić M (2016) Financial Stability Indicators – The Case of Croatia. Journal of Central Banking Theory and Practice 1:113–140. DOI: https://doi.org/10.1515/jcbtp-2016-0006

Dumičić M (2017) Effectiveness of Macroprudential Policies in Central and Eastern European Countries. Working Papers W-48, Croatian National Bank

ECB (2010) The impact of the financial crisis on the central and eastern European countries. Monthly Bulletin, 2010

ECB (2016) Recent trends in euro area banks' business models and implications for banking sector stability. Financial Stability Review, May

ECB (2018) Financial Stability Review, May

Efthyvoulou G, Yildirim C (2014) Market Power in CEE Banking Sectors and the Impact of the Global Financial Crisis. J Bank Financ 40(C):11–27. https://doi.org/10.1016/j.jbankfin.2013.11.010

Égert B, Kočenda E (2007) Interdependence between Eastern and Western European stock markets: Evidence from intraday data. Econ Syst 31(2):184–203. https://doi.org/10.1016/j.ecosys.2006.12.004

End van den JW (2006) Indicator and boundaries of financial stability. DNB Working Paper, No. 97

Epstein RA (2013) When do foreign banks 'cut and run'? Evidence from west European bailouts and east European markets. Rev Int Polit Econ 21(4):847–877. DOI: https://doi.org/10.1080/09692290.2013.824913

ESRB (2018) ESRB risk dashboard. Issue 23, March

European Banking Authority (2015) Guidelines on methods for calculating contributions to deposit guarantee schemes. EBA/GL/2015/10

European Commission (2017) Coping with the international financial crisis at the national level in a European context. Impact and financial sector policy responses in 2008 – 2015. Commission Staff Working Document, SWD(2017)373, Brussels

Fang, Y, Hasan I, Li L (2014) Banking reform, risk-taking and earnings quality-evidence from transition countries. Discussion paper 19/2014, BOFIT, Bank of Finland

Financial Stability Report, No. 25 June, OENB

Foos D, Norden L, Weber M (2010) Loan growth and riskiness of banks. J Bank Financ 34(12):2929–2940. https://doi.org/10.1016/j.jbankfin.2010.06.007
Fries S, Taci A (2005) Cost Efficiency of Banks in Transition: Evidence from 289 Banks in 15 Post-Communist Countries. J Bank Financ 29(1):55–81. https://doi.org/10.1016/j.jbankfin.2004.06.016
Frey R, Kerl C (2015) Multinational banks in the crisis: Foreign affiliate lending as a mirror of funding pressure and competition on the internal market. J Bank Financ 50. https://doi.org/10.1016/j.jbankfin.2014.06.005
Gächter M, Macki P, Moder I, Polgár EK, Savelin L, Żuk P (2017) Financial stability assessment of EU candidate and potential candidate countries. Developments since 2014. EBC Occasional Paper Series, No.190
Gadanecz B, Jayaram K (2009) Measures of financial stability – a review. IFC Bulletin, No.31, BIS
Galati G, Moessner R (2013) Macroprudential Policy – A Literature Review. J Econ Surv 27(5):846–878. https://doi.org/10.1111/j.1467-6419.2012.00729.x
Gallego S, Gardo S, Reiner M, Sánchez LM, Garralda JMS (2010) The Impact of the Global Economic and Financial Crisis on Central Eastern and SouthEastern Europe (CESEE) and Latin America. Occasional Papers, No.1002, Banco de España
Gardo S, Martin R (2010) The Impact of the Global Economic and Financial Crisis on Central, Eastern and South-Eastern Europe: A Stock-Taking Exercise. ECB Occasional Paper, No. 114
Geršl A, Heřmánek J (2006) Financial stability indicators: advantages and disadvantages of their use in the assessment of financial system stability. Financial Stability Report, CNB
Geršl A, Jašova M (2014) Measures to Tame Credit Growth: Are They Effective. Econ Syst 38(1):7–25. https://doi.org/10.1016/j.ecosys.2013.10.001
Geršl A, Seidler J (2015) Countercyclical Capital Buffers and Credit-to-GDP Gaps: Simulation for Central, Eastern, and Southeastern Europe, Eastern Eur Econ 53(6):439–465. doi:https://doi.org/10.1080/00128775.2015.1102602
Ghosh S (2012) Foreign Banks in India: Liabilities or Assets? Economic Papers 31(2): 225–243. https://doi.org/10.1111/j.1759-3441.2011.00143.x
Goldberg LS (2009) Understanding Banking Sector Globalization. IMF Staff Papers 56(1):171–197
Green D, Petrick K (eds) (2002) Banking and financial stability in Central Europe. Integrating transition economies into the European Union. Edward Elgar, Cheltenham
Hakkio CS, Keeton WR (2009a) Financial Stress: What Is It, How Can It Be Measured, and Why Does It Matter? Economic Review, Second Quarter, Federal Reserve Bank of Kansas City

Hakkio SC, Keeton WR (2009b) Financial stress: what is it, how can it be measured, and why does it matter? Federal Reserve Bank of Kansas City Economic Review, Second Quarter

Hameter M, Lahnsteiner M, Vogel U (2012): Intra-Group Cross-Border Credit and Roll-Over Risks in CESEE – Evidence from Austrian Banks. Financial Stability Report, June 2012, Oesterreichische Nationalbank

Hanschel E, Monnin P (2005) Measuring and forecasting stress in the banking sector: evidence from Switzerland. In: Investigating the relationship between the financial and real economy, BIS Papers, No. 22

Haselmann R, Wachtel P (2007) Risk Taking by Banks in the Transition Countries. Comp Econ Stud 49(3):411–429. https://doi.org/10.1057/s41294-017-0050-4

Hassan MK, Sanchez B, Ngene GM, Ashraf A (2012) Financial Liberalization and Foreign Bank Entry on the Domestic Banking Performance in MENA Countries. Afr Dev Rev 24(3):195–207

Hilbers P, Otker-Robe I, Pazarbasioglu C, Johnsen G (2005) Assessing and Managing Rapid Credit Growth and the Role of Supervisory and Prudential Policies, IMF Working Paper, No. 05/151

Holló D, Lo Duca M, Kremer M (2012) CISS – a composite indicator of systemic stress in the financial system. ECB Working Paper Series, No. 1426

Horvath R, Petrovski D (2013) International stock market integration: Central and South Eastern Europe compared. Econ Syst 37(1):81–91. https://doi.org/10.1016/j.ecosys.2012.07.004

Hsieh M-F, Chen P-F, Lee Ch-Ch, Yang S-J (2013) How Does Diversification Impact Bank Stability? The Role of Globalization, Regulations, and Governance Environments. Asia Pac J Financ Stud 42:813–844. doi:https://doi.org/10.1111/ajfs.12032

Illing M, Liu Y (2006) Measuring financial stress in a developed country: An application to Canada. J Financ Stabil 2(3):243–265. https://doi.org/10.1016/j.jfs.2006.06.002

IMF (2006) Financial Soundness Indicators Compilation Guide

IMF (2016) How to Get Back on the Fast Track. Regional Economic Issues: Central, Eastern, and Southeastern Europe, May, IMF

Impavido G, Rudolph H, Ruggerone L (2013) Bank Funding in Central, Eastern and South Eastern Europe Post Lehman: a "New Normal"? IMF Working Paper, No. 13/148

Islami M, Kurz-Kim J-R (2014) A single composite financial stress indicator and its real impact in the euro area. Int J Fin Econ 19(3):204–211. doi: https://doi.org/10.1002/ijfe.1483

Iwanicz-Drozdowska M (2011) Deposit Insurance Systems – Lessons from the Crisis for CESEE Banking Systems. In: Csajbók A, Gnan E (ed) The Future Of Banking In CESEE After The Financial Crisis, SUERF Studies: 2011/1

Iwanicz-Drozdowska M (eds.) (2016) European Bank Restructuring During the Global Financial Crisis. Palgrave Macmillan Studies in Banking and Financial Institutions

Iwanicz-Drozdowska M, Smaga P, Witkowski B. (2017) Role of Foreign Capital in Stability of Banking Sectors in CESEE Countries. Financ Uver 67(6):492–511

Jahn N, Kick T (2012) Early warning indicators for the German banking system: a macroprudential analysis. Bundesbank Discussion Paper, No. 27/2012

Jakubík P, Slačík T (2013) Measuring Financial (In)Stability in Emerging Europe: A New Index-Based Approach.

Jeon BN, Olivero MP, Wu Ji (2011) Do foreign banks increase competition? Evidence from emerging Asian and Latin American banking markets. J Bank Financ 35(4):856–875. https://doi.org/10.1016/j.jbankfin.2010.10.012

Josifidis K, Allegret JP, Gimet C, Pucar EB (2014) Macroeconomic policy responses to financial crises in emerging European economies. Ecol Model 36(C):577–591. https://doi.org/10.1016/j.econmod.2013.09.035

Karanovic G, Karanovic B (2015) Developing an Aggregate Index for Measuring Financial Stability in the Balkans. Proc Econ Financ 33:3–17. https://doi.org/10.1016/S2212-5671(15)01690-1

Karkowska R, (2014) Analyzing Systemic Risk in CEE Markets in 2007–2008 Financial Crisis. Management 8(1):37–47

Kliesen KL, Owyang MT, Vermann EK (2012) Disentangling diverse measures: A survey of financial stress indexes. Federal Reserve Bank of St. Louis Econ Rev Sep:369–397

Klomp J, de Haan J (2012) Banking risk and regulation: Does one size fit all? J Bank Financ 36(12):3197–3212. https://doi.org/10.1016/j.jbankfin.2011.10.006

Kolev A, Zwart S (eds) (2013) Banking in Central and Eastern Europe and Turkey – Challenges and Opportunities. European Investment Bank

Kota V, Saqe A (2013) A Financial Systemic Stress Index for Albania. Working Paper, No 03 (42), Bank of Albania

Kurowski Ł, Rogowicz K (2017) Negative interest rates as systemic risk event. Finance Research Letters 22:153–157. https://doi.org/10.1016/j.frl.2017.04.001

La Porta, R, Lopez-de-Silanes F, Shleifer A, Vishny RW (1998) Law and finance. J Polit Econ 106(6):1113–1155.

Laeven L, Levine R (2009) Bank governance, regulation and risk taking. J Financ Econ 93:259–275. https://doi.org/10.1016/j.jfineco.2008.09.003

Lee Ch-Ch, Hsieh M-F, Dai H-W (2012) How does foreign bank ownership in the banking sector affect domestic bank behaviour? A dynamic panel data analysis. B Econ Res 64:S1:0307–3378. doi: https://doi.org/10.1111/j.1467-8586.2011.00418.x

Lepetit L, Strobel F (2013) Bank insolvency risk and time-varying Z-score measures. J Int Financ Mark I 25:73–87. https://doi.org/10.1016/j.intfin.2013.01.004

Lepetit L, Strobel F (2015) Bank insolvency risk and Z-score measures: A refinement. Financ Res Lett 13:214–224. https://doi.org/10.1016/j.frl.2015.01.001

Llaudes R, Salman F, Chivakul M (2010) The Impact of the Great Recession on Emerging Markets. IMF Working Paper, No. 10/237

Maecheler A, Srobona M, DeLisle W (2007) Decomposing financial risks and vulnerabilities in Eastern Europe. IMF Working Paper, No. 07/248

Maloku Bakija K, Mustafa A (2016) Financial Stability Map in Kosovo, CBK Working paper, No. 6.1, Central Bank of the Republic of Kosovo

Manolescu CM, Manolescu E (2017) The Financial Stability Index–An Insight into the Financial and Economic Conditions of Romania. Theoretical and Applied Economics, Volume XXIV, No 4(613), The Bucharest University of Economic Studies, Romania, p 5–24

Miklaszewska E, Kil K (2015) The impact of the 2008 crisis on the banking sectors of the CEE-11 countries: Multi Level Performance (MLP) score as a synthetic measure of bank risk adjusted performance. Econometrics 4(50), Wydawnictwo Uniwersytetu Ekonomicznego we Wrocławiu, Wrocław, p 126–141

Minoiu C, Reyes JA (2013) A network analysis of global banking: 1978–2010. J Financ Stabil 9(2):168–184. https://doi.org/10.1016/j.jfs.2013.03.001

Moorhouse A (2004) An introduction to Financial Soundness Indicators. Monetary & Financial Statistics, Bank of England

Mörttinen LM, Poloni P, Sandars P, Vesala JM (2005) Analysing Banking Sector Conditions: How to Use Macro-Prudential Indicators. ECB Occasional Paper, No. 26

Muceva-Mihajlovska E, Petreski A (2016) Aggregate Indices for Financial Stability as Early Warning Indicators for the Monetary Measures in the Republic of Macedonia. Paper presented at the 5th Research Conference "Economic and Financial Cycle Spillovers: Reconsidering Domestic and Cross-Border Channels and Policy Responses", National Bank of the Republic of Macedonia, Skopje, 7–8 April 2016

National Bank of Poland (2016) Antycykliczny bufor kapitałowy i modele wczesnego ostrzegania przed kryzysami bankowymi – zastosowanie dla Polski [Countercyclical capital buffer and early warning models of banking crises – application for Poland]

National Bank of Serbia (2012) Annual Financial Stability Report

National Bank of Serbia (2014) Annual Financial Stability Report

National Bank of Serbia (2018) Quarterly Review of the Dynamics of Financial Stability Indicators for the Republic of Serbia – Fourth Quarter 2017, April

National Bank of Slovakia (2011) Financial Stability Report For The First Half Of 2011

National Bank of the Republic of Belarus (2017) Financial Stability in the Republic of Belarus 2016

National Bank of the Republic of Macedonia (2016) Financial Stability Report for the Republic of Macedonia in 2015. Annex 3, July

National Bank of Ukraine (2017) Financial Stability Report, Issue 4, December

Oosterloo S, de Haan J (2003) A Survey of Institutional Frameworks for Financial Stability. Occasional Studies, Vol.1/Nr.4, De Nederlandsche Bank

Pawłowska M, Serwa D, Zajączkowski S (2014) International transmission of liquidity shocks between parent banks and their affiliates: the host country perspective. NBP Working Paper, No. 172

Plašil M, Seidler J, Hlaváč P (2016) A New Measure of the Financial Cycle: Application to the Czech Republic. Eastern Eur Econ 54(4)296–318. doi:https://doi.org/10.1080/00128775.2016.1192950

Poghosyan T, Cihak M (2011) Distress in European banks: An analysis based on a new dataset. J Financ Serv Res 40(3):163–184. doi:https://doi.org/10.1007/s10693-011-0103-1

Poghosyan T, Poghosyan A (2010) Foreign bank entry, bank efficiency and market power in Central and Eastern European Countries. Econ Transit *18*(3):571–598. doi:https://doi.org/10.1111/j.1468-0351.2009.00378.x

Raiffeisen Research (2014) CEE Banking Sector Report

Raiffeisen Research (2017) CEE Banking Sector Report

Roaf J, Atoyan R, Joshi B, Krogulski K and an IMF Staff Team (2014) 25 Years of Transition Post-Communist Europe and the IMF. Regional Economic Issues, Special Report, IMF

Schinasi JG (2005) Preserving Financial Stability. Economic Issues, No. 36, IMF

Simor A (2011) Micro to Macro: New Focus in Financial Stability. In: Csajbók A, Gnan E (ed) The Future Of Banking In CESEE After The Financial Crisis, SUERF Studies: 2011/1

Sinenko N, Lielkalne O (2015) Cobweb diagram as a tool for assessing changes in the most important financial stability risks. Discussion Papers, No. 2015/01, Latvijas Banka

Siņenko N, Titarenko D, Āriņš M (2014) The Latvian financial stress index as an important element of the financial system stability monitoring framework. Balt J Econ 13(2):87–112. DOI: https://doi.org/10.1080/1406099X.2013.10840534

Sinkey J (1979) Problem and failed institutions in the commercial banking industry. Cont Stu Ec, Vol. 4, JAI Press, Amsterdam

Slingenberg JW, de Haan J (2011) Forecasting financial stress. De Nederlandsche Bank Working Paper, No 292

Smaga P (2013) Assessing Involvement of Central Banks in Financial Stability. Center for Financial Stability Policy Paper

Smaga P (2014) The Concept of Systemic Risk. Systemic Risk Centre Special Paper No 5, The London School of Economics and Political Science

Smaga P, Wiliński M, Ochnicki P, Arendarski P, Gubiec T (2018) Can Banks Default Overnight? Modelling Endogenous Contagion on the O/N Interbank Market. Quant Financ 18(11):1815–1829. https://doi.org/10.1080/14697688.2018.1438641

Steiner K (2011) Households' Exposure to Foreign Currency Loans in CESEE EU Member States and Croatia. Focus on European Economic Integration Q1/11, OENB

Stremmel H, Zsámboki B (2015) The relationship between structural and cyclical features of the EU financial sector. ECB Working Paper Series, No. 1812

Sundararajan V, Enoch C, San Jose A, Hilbers P, Krueger R, Moretti M, Slack G (2002) Financial soundness indicators: Analytical aspects and country practices. IMF Occasional Paper, No. 212

Swiss National Bank (2006) Financial Stability Report

Szendrei T, Varga K (2017) FISS – A Factor Based Index of Systemic Stress in the Financial System. MNB Working Papers 9, Magyar Nemzeti Bank

Temesvary J, Banai A (2017) The drivers of foreign bank lending in Central and Eastern Europe: The roles of parent, subsidiary and host market traits. J Int Money Financ 79:157–173. https://doi.org/10.1016/j.jimonfin.2017.08.005

Tressel T (2010) Financial Contagion through Bank Deleveraging: Stylized Facts and Simulations Applied to the Financial Crisis. IMF Working Paper, No. 10/236

Tyshchenko L, Csajbok A (2017) A Financial Stress Index for Ukraine. Visnyk of the National Bank of Ukraine 240: 5–13

Unite AA, Sullivan MJ (2003) The effect of foreign entry and ownership structure on the Philippine domestic banking market. J Bank Financ 27:2323–2345. doi:https://doi.org/10.1016/S0378-4266(02)00330-8

Vandenbussche J, Vogel U, Detragiache E (2015) Macroprudential Policies and Housing Prices: A New Database and Empirical Evidence for Central, Eastern, and Southeastern Europe. J Money Credit Bank 47(S1):343–377. doi:https://doi.org/10.1111/jmcb.12206

Vandenbussche J, Kongsamut P, Dimova D (2018) Macroprudential Policy Effectiveness: Lessons from Southeastern Europe. Journal of Banking and Financial Economics 1(9)2018:60–102. DOI: https://doi.org/10.7172/2353-6845.jbfe.2018.1.4

Vermeulen R, Hoeberichts M, Vašíček B, Žigraiová D, Šmídková K, Haan J (2015) Financial Stress Indices and Financial Crises. Open Econ Rev 26:383–406. https://doi.org/10.1007/s11079-015-9348-x

Vujić V (2015) Internal capital markets and crisis transmission: evidence from foreign bank subsidiaries in CESEE. Focus on European Economic Integration Q3/15, OENB

Yeyati EL, Micco A (2007) Concentration and foreign penetration in Latin American banking sectors: Impact on competition and risk. J Bank Financ 31:1633–1647. doi:https://doi.org/10.1016/j.jbankfin.2006.11.003

CHAPTER 6

Impact of Foreign-Owned Banks on Economic Development

Małgorzata Iwanicz-Drozdowska, Paola Bongini, Paweł Smaga, and Bartosz Witkowski

6.1 Economic Growth and Financial Development: Theory and Evidence

Two main paradigms characterize growth economics: the neoclassical or exogenous growth theory (better known as the Solow model) and the endogenous growth theory.

In the neoclassical paradigm, the growth process is described by only two equations: (i) a production equation that expresses the current flow of output goods as a function of the current stocks of capital and labour, and (ii) a law of motion that shows how capital accumulation depends on investments and capital depreciation. The main idea of the Solow model is that per capita GDP (the measure of economic growth) cannot grow in the long run, unless we assume that productivity—an important component of the production equation—also grows over time, thanks, for instance, to some sort of "technical progress" which can drive economic growth. Such technical progress is totally exogenous and cannot be explained.

Endogenous growth theories are, instead, theoretical frameworks in which productivity growth is endogenous and dependent upon certain characteristics of the economic environment. As Rodrik (2011) highlights,

M. Iwanicz-Drozdowska et al.,
Foreign-Owned Banks, Studies in Economic Transition,
https://doi.org/10.1007/978-3-030-01111-6_6

economic convergence "depends on policies, institutions and other country specific circumstances" such as the saving rate or the demographic rate. Institutions, in particular, may include a wide variety of formal and informal rules, such as property rights, contract enforcement, judicial system's effectiveness, the quality of regulation and governance, political stability, and financial stability (Rodrik 2000).

Among these models, the one that considers and incorporates the role of the financial system is known as the Schumpeterian growth theory as it involves the force that in the early 1900s economist Joseph Schumpeter called "creative destruction". In particular, Schumpeter argued that the services provided by financial intermediaries are essential for technological innovation and economic development. The studies of Aghion and Howitt (1992, 1998) and King and Levine (1993a, b) are the most prominent attempts to incorporate Schumpeter's qualitative ideas into a quantitative model, which could also be used for empirical tests of the influence of finance on economic growth.

In order to see the role that finance plays in the growth process, one needs to take market frictions into account: for instance, the difficulties that a firm/entrepreneur might have financing investments that drive growth. When market frictions are taken into account, then financial markets and intermediaries might have a causal impact on economic development. Indeed, theory provides that effective financial institutions (markets and intermediaries) help overcome market frictions introduced by asymmetric information and transaction costs; in this way, they foster economic growth through five main channels (Levine 2005).

Specifically, financial systems (1) produce ex ante information about possible investments and allocate capital; (2) monitor investments and exert corporate governance after providing finance; (3) facilitate trading, diversification, and management of risk; (4) mobilize and pool savings; and (5) ease the exchange of goods and services.

Table 6.1 reports and describes the above functions, highlighting which financial institutions provide them; it explains the effects on economic growth and the conditions under which financial institutions can foster growth; finally, it quotes relevant literature that theorizes the link between finance and growth.

In sum, theoretical literature on financial intermediation predicts that an efficient and well-developed financial system can help increase economic growth rates through improved capital accumulation and higher productivity growth.

Table 6.1 Review of theoretical literature on finance and growth

Functions	*Description*	*Main characteristics of intermediaries/markets*	*Effects on growth*	*References (in bold studies that directly theorize the link between finance and growth)*
Evaluate projects	Financial intermediaries (FIs) reduce the cost of acquiring and processing information	Efficiency in screening	Improving the ex ante assessment of investment opportunities has a positive spillover effect on resource allocation (and therefore accelerate economic growth)	Greenwood and Jovanovic (1990)
		Efficiency in venture capital investment	Boost the rate of technological innovation by identifying those entrepreneurs with the best chances of successfully initiating new goods and productions	King and Levine (1993a, b), Galetovic (1996), Blackburn and Hung (1998), Morales (2003), Acemoglu et al. (2003)
	Financial markets (FMs) stimulate the production of information about firms	Large size and liquidity; market efficiency	Valuable information has positive implications for capital allocation	Grossman an Stiglitz (1980), Kyle (1984), Holmstrom and Tirole (1993), Aghion and Howitt (1998)

(*continued*)

Table 6.1 (continued)

Functions	*Description*	*Main characteristics of intermediaries/markets*	*Effects on growth*	*References (in bold studies that directly theorize the link between finance and growth)*
Exert corporate control (which is central to understanding economic growth)	Liquid equity markets	Stock options to align manager compensation to firm performance Easiness of takeovers	Well-functioning stock markets foster corporate governance which directly impact firm performance	Jensen and Meckling (1976), Diamond and Verrecchia (1982), Jensen and Murphy (1990) Scharfstein (1998), Stein (1988)
	Debt contracts	Debt instruments used by firms	Debt contracts arise to lower the cost of monitoring firm insiders; reduce managerial slack and accelerate the rate of firm innovation	Gale and Hellwig (1985), Boyd and Smith (1994), Aghion et al. (1999)
	Banks	Economize on monitoring costs and reduce credit rationing	Specialize in ex post monitoring (delegated monitors of dispersed investors)	Diamond (1984), Bencivenga and Smith (1993), Sussman (1993), Harrison et al. (1999), Boyd and Smith (1992), De La Fuente and Marin (1996)
Facilitate risk management	FIs and FMs ease the trading, hedging, and pooling of risks with implications for resource allocation and growth	Markets allow agents to hold diversified portfolios	Cross-sectional risk diversification services can affect long-run EG by altering resource allocation and saving rates	Acemoglu and Zilibotti (1997), King and Levine (1993a, b)
			Intertemporal risk sharing by FIs which invest with a long-run perspective and smooth interest rates across business cycles	Allen and Gale (1997)
		Secondary market trading costs	Liquidity risk is associated with projects requiring a long-run commitment of capital; both stock market and banks may enhance liquidity and influence EG	Levine (1991), Diamond (1991), Bencivenga and Smith (1993)

Ease the mobilization (pooling) of savings	Pooling of resources helps overcoming transaction costs (firms mobilizing savings from different individuals) and information asymmetries associated with making savers feel comfortable in relinquishing control of their savings	FIs invest in their reputation as safe haven; diversification applies to FIs portfolios	Effective pooling individuals' savings affects EG by increasing savings, exploiting economies of scale and overcoming investment indivisibilities	Sirri and Tufano (1995), Acemoglu and Zilibotti (1997)
Facilitate exchange	Financial arrangements which lower transaction costs can promote specialization, tech innovation and growth		Markets that promote exchange encourage productivity gains	Greenwood and Smith (1997)

Source: Own work

However, theory also host contrarian voices which warn against potential negative effects on economic growth from an "excess" of financial deepening; better resource allocation and lower risks may depress saving rates to such an extent that the overall growth rates actually drop with enhanced financial development (King and Levine 1993a, b; Bencivenga and Smith 1993). Besides, a well-functioning and large financial sector will compete with the real sector in attracting resources—for instance, the best human resources—with potential negative repercussion for growth (Philippon 2010; Bolton et al. 2011). More recently, financial instability stands in the dock as the main cause of the economic depression that advanced countries are experiencing since the burst of the financial crisis in 2007.

Another point under discussion is whether finance is an important driver of economic growth at any stage of economic development or it instead plays a role up to a certain level of income per capita, with the positive relationship being the strongest among low- and middle-income countries which are catching up with high-income countries. Besides, considering that after reaching the status of a middle-income economy, many developing economies have failed to converge to their high-income peers and a "middle-income trap" has been theorized (Eichengreen et al. 2011, 2013; Agénor et al. 2012); the initial advantages of a catching-up economy may disappear once a certain level of development has been reached, that is, when the fuel for economic growth is innovative and technologically advanced production for which the economy does not have the level of capital and the quality of human capital necessary to sustain such a process.

Finally, financial innovation seems to be a relevant ingredient of economic growth as long as financiers themselves innovate. Laeven et al. (2015) theorize and empirically test the conjectures that: (i) technological and financial innovations are positively correlated; and (ii) economic growth will eventually stagnate unless financiers innovate. Obviously, not all financial innovations promote economic growth. Financial innovation has played an important role in triggering the recent global financial crisis (GFC). However, the model stresses the idea that financial innovation is necessary for sustaining economic growth.

The empirical research on the finance and growth nexus has produced a substantial body of studies growing constantly since the seminal work of Goldsmith (1969), who was the first to empirically show the positive correlation between financial development and GDP per capita, on a sample of 35 countries over the 1860–1963 period. Yet the strand of research linking finance to growth in a methodologically robust manner can be traced back to the pioneering works by King and Levine (1993a, b). The authors, using panel data for 80 countries over 1960–1989, were the first to prove that various measures of financial development levels were positively related to GDP per capita growth via productivity improvements. Using a different methodology—vector error correction models (VECM)—Rousseau and Wachtel (1998) proved, for the main industrialized economies, the long-run causality between the measures of financial intensity and real per capita levels of output. The positive relationship between the exogenous components of financial development and economic growth was later confirmed by Levine et al. (2000) for a panel of 74 countries over the extended period of 1960–1995. In addition to banks, Levine and Zervos (1998) showed that stock markets also contribute to long-run growth, capital accumulation and productivity improvements. Therefore, they should be analysed simultaneously. The long-run equilibrium relationship between development of banking and stock markets and economic growth was confirmed for a sample of 13 EU countries during 1976–2005 (Wu et al. 2010), though the study also uncovered a negative short-run effect between liquidity and economic development.

Advances in computational capacity and availability of large cross-country data sets with relatively large time dimensions helped in making progress in the methodological aspects of the empirical research, whose efforts were mainly devoted to say a final word, in sound and sophisticated econometric models, about the causal links between finance and growth, so as to address biases introduced by measurement errors, reverse causation and omitted variables' problems (Beck 2008). Although complete unanimity does not exist, the bulk of empirical research on the mechanisms through which finance affects growth suggests that (Levine 2005): (a) countries with better functioning banks and markets grow faster; (b) simultaneity bias does not seem to drive these conclusions; and (c) better functioning financial systems ease the external financing constraints that impede firm and industrial expansion.

Prominent qualitative surveys of this empirical literature are that of Levine (2005), Beck (2008, 2011, 2013) and Popov (2017), acknowledging that countries with better functioning banks and markets grow faster since the financial system, when working efficiently, can ease the external financing constraints that impede firm and industrial expansion. More recent quantitative surveys based on meta-analysis (Valickova et al. 2015; Arestis et al. 2015) attempted to address and uncover the reasons why the empirical literature has yet reached a unanimous consensus after almost five decades of extensive research.

The ambiguity in the direction and strength of the finance and growth nexus might indeed have several causes: (i) the choice of proxies for financial variables; (ii) the scope of data used; or (iii) the estimation approach applied (e.g. addressing or ignoring the issue of endogeneity).

As far as the first motivation, notwithstanding the methodological achievement in investigating the link between finance and growth, measures of financial development used in the literature (i.e. private credit to GDP, stock market capitalization to GDP) are mainly those traditionally proposed since the seminal works by King and Levine (1993a, b) and Atje and Jovanovic (1993). This choice has a main drawback as pointed out by Levine (2005), which is that the empirical literature on finance and growth suffers from an insufficiently precise link between theory and measurement. In fact, if theory focuses on particular functions provided by the financial sector—producing information, exerting corporate governance, facilitating risk management, pooling savings and easing exchange (see Table 6.1)—and how these functions influence resource allocation decisions and economic growth, empirical works too frequently fail to directly measure these financial functions and employ the simple "size" of the financial system as a proxy for financial development. To overcome these shortcomings, a new comprehensive index, capturing both financial institutions and markets, has been constructed based on a new database made publicly available by the IMF and the World Bank (Čihák et al. 2012; Sahay et al. 2015) and a number of other important sources of data.[1] Financial institutions include banks, insurance companies, mutual funds, pension funds, and other types of non-bank financial institutions. Financial markets include mainly stock and bond markets. Different dimensions of the financial system are measured: depth, access, efficiency and stability (see Table 6.2). As Sahay et al. (2015) show, banking system credit to the private sector, while still being a relevant component of financial development, reflecting the role of banks in many financial systems, is far from being the only driver of the economic growth. In the following years, this new index will prove relevant in advancing our knowledge on the finance and growth nexus, when long series of data will be available for emerging countries on various aspects of their financial architecture.

As regards the second issue, that is the number of countries or time periods under investigation, Arestis et al. (2015) highlight how these aspects of data characteristics can impact the results and explain the observed heterogeneity in the literature. The growth-finance literature reveals large differences in the number of countries examined by each

Table 6.2 Financial development index

	Depth	*Access*	*Efficiency*	*Stability*
Financial institutions	Private sector credit to GDP; Financial institutions' assets to GDP; M2 to GDP; Deposits to GDP; Gross value-added of the financial sector to GDP	Accounts per thousand adults; branches per 100,000 adults; per cent of people with a bank account; per cent of firms with line of credit (small); per cent of firms with line of credit (all)	Net interest margin; lending-deposits spread; non-interest income to total income; overhead costs (% of total assets) profitability (return on assets, return on equity); Boone indicator (or Herfindahl or H-statistics)	Z-score (or distance to default) capital adequacy ratios; asset quality ratios; liquidity ratios; other
Financial markets	Stock market capitalization plus outstanding domestic private debt securities to GDP; private debt securities to GDP; public debt securities to GDP; international debt securities to GDP; stock market capitalization to GDP; stocks traded to GDP	Per cent of market capitalization outside of top ten largest companies; per cent of value traded outside of top ten traded companies; government bond yields; ratio of domestic to total debt securities; ratio of private to total debt securities (domestic); ratio of new corporate bond issues to GDP	Turnover ratio (turnover/capitalization) for stock market; price synchronicity (co-movement); private information trading; price impact; liquidity/transaction costs; quoted bid-ask spread for government bonds; turnover of bonds on securities exchange; settlement efficiency	Volatility of stock price index, sovereign bond index; skewness of those indices; vulnerability to earnings manipulation; price/earnings ratio; duration; ratio of short term to total bonds; correlation with major bond returns

Source: Based on Čihák et al. (2012)

study, with some studies focusing only on one country and others using extended set of economies pertaining to different regions (also diverse as far as their level of development, in terms of per capita GDP); differences also exist between studies that rely on cross-sectional data or time series data or finally make use of panel data. According to the authors' meta-regressions based on 118 empirical papers published between 1993 and 2013, using either panel data or time series tends to produce lower partial correlation than using cross-sectional data. This is robust evidence that the kind of input used plays an important role in explaining heterogeneity in the studies. Furthermore, the coefficient of the "number of countries" variable and of the "homogenous" variable (i.e. whether the examined set of countries are homogeneous in terms of per capita GDP) comes with a different sign according to the specific statistical methodology used (OLS, fixed effects, or random effects estimations). However, their magnitude is quite low, suggesting that their influence is not economically meaningful.

Similar findings are uncovered by Valickova et al. (2015), who also apply meta-analysis on 67 empirical studies. In particular, studies that combine different regions should be carefully interpreted as the growth effects appear to depend on the level of economic development, as stressed by Rioja and Valev (2014) and Rousseau and Wachtel (2011) or Beck (2013), who showed that the positive finance and growth relationship is most evident in low- and middle-income countries. The meta-analysis results suggest that the number of countries as well as the sample size included in the analysis matters for the reported results; cross-sectional studies and time series studies report, on average, larger effects than studies using panel data, partially confirming the results by Arestis et al. (2015). Besides, the variable capturing the number of years in the data set is found to be positive and significant, that is, studies examining longer time horizons generally report larger effects of finance on economic growth.

What a non-negligible body of recent empirical studies put under question is the presence of a linear relationship between finance and growth. A growing number of studies started to point to the existence of a threshold of growth-enhancing impact of financial development. Rousseau and Wachtel (2011) show that, when the post-1990 data are used, the positive relationship between finance and growth is not as strong as it was in the past. In a similar vein, Demetriades and Rousseau (2016) show on a sample of 91 countries over 1973–2004 that financial depth is no longer a significant determinant of long-run growth. Valickova et al. (2015) support this evidence, adding that the effect of finance on growth weakens in the 1990s and is generally stronger in wealthier countries. Further, Arcand et al. (2015), using different data sets and empirical approaches, provide evidence that there can be a limit to the positive effects of the expansion of finance, after which there is indeed "too much" finance. In particular, their results show that the marginal effect of financial depth on output growth becomes negative when credit to the private sector reaches 80–100% of GDP.

As for the differences in the research design due to the estimation approach adopted, the interested reader can refer to Beck (2008) as the main reference to review different econometric methodologies used in the literature to assess the relationship between financial development and growth. The study illustrates the identification problem, which is at the centre of the finance and growth literature. The meta-analysis studies suggest that it is important to control for endogeneity when estimating the effect of finance on growth. Studies using OLS find on average larger effects than studies that account for endogeneity—for example, using instrumental variables or panel data methods, with generalised method of moments (GMM) being nowadays the most popular econometric method employed in the most recent studies on finance and growth. Indeed, just some older studies from the 1990s of the previous century and the initial years of 2000s are cross-sectional analysis, based on OLS estimations only; virtually, all contemporary research is on the country level and is based on panel data. Basically, three main subtypes of analyses can be pointed out: VAR approach, cointegration analyses and "Barro-type" approach, while other types of approach are quite rare. The VAR or Error Correction Model (ECM) approach (Shan 2005; Tennant and Abdulkadri 2010) is the least theoretically motivated one. The cointegration-type analyses (de Mello 1999; Buch et al. 2003; Handa and Khan 2008), make use of cointegrating equation to find whether a long-run equilibrium exists between the independent and the dependent variables. This is supposed to answer the question of whether the relation between them is not spurious, especially if the variables of interest are integrated of order higher than one—recent developments in the panel data analysis that include second-generation tests of cointegration facilitate this aim. Nevertheless, the short time series which constitute most panels have a very negative influence on the power of the tests used. Given that typical research in this field is based on the country-level panel data with a group of at least a few countries included in the analysis, the natural approach to the GDP growth equation is based on the so-called Barro regression, which stems from Solow's model. It is assumed that the growth of GDP is a (log linear) function of the earlier GDP level and a group of potential growth factors. The latter include a wide variety of variables (with hundreds of possibilities considered in the literature); some of which are related with the banking sector. Such a type of regression is easily estimated if cross-sectional data are used, as it is the case in the 1990s of the previous century (and still can be found, mostly in the form of robustness check, but sometimes also as the main tool—for example, Alfaro et al. 2004 or Buch and Toubal 2003). The use of panel data complicates the estimation process significantly. Some authors still apply the more traditional estimation approaches, such as the fixed effects (Eller et al. 2005; Chee and Nair 2010) or random effects (Bevan and Estrin 2004; de Haas and van Lelyveld 2006), although these are not statistically correct in view of the dynamics of the model of interest. A step forward includes instrumental variables (Borensztein et al. 1998). Nowadays, however, the most popular approach is based on the general method of moments. The Arellano and Bond's "difference estimator" can be found as a tool (Carkovic and Levine 2002; Akimov et al. 2009); however, the theoretical papers published at the end of the previous century suggest that such an estimator lacks efficiency and—most importantly—suffers from the small sample bias, especially if strong autoregression is incurred. While the latter is almost surely present due to the existence of strong GDP beta convergence, Blundell and Bond's GMM estimator is currently the most popular one. Its use can be found in papers by Carstensen and Toubal (2004), Carkovic and Levine (2002), or Compton and Giedeman (2011). Still, some criticize GMM on the basis of too little sample size. Indeed, this method was invented typically for microeconomic data. Although it is widely applied in macroeconomic research, some authors prefer to use methods which do not require the large number of units for asymptotics, such as the pooled mean group estimator (Cheng et al. 2014) and group mean dynamic OLS (Herzer 2012). Although the above-discussed (log) linear models dominate, some partly non-linear approaches can be found in the literature. Those include threshold models estimated with conditional OLS (Lensink and Hermes 2004; Lensink and Murinde 2006); however, this group of models has not gained much popularity.

Having briefly depicted the current status of the theoretical literature on the finance and growth nexus, we now turn our attention to the main findings of studies, specifically focused on investigating such a link in our sample of transition economies.

6.2 Finance and Growth in CESEE Countries

Focusing on studies specifically investigating the issue of growth and finance in transition economies or subregions such as the CESEE countries, we can highlight that this link is significantly weaker with respect to developed and high-income economies; in fact, in catching-up countries with younger and relatively less developed financial systems, the finance and growth nexus is less evident.

Table 6.3 presents a summary of the main results of these studies that in the last 15 years focused on the CESEE countries.

Berglof and Bolton (2002) investigated the experience of the transition economies in the first decade of their transformation from a centrally planned to a market economy to derive evidence on the link between finance and economic growth, that is, to give answers to the questions of whether it is possible "*to engineer a development take-off by creating a modern financial architecture from scratch*" or whether "*financial institutions and markets are just a reflection of underlying conditions in the real sector*" (p. 78). The authors analysed the great divide between transition countries where economic development had already taken off (Czech Republic, Estonia, Hungary, Latvia, Lithuania, Poland, Slovenia and Slovakia) and those caught in a vicious circle of institutional backwardness and macro instability (Bulgaria, Romania, Russia, and Ukraine). This great divide was present in every measure of economic performance: GDP growth, investment, government finances, growth in inequality, and general institutional infrastructure. These measures were weakly linked to measures of financial development, like domestic credit to the private sector to GDP, index of financial reforms, concentration ratio in the banking sector, the loan-deposit rate spread or the number of companies listed on the stock market. As a matter of fact, the authors illustrate that the reason why some countries were able to cross the "great divide" while others did not was to be found to a large extent outside their financial systems. Differences in fiscal and monetary discipline and low enforcement capacity of governments, excessively committed to bailout policies, were indeed considered by the authors as the leading explanations for the observed variation in economic development across transition economies.

However, more advanced transition economies shared the following three key features. First, they all have converged to mainly bank-based financial systems with a significant fraction of foreign bank ownership. These banks were playing a limited role in financing investments and firms

Table 6.3 Review of empirical literature in CESEE countries

Authors (year)	*Sample*	*Period*	*Economic growth variables*	*Financial development variables*	*Research method*	*Effects of finance on economic growth*	*Key findings*
Berglof and Bolton (2002)	CZ, EE, HU, PL, LT, LV, SI, SK, BG, RO, UK	1993–1997	GDP growth, investments, inequality, government finances	Domestic credit to the private sector/GDP; C3assets/total banking sector assets; number of banks; bad loans/total loans; interest rate spread; number of listed companies	Correlation between relevant variables	Weak correlation	Countries on the prospering side had converged to a bank-based financial system, with a significant fraction of foreign bank ownership. Local markets declined and local firms preferred to be listed in foreign well-known stock exchanges
Koivu (2002)	AL, RO, HU, SK, Belarus, SI, BG, LT, HR, CZ, LT, Moldova, UK, EE, PL, Macedonia + other transition countries	1993–2000	Real GDP growth	Interest rate margin, domestic credit to the private sectors/GDP	Fixed effects panel model	Interest rate margin (−); credit (−)	The relationship between the amount of credit to the private sector and economic growth is not clear; causality seems to run mostly from economic growth to credit growth

Mehl and Winkler (2003)	SEE	1993–2001	Real GDP per capita growth	Domestic credit to the private sector/GDP; broad money/GDP	OLS, 2SLS, 2SLS and country fixed effects	None statistically significant	Reforms failed to prevent inflationary finance and crises, contributing to large output losses. Subsequent tightening of regulation and supervision, as well as the opening of domestic banking sectors to foreign investors positively changed the environment of the SEE financial sectors
Dawson (2003)	BG, RO, HU, SK, SI, LT, CZ, LT, Moldova, UK, EE, PL, Russian Federation	1994–1999	Real GDP growth	Liquid liabilities (M3)/GDP	Panel model	Positive but not significant	Economic growth in CEECs was not constrained by underdeveloped financial sectors (as they are at the time of investigation)
Fink et al. (2009)	BG, CZ, HU, SI, SK, PL, RO, MT, TK plus mature economies	1996–2000	Real GDP per capita growth	Domestic credit /GDP; private credit/GDP; stock market capitalisation/GDP; bond outstanding/GDP	Panel model	Domestic credit (+); bond outstanding (+); capital stock (+); all other variables non-significant impact on growth	Some evidence that total financial intermediation contributed to economic growth and stability. Unlike private credit, which was never significant, domestic credit made an important contribution to economic growth

(*continued*)

Table 6.3 (continued)

Authors (year)	*Sample*	*Period*	*Economic growth variables*	*Financial development variables*	*Research method*	*Effects of finance on economic growth*	*Key findings*
Akimov et al. (2009)	AL, Belarus, Bosnia H, CZ, Macedonia, EE, HU, LT, LV, Moldova, PL, RO, Russia, SK, SI, UK + other transition countries from Central Asia and East Asia	1989–2004	Real GDP growth	M2/GDP, claims on the non-financial sector/total domestic credit; credit to private sector/GDP; commercial bank assets/commercial bank + central bank assets	Fixed effect panel model; dynamic panel model	Positive and significant	The positive link that exists between financial development and economic growth is invariant with the choice of financial proxies
Carp (2012)	Romania	1995–2010	Real GDP growth	Stock market capitalization/GDP; turnover ratio; stock value traded/GDP	VAR model	GDP growth rate and turnover ratio show positive bidirectional Granger correlation	No effect in the long run, except for bidirectional correlation between GDP growth rates and turnover ratio

Hassan et al. (2011)	EE and Central Asia, among many other regions	1980–2007	Real GDP growth	Domestic credit to the private sector/GDP; domestic credit by bank sector/GDP; M3/GDP; gross domestic savings/GDP, stock market cap/GDP; stock market total value traded/GDP	Fixed effects panel estimation; VAR model	No statistically significant effects	Domestic credit and growth show bidirectional correlation; a shock in gross domestic savings cause growth to increase
Yu et al. (2012)	EE and Central Asia, among many other regions	1980–2009	Real GDP growth	Domestic credit to the private sector/GDP; domestic credit by bank sector/GDP; M3/GDP; gross domestic savings/GDP, stock market cap/GDP; stock market total value traded/GDP	Fixed effects panel estimation; VAR model	No statistically significant effects	No Granger causality between GDP growth rates and financial development proxies
Barajas et al. (2013)	150 countries including AL, BG, LT, Moldova, RO, UK and other Central Asia economies	1975–2005	Real GDP per capita growth	Private credit/GDP; stock market cap/GDP, stock market turnover/GDP	Dynamic panel model		Positive and significant effect of credit on growth

(*continued*)

Table 6.3 (continued)

Authors (year)	*Sample*	*Period*	*Economic growth variables*	*Financial development variables*	*Research method*	*Effects of finance on economic growth*	*Key findings*
Petkovski and Kjosevski (2014)	16 transition economies from Central and SEE	1991–2011	Real GDP growth	Net interest margin, private credit/GDP	Dynamic panel model	Interest margin (−) not significant; Private credit (−) and significant	The large stock of NPLs and the banking crises experienced at the beginning of the transition period hindered the growth-enhancing role of the banking sector. It is relevant to implement an institutional environment where banks and bank credit can deliver their positive effects
Caporale et al. (2015)	Ten new EU members (BG, CZ, EE, Hu, LT, LV, PL, RO, SK, SI)	1994–2007	Real GDP per capita growth	Domestic credit to the private sector /GDP, stock market cap/GDP, Net interest margin, Liquid liabilities/GDP	Dynamic panel model	Stock market cap (+); liquid liabilities (+); NIM (−) and significant	The underdevelopment of stock and credit markets, with the consequent lack of financial depth, remains one of the main features of these economies

Source: Own work

could finance their investments almost exclusively from retained earnings or through foreign direct investments, which corroborates the evidence that finance was not strongly correlated to economic growth. Second, the ownership structure of banks and firms was concentrated and turnover of shares in the stock market was low, while the number of listed companies was diminishing as a result of foreign acquisitions, mergers and subsequent delisting. Besides, most of the best firms showed a preference in listing abroad, in more liquid and attractive US or EU markets. Finally, bank spreads showed a declining path, in the level and volatility, though they remained high by the standards of developed market economies, which explained, as we showed in Chap. 3, the great interest of foreign banks to enter these banking markets.

In the same year, Koivu (2002) reached a similar conclusion, using panel data from 25 transition countries over the 1993–2000 period. He measured the level of financial development by means of two variables: the margin between lending and deposit interest rates and the amount of bank credit allocated to the private sector as a share of GDP. According to his results, the interest rate margin was significantly and negatively related to economic growth, supporting the view that the presence of an efficient banking sector boosts economic growth and so it did in transition economies. Indeed, as banking sector reforms and the interest rate margin were negatively correlated in the sample countries, the policy implications of the study were quite relevant and in line with Berglof and Bolton (2002) conclusions; countries with evolved banking sectors (in terms of banking reforms) had smaller interest margins and higher economic growth than countries struggling with banking sector reforms. However, in contradiction to the general literature, a rise in the amount of credit did not seem to accelerate economic growth in transition economies. The main reasons behind this result were traced back to the numerous banking crises the transition countries experienced in the years under investigation and the soft budget constraints that were still prevalent in many of these countries, encouraging private sector agents to make counterproductive investments. Due to these specific characteristics of transition economies, the growth in credit had not always been sustainable and, in some cases, it may have led to a decline in growth rates. The author warned against the use of the "size" of the financial sector as a good variable to measure the effectiveness of the financial system in inducing real growth.

In such an environment, Mehl and Winkler (2003) confirmed a relatively weak contribution of the financial sector (domestic credit and broad money as a share of GDP) to economic growth in SEE in the first decade of transition (1993–2001), interpreting their results in the light of the socialist legacy, as well as the failure to establish robustly and prudently functioning regulatory and legal frameworks. In the early years of transition, the financial sectors in Southeast Europe were characterized by relative depth and yet a poor environment which was not able to prevent inflationary finance and crises in many countries of the region, ultimately contributing to large output losses. Indeed, the main deficiencies of the financial sector were: (i) insufficient restructuring of state-owned banks and poor governance, which led the state-owned banks to be subject to political pressures to continue extending loans to non-profitable state-owned enterprises, triggering a rise in bad loans and resource misallocation; (ii) lax regulation on licensing new private banks and corresponding lending which implied the foundation of banks as "agent" or "pocket" banks of their parent (non-financial) companies; (iii) lack of human capital and credit technology, such as risk assessment and risk management; (iv) inadequate banking supervision. In most cases, banking regulation and supervision had to be created from scratch, and as banks lacked the skills necessary to guarantee sound credit policies and procedures, the same happened in most supervisory departments, not able to set out and reinforce international supervisory standards; and (v) a poor institutional and legal environment, unable to put into practice the regulations pertaining to financial contracts, is mainly in the areas of insolvency, bankruptcy and collateral collection. As a result, rather than promoting growth, bank credit led to misallocation of resources and lack of confidence in the whole banking sector in Southeast transition economies.

As before, the study concluded that the subsequent phase of tightened regulations and supervisions as well as of opening of domestic banking sectors to foreign investors could positively change the environment of Southeast Europe's financial sectors with potential positive effects on economic growth. It also reckoned that domestic policymakers and international institutions should take the evidence from transition economies as a recommendation to promote lending activities, especially to micro-, small-, and medium-sized businesses, that up to that period did not obtain much support from the banking sector, as the financial deepening materialized mainly through monetization than intermediation.

Testing a different measure of financial development (liquid liabilities, M3, as a share of GDP) did not help Dawson (2003) to find a positive and significant relationship between financial development and economic growth in 13 CESEE countries over the 1994–1999 period. The conclusion was that economic growth in the CEECs was not constrained by underdeveloped financial sectors (as they were at the time of investigation).

Also Fink et al. (2009) developed further measures of financial development by expanding the scope of their investigation to include various financial market segments, including stock and bond markets in addition to the banking sector. In particular, the authors used an aggregate measure of financial development covering credit, bond, and stock markets, so that the measure could be less influenced by differences in the financial market structures between countries, and changes of the financial market structures within countries. Further, they analysed the causal links between single financial market segments and economic development in order to determine interdependencies between the structure of financial markets and economic growth. They found that one measure of overall financial sector development (i.e. domestic credit expansion) and one single segment of the financial sector (i.e. bond markets) stimulate economic growth and thus enhance economic stability over early years of transition (1996–2000). Without a proper legal, institutional, and corporate governance framework, the stock market seemed to have introduced rather instability to the financial sector than have contributed to economic growth in the early phase of transition. As before, no significant influence of private credit on growth was found.

Interestingly, their results indicated a clear distinction between the growth effects of the financial funds channelled to/through the public sector and those directed to the private sector. The authors explained these different findings for the two measures of bank credit as a direct effect of the bad loans that were lingering private banks and were only gradually removed from the banks' balance sheets. This made the contribution of private credit to stability and growth relatively weak compared with domestic credit, which also included bank credits to central and local governments, for which there was very low default probability. In addition, they supported the conclusion by Berglof and Bolton (2002), for whom banks in transition economies were mostly providing working capital finance to enterprises, while investment finance came predominantly from retained earnings and foreign direct investment. Similar arguments about a different impact of financing the private and the public sectors were applied in interpreting the results of the impact of bond markets on growth, since these markets were heavily dominated by government issues in all accession countries.

The issue of separating credit extended to the private sector from credit allocated to state-owned companies is also investigated by Akimov et al. (2009), where four measures of bank sector development are included: liquid liabilities as a share of GDP; the ratio of claims on the non-financial private sector by total domestic credit and as a share of GDP; and the ratio of commercial bank assets divided by commercial plus central bank assets. In contrast to existing studies on transition economies, and yet in accordance with empirical evidence in advanced and developing economies, the authors deliver robust evidence on the positive relationship between all selected financial development measures and economic growth. Their findings support the previous suspicion of Mehl and Winkler (2003) that proper financial development in a conductive environment may have just started in the CESEE economies.

More recent regional studies which also include a number of CESEE countries are those by Hassan et al. (2011), Yu et al. (2012), and Barajas et al. (2013). In the two companion papers, Hassan et al. (2011) and Yu et al. (2012) analysed a large set of countries over the 1980–2007 and 1980–2009 periods respectively, including EE and Central Asia. They did not find, for that region, any specific relationship between bank development, stock market development and economic growth. They concluded that in order to achieve a long-run positive finance and growth relationship, as established by Levine and Zervos (1998), those countries needed to increase domestic credit to the private sector and domestic savings to attract a higher level of investments for the long-run economic growth. Barajas et al. (2013) proved, on a sample of 146 countries with data for 1975–2005 period, that the finance-growth nexus has a heterogeneous impact across regions, that is, it is weaker for low-income countries. In the Middle East and North Africa countries, the banking sector provides a lower contribution to economic growth than in the rest of the world, while in Europe and Central Asia, the impact is greater and generally positive. Those differences are partly due to the varied access to financial services and the degree of banking competition. However, as shown by Rousseau and Wachtel (2011), the authors warn that the empirical link between finance and growth weakens considerably once post-1990 data are introduced, primarily as a result of the proliferation of financial crises and their adverse effects on economic activity.

Finally, Caporale et al. (2015), concentrating on the ten new EU members in the 1994–2007 period, supported the evidence that the stock and credit markets were still underdeveloped in these economies, so that their contribution to economic growth was limited. Indicators of efficiency of the financial sector (the net interest margin and the EBRD index of institutional development, measuring the progress in reforming the financial sector) yielded better results, supporting the theoretical expectation that an efficient banking sector plays an important role in economic growth. As seen in Chap. 3, achieving higher efficiency was a challenge for all the groups of countries under investigation which policymakers faced and tried to solve by "importing" the needed skills from abroad.

As the process of financial deepening was delegated to foreign banks, it is now time to investigate their role in influencing economic growth in host countries.

6.3 Is Foreign Bank Credit Growth-Enhancing?

The majority of the studies analysed in the previous section tended to hint at a positive role played by foreign-owned banks which in the years under investigation were entering these markets, taking control of relevant market shares. Even those studies pointing to the lack of significance of the finance and growth nexus regarded the entry of foreign bank as a potential (future) trigger of economic growth by means of increased efficiency in the banking sector, which in turn could deliver reduced transaction costs and increased credit availability.

Few are the papers specifically focused on investigating the "real effects" of significant foreign ownership in banking. Eller et al. (2005) represent one of the first attempts to deliver empirical evidence on the effect of sectoral FDI (e.g. in the financial sector) on economic performance of the CESEE economies. The authors, through an extensive literature review, identify four different channels through which foreign ownership in banking may affect economic development, namely (i) efficiency, (ii) credit volume, (iii) corporate governance and institution building, and (iv) signal effects (see Fig. 6.1). They also try to incorporate one of these channels (e.g. the efficiency channel) in a formal theoretical model that could be econometrically tested as well.

Financial sector FDI (FSFDI) strategically reorientate the host target bank with respect to the parent bank's typical market and activities. This implies the supply of products and services new to the host banking market, the availability of fresh capital and liquid resources which in turn increase foreign banks' lending supply, and the implementation of internal group standards for risk assessment and management, which also play an

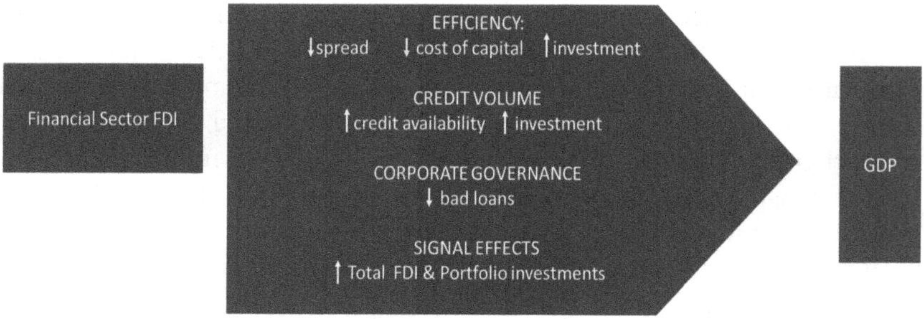

Fig. 6.1 Financial Sector Foreign Direct Investments and transmission channels that affect GDP growth. (Source: Adapted from Eller et al. 2005)

important role in clearing the credit portfolio and reducing the share of bad loans, again with positive effects on their lending ability. These changes point to a higher management and operational efficiency of foreign banks as opposed to domestic-owned banks (Claessens et al. 2001) that produce positive spillovers on the whole financial sector. Better risk management and lower operating costs allow for more efficient capital allocation, which translates into narrower interest margins and an offer of products and services at lower prices. The increased competition in the banking industry should induce the overall financial system to reach higher efficiency, resulting in an overall reduction of transaction costs. The lower cost of borrowing for non-financial firms should facilitate investment and ultimately deliver growth-enhancing effects. In addition, well-capitalized foreign banks may provide a higher volume of loans to the host country's private sector, in particular businesses. Deeper financial intermediation might contribute to investment and thus to growth. As acquired banks are subject to strategic reorientation and receive capital injection from their parent banks, their technologies, know-how and operational practices are also upgraded, with positive effects on the reduction of bad loans. Foreign-owned banks are also less involved in connected lending, and their better loan portfolios and risk management should contribute to financial stability (especially when foreign-owned stake in the banking market is high) which is important for economic development. The higher know-how and technology can be transferred to other industries: non-financial companies in search for external finance will need to comply with the higher and stricter credit requirements by foreign banks, so that businesses themselves stick to international standards in terms of accounting, auditing, and corporate governance practices. In the long run, these spillover effects could permeate all industries as well as the whole infrastructure (including regulation, legislation, and supervision) with positive returns on stable economic development. Indeed, foreign-owned banks act as a catalyst for regulatory changes and implementation of international standards also in legislation and supervision (Soussa 2004). Finally, financial services FDI might have signal effects for total FDI and portfolio investments. Product innovation, such as in the field of asset management, can foster capital market development, which in turn enlarges the range of funding possibilities for corporate investors, spurring investment and economic growth. At the same time, FSFDI can act as a catalyst for FDI from other industries with again further positive influences on economic growth.

Among the briefly described diverse microstructure changes that foreign banks induce in host countries, Eller et al. (2005) analyse the potential efficiency improvements for the whole financial sectors and their effects on economic growth. They test this hypothesis (economic growth is led by FSFDI-induced efficiency gains) in 11 CEECs from 1994 to 2003, by means of a cross-country growth accounting model and employ fixed effects' panel data estimations. Their empirical results indicate that there can be a positive relationship between FSFDI and economic development, although with certain limits; as a matter of fact, modelling the impact of inward FSFDI to represent a hump-shaped impact on economic growth helps the authors to detect potential non-linearities between FSFDI and growth. In particular, FSFDI seems to spur economic growth depending on higher human capital stock, while the interaction of the FSFDI stock with the stock of domestic physical capital is negatively associated to growth. In other terms, the contribution of FDI to growth holds when the host country has a minimum stock of human capital to activate knowledge spillovers as argued by Borensztein et al. (1998).

A similar conclusion is also supported by the study of Lensik and Murinde (2006), who investigate the relationship between the entry of foreign-owned private banks and changes in gross domestic investment in 54 countries, both advanced and developing economies, for the 1990–1997 period. The sample included Hungary and Poland as representative of EE transition economies. A standard model of aggregate investment behaviour was estimated in which an indicator of foreign banks' presence (e.g. the share of foreign bank assets in total banking sector assets and the number of foreign banks in total banks in the host country) was included as one of the determinants of the ratio of investment to GDP. As the authors argued, foreign banks' entry can induce positive and negative effects on the host country's economic performance. On the positive side, as argued by Eller et al. (2005, see Fig. 6.1), foreign banks are expected to improve the quality, pricing and availability of financial products and services, in particular credit; they induce higher competition and efficiency in the whole banking sector and reduce the (negative) influence of the government on the domestic financial sector, limiting the importance of directed credit policies; they accelerate the process of building up supportive systems, such as accounting, auditing, transparency and financial regulations; they facilitate knowledge spillover in key areas such as regulation and supervision and risk management. On the negative side, it is argued that foreign-owned banks tend to adversely affect the stability of the host country for various reasons.

Therefore, Lensik and Murinde (2006) specifically considered the potential non-linear relationship between investment and foreign banks' presence. Indeed, econometric results supported the hypothesized non-linear relationship and a threshold level of foreign bank entry is determined to distinguish between the effects of a high versus low degree of foreign bank ownership on aggregate investment. The authors support the evidence of a U-shaped curve which highlights that a foreign bank entry stimulates domestic investment not until foreign ownership has gained a substantial size (over and above the critical value).

This has important policy implications as it suggests that the policy followed by CESEE countries in letting foreign banks hold increasingly high shares in banking assets was the right choice.

A recent study by Bruno and Hauswald (2014), on a wide sample of developing and advanced economies for the 1995–2003 period examined overall consequences of a foreign bank entry (and the mode of entry, as well) for real economic activity, including the competitive reaction of local lenders. It identified three distinct channels through which foreign-owned lenders improve access to credit and industry growth, namely the lessening of external financing constraints, the overcoming of informational constraints and the overcoming of contracting legal constraints. Domestic lending by foreign banks stimulates the growth of financially constrained industries even after controlling for credit to the industrial sector by local banks. As the mode of entry (acquisitions vs greenfield) implies different informational dynamics, Bruno and Hauswald (2014) show that foreign banks can overcome informational obstacles to lending through acquisitions; acquiring domestic banks allows new entrants to combine their own superior credit assessment policy and procedures with access to local data and borrower-specific information. Indeed, entry by M&A has a highly statistical and economic effect on local economic activity, especially in developing countries where borrower information is less easily and readily available. Finally, as foreign banks appear to mitigate the consequences of local banking crises, the authors interpret this finding as a better ability by foreign banks to commit to more stable lending relationship, which in turn incentives borrowers to keep honouring their contractual obligations, despite the lack of local legal recourse and adequate contract enforcement that in many developing countries is still a pervasive problem. In other words, the promise of a stable lending relationship, even in time of local crises, gives foreign banks more authority and power with borrowers which translate into a natural advantage in enforcing debt contracts. To sum up, thanks to foreign-owned banks, external financing constraints are relaxed and informational barriers and legal obstacles are diminished.

All these studies share two main features that may limit their analysis and evidence: their time horizon—which mainly covers the initial transition period up to the GFC[2]—and the fact that they did not fully measure the impact of foreign-owned banks in the credit allocation process.

As for the first point, the GFC and the subsequent sovereign debt crisis, which exerted significance influence on the home country parent bank, are important factors which need to be carefully taken into consideration when studying the role of foreign banks in CESEE. The majority of these foreign-owned banks are in fact parts of large Western European financial groups, which faced idiosyncratic and/or systemic risk at home country. These recent crises challenged the idea that multinational banks play a positive role as shock absorbers in local markets and a new stream of research emerged, specifically investigating the "exit" of foreign-owned banks from the local market.

Considering the second feature, as foreign banks hold high shares in banking assets in the CESEE economies, it is crucial to look at the role they play in credit allocation. The quality of lending and the efficient credit allocation seem to be significantly more important for economic performance than mere lending volumes (Giannetti and Ongena 2005). The lack of readily available data has hindered such an analysis so far; however, although still limited, a number of studies are appearing which take into consideration the issue of credit allocation and the credit supply to different target groups within the private sector, that is, distinguishing between household credit and business credit. Beck et al. (2012) highlighted that the banking sector can play a growth-supporting role to the extent that it lends to enterprises and not to households. Household credit has a negative impact on growth prospects since it is usually deemed to finance consumption and demand for goods and services, whereas business credit is usually directed at productive purposes, that is, to increase investments and labour demand—the true engine of growth, according to Solow (1956). Further evidence has recently appeared, specifically concerning a number of transition economies, for example, Gaffeo and Garalova (2014), Sassi and Gasmi (2014), Sahay et al. (2015), and Léon (2018). As highlighted by Sahay et al. (2015), in a sample of 34 countries with data available on credit composition, credit to households is likely to result in lower savings and, therefore, in lower growth. With specific reference to 27 European countries, Sassi and Gasmi (2014) provided evidence that household credit undermines economic growth. Léon (2018), with a hand-collected database covering 143 countries for the period of 1995–2014, also documented the absence of any positive effect of total credit on growth, while his findings also showed that household credit has a negative effect on growth (yet the study failed to provide robust support for a positive effect of business credit). Using a panel of 13 CESEE countries, Gaffeo and Garalova (2014) found that the financial system is more likely to improve economic growth when the process of financial intermediation channels funds not to publicly owned enterprises or households but rather to private businesses.

In the next section, we tackle these issues to further explore the role of credit as a growth-enhancing or diminishing factor and the related effect of the credit extended by foreign banks.

6.4 Foreign Ownership in CESEE Countries: Evidence from a Large Sample and Extended Sample Period

We studied the role of financial development in economic growth in CESEE countries starting after the transformational recession (1995) until 2015.

We collected data from World Bank database, Barro and Lee database, Bankscope, Factset, and HelgiLibrary. We also used hand-collected data on banks' ownership structure. Initially, we cover all 20 post-communist countries. However, due to the lack of data on the development of human capital, our sample had to be reduced to 14 countries from CESEE, namely Bulgaria, Croatia, Czech Republic, Estonia, Hungary, Latvia, Lithuania, Moldova, Poland, Romania, Serbia, Slovenia, Slovakia, and Ukraine.

As shown in the previous chapters, the transformation period was marked, after a deep decline, by dynamic development. One of the key challenges was the privatization of state-owned banks and enterprises, as well as the liberalization of market entry for private investors, both domestic and foreign. Foreign bank entry was particularly high in these economies in the late 1990s and early 2000s, which contributed to the growth of nascent banking systems. According to Claessens and Van Horen (2014), this partly reflected waves of reforms, including the opening-up of transition economies, as well as rapid financial globalization before the GFC. This trend peaked in 2007 and slowed markedly after the outbreak of the crisis. The share of foreign-owned banks in banking sector assets in the CESEE countries in 2017 (see Table 6.4.) ranges from 29% in Ukraine to 99% in Slovakia. As of 2017, the stake of foreign-owned banks is below 50% only in 5 out of 20 countries (Belarus, Hungary, Poland, Slovenia, and Ukraine). Since 2015 (the end of our sample), further reduction of foreign-owned banks' engagement in the region is especially visible in Albania, Estonia, Poland, Romania, and Ukraine, mainly due to parent banks selling (stakes in) their subsidiaries in those countries.

Our variables of interest are listed and explained in Table 6.5. They belong to three main groups depicting the macroeconomic, institutional, and financial system characteristics of the investigated economies.

Table 6.4 Share of foreign ownership in CESEE countries as of 2015 (2017)

Albania	86% (78%)	Latvia	47% (52%)
Belarus	32% (32%)	Lithuania	92% (92%)
Bosnia and Herzegovina	84% (86%)	Moldova	81% (81%)
Bulgaria	76% (77%)	Montenegro[b]	79%
Croatia	89% (88%)	Poland	61% (45%)
Czech Republic	84% (87%)	Romania	90% (77%)
Estonia	94% (88%)	Serbia	76% (76%)
FYR Macedonia[a]	75% (75%)	Slovakia	99% (99%)
Hungary	44% (45%)	Slovenia[a]	33% (46%)
Kosovo	90% (88%)	Ukraine	35% (29%)

Note: the share of assets held by foreign-owned banks in banking sector assets; data for 2017 in brackets: [a]in brackets data for 2016; [b]no data for 2017

Source: Helgi Library, Raiffeisen Research, European Central Bank, and National Central Bank Data

Table 6.5 Definition of variables

Variables	*Definition*	*Expected sign for economic development*	*Source of data*
GDP	Gross domestic product, current prices (m EUR)	Dependent variable	WB database
Inflation	Inflation annual data: average rate of change	–	WB database
Government size	General government final consumption to GDP	–	WB database
Country's openness to trade	(Exports + imports) to GDP	+	WB database
Country's openness to investments	FDI inflows to GDP	+	WB database
Human capital	(1) % of population (>15 years) with tertiary education (2) Average years of schooling and rate of return to education; the average years of schooling are taken from the Barro and Lee database, while the assumed rate of return to education is based on Mincer equation estimates around the world	+	(1) Barro and Lee database (2) Penn World Table 9.0
Credit-to-GDP	Domestic credit to private sector (outstanding amount) to GDP	+	WB database
Stock market capitalization	Stock market capitalization to GDP	+	WB database
Governance indicator	(1) Rule of law index (2) Regulatory quality index	+	WGI database
Foreign banks relevance	Share of the outstanding credit by foreign-owned banks in domestic credit to private sector	+/–	Own calculation based on Bankscope[a] and hand-collected data

Source: Own work

[a]All banks in a given year in a given country; consolidated financial statements; if not available—stand-alone financial statements

6.4.1 *Measures of Macroeconomic Environment*

The first group includes variables typically used in growth models to analyse the impact of the macroeconomic context on economic growth—see among the many Mankiw et al. (1992) and Barro and Sala-i-Martin (2003). The empirical literature supports negative effects of inflation—a measure of monetary discipline—and government expenditure—a measure of government burden—on economic growth; trade and investment openness, instead, are expected to be positively correlated to growth: on the one hand, by facilitating the exchange of goods and services, trade openness can foster economic growth; on the other hand, FDI inflows are expected to produce positive externalities in the form of technology transfer and spillovers.

6.4.2 *Measures of Institutional Environment*

The second group includes variables that highlight the institutional characteristics of a country. Mankiw et al. (1992) showed that the accumulation of human capital improves the empirics of economic growth modelling; for this reason, higher educational attainment among the population is included in our finance and growth models, with the expectation of positive effects on economic growth. The proxies used to measure human capital are the percentage of population with tertiary education (from the Barro and Lee database 2013) and, alternatively, an index of the "rate of return" to education extracted from the Penn World Table (PWT version 9.0) on human capital.[3]

Following Acemoglu et al. (2001, 2002), Claessens and Laeven (2003), and Eicher and Leukert (2009), who provided evidence that differences in institutions can extensively affect economic growth and financial deepening, we also controlled for the institutional quality of our sample economies. For this reason, we included the Rule of Law Index and the Regulatory Quality Index, extracted from the World Bank's Worldwide Governance Indicators database, as proxies for the quality of the institutions in our sample countries.[4]

6.4.3 *Measures of Financial Development and Foreign Ownership*

We include traditional measures, such as credit to the private sector, as a share of GDP (King and Levine 1993b) or stock market capitalization to

GDP (Atje and Jovanovic 1993; Levine and Zervos 1998), into our model. To control the role of foreign-owned banks within the local financial systems, we introduced the ratio of foreign-owned banks' lending to total domestic credit. This second variable captures the actual capability of foreign banks to impact the local financial system. Foreign banks can play a leading role—which does not necessarily translate into a positive judgement of their behaviour—to the extent that they hold an important share in the local credit market, as already underlined by the review of the empirical literature.

6.4.4 *The Model*

The theme of modelling GDP growth has been profoundly discussed in economic literature. Most empirical research is based on an augmented form of Solow's model, operationalized via the so-called Barro regression. Given that the data used in this research are a set of countries observed over time, those can be viewed as a panel. The general form of the Barro regression for panel data can be written as:

$$\Delta \ln \mathrm{GDP}_{it} = \beta_1 \ln y\mathrm{GDP}_{i,t-1} + x_{it}'\beta + \alpha_i + \varepsilon_{it} \tag{6.1}$$

where $\Delta \mathrm{GDP}_{it}$ is the GDP growth of country i in period t, x_{it} is the vector of independent variables, α_i is the country-specific individual effect, and ε_{it} is the error term (assumed to be the white noise), while β and β_1 are the parameters of the model.

The variables included in the x_{it}' vector represent two types of potential growth determinants: well-recognized potential growth factors that can be attributed to physical or human capital and, additionally, characteristics of the financial market, which are considered as potential growth factors. These are presented in Table 6.5.

Given the autoregressive character of Eq. (6.1) and the related endogeneity issues, the specification needs to be transformed into the equivalent form before estimation:

$$\ln y_{it} = (\beta_1 + 1)\ln y_{i,t-1} + x_{it}'\beta + \alpha_i + \varepsilon_{it} \tag{6.2}$$

In order to avoid inconsistency of the estimator, we use Blundell and Bond's (1998) system GMM approach to assess the impact of the regressors on the GDP growth, treating most of the regressors as potentially endogenous. In most of the literature, this approach has replaced the earlier Arellano and Bond's (1991) estimator, which was found to possess a notable small sample bias. It should be noticed that allowing for endogeneity does not necessarily mean that these variables need to be endogenous; this can be viewed as a precaution, adopted by most authors, which secures the consistency of the estimator, in view of the endogeneity threat, at the relatively low price of a minor efficiency decrease.

We use the Arellano-Bond test for autocorrelation and Sargan's test for overidentifying restrictions, given that no autocorrelation in the error term ε_{it} and exogeneity of the instruments are essential for the estimator to maintain its consistency. We used annual data in this study and, as a result, specific observations might be located in different phases of the economic cycles and be influenced by temporary shocks. To limit this issue, we introduced fixed time effects into one of the models to eliminate the global shocks.

Empirical results are presented in Table 6.6. Five models were estimated. The differences between models consist in the methodology applied (no fixed time affect vs fixed time effects, limited number of instruments vs full instruments) and the set of regressors, among which we used different measures of human capital and regulatory quality. In the discussion, wherever we use the concept of significance of a variable, we assume 10% level of significance for brevity.

Having focused our analysis on the role of foreign-owned banks and their effect on growth, we find that the market share of these financial institutions in local credit markets is never significantly associated with economic growth in all the models estimated. The findings lead us to conclude that the strategy of a considerable entry of foreign banks in local credit markets has not guaranteed the supposed positive effects on financial innovation and development and, ultimately, economic growth that were expected. Economic growth was supported by openness to investment and the development of the stock market, while it was reduced by the increasing role of bank credit to GDP. While the estimates of the fixed time effects model (Model 1.5) undoubtedly confirm the relevance of the credit-to-GDP, other revealed discrepancies (for variables such as the regulatory quality index and country openness to investment) might be due to the fact that other factors are related with the phases of the economic cycles and as such are at least to some extent covered by the time dummies included in Model 1.5.

Table 6.6 Estimates of Eq. (6.2)—models 1.1–1.5

Regressor	*Model 1.1*	*Model 1.2*	*Model 1.3*	*Model 1.4*	*Model 1.5*
	Coefficient[a]	*Coefficient*[a]	*Coefficient*[a]	*Coefficient*[a]	*Coefficient*[a]
lnGDP (−1)[b]	0.9759***	0.9798***	0.9753***	0.9788***	0.9752***
Inflation	0.0040	0.0058	0.0036	0.0034	0.0011
Government size	−0.6482	−0.6522	−0.6168	−0.6283	−0.0156
Country's openness to trade	0.0154	0.0494	0.0131	0.0328	−0.0495
Country's openness to investments	0.3293**	0.2958*	0.3211**	0.3033*	0.0288
Human capital (BARRO_LEE)	0.0009		0.0003		
Human capital (PENN_STAT)		−0.0344		−0.0474	0.0159
Stock market capitalization	0.1499***	0.1573***	0.1452***	0.1520***	0.0070
Credit-to-GDP	−0.1339***	−0.1512***	−0.1213***	−0.1151***	−0.1154***
Rule of law index	0.0032		0.0028	0.0106	0.0198**
Regulatory quality		0.0010			
Foreign banks relevance	0.0129	0.0180	0.0156	0.0183	0.0044
Constant	0.4244	0.4701	0.4305	0.5241	0.3007
Fixed time effects	NO	NO	NO	NO	YES
Instruments[c]	Limited	Limited	Full	Full	Limited
Number of observations[d]	299	299	299	229	229

Arellano-Bond test of autocorrelation of the 2nd order[e]	−1.7630	0.0779	−1.7242	0.0847	−1.7749	0.0759	−1.7557	0.0791	−1.8378	0.0661
Sargan-Hansen test[f]	391.7189	0.0761	387.2103	0.1082	401.9431	0.1622	402.2284	0.1687	222.6136	0.0007

Note: All equations are estimated with annual data from 1995 to 2015 with the use of one-step system GMM estimator; p-values of t statistics obtained with the use of robust standard errors are reported with $^{*}p < 0.1$; $^{**}p < 0.05$; $^{***}p < 0.01$

[a]In the rows for the Arellano-Bond and Sargan-Hansen tests, the value of test statistic is provided in this column

[b]The one-year-lagged lnGDP estimates are provided in this row corresponding to the $\beta_1 + 1$ joint estimate in formulas (1) and (2). The $\beta_1 + 1$ is found significantly different from 0 as well as significantly lower than 1 with $p < 0.01$

[c]"Limited" instruments means that at most two lags of the regressors were used as instruments, "full" means that all the available lags of the regressors were used for that purpose

[d]Total number of observations used to estimate the model (in each case $n = 14$)

[e]Under H0 the $\Delta\varepsilon_t \sim AR(2)$ which corresponds to the $\varepsilon_t \sim AR(1)$

[f]Under H0 the instruments are considered as exogenous

Banks can positively affect economic performance as long as they efficiently perform their primary function of allocating resources to their most productive opportunities. Indeed, while lacking information on the composition of credit in banks' portfolios, Koivu (2002) provided a different explanation for the lack of a positive impact of bank credit on growth and that refers to the soft budget constraints prevalent among the CESEE companies after the economic transformation; lending to enterprises which apply soft budget constraints is likely to end up financing inefficient investment projects and generating financial losses. As a result, credit is neither profitable nor enhances productivity in the economy, even though it is channelled to enterprises and not to households. The capital markets in the CESEE countries started to develop in the early 1990s. The removal of capital controls (financial liberalization), perspective of EU accession and receding political risks have boosted their development with increased interest from investors. The empirical literature on the effects of stock market development on growth suggests the existence of a positive link; yet there is paucity of such studies on the CESEE countries.[5] Our study has confirmed its positive impact.

6.5 Conclusions

This chapter investigated the link between foreign bank penetration in CESEE and the economic growth of the region. The enormous changes and transformations occurring in the last 25 years in the real economy and in the institutional setting do not seem to be driven nor facilitated by a development of the banking sector. The finance and growth nexus in the region is at best weak, if not negative, and foreign-owned banks do not seem to have delivered the supposed positive effects on financial innovation and development and, ultimately, economic growth as expected.

A future step of the analysis, worth investigating for our sample of countries, should consider the link between (1) foreign bank penetration and the bilateral trade of the host country with home countries of the parent banks and (2) credit portfolio composition (households vs businesses). In this respect, the CESEE countries could represent an interesting case study as, on the one hand, foreign banks dominate their banking sectors while, on the other hand, being small and open economies trade liberalization during transition, increasing the scale of their foreign trade exchange, helped their development significantly. Moreover, observing the credit policies of foreign-owned banks, their focus—for a long time—has been on the credit to households, so maybe this kind of approach will explain why bank credit does not support economic growth.

Notes

1. The dataset contains annual data starting from 1980 for 176 advanced, emerging and low-income economies from the World Bank Global Financial Development database and World Bank FinStat, IMF's Financial Access Survey, Dealogic corporate debt database, and Bank for International Settlements debt securities database.
2. Only two studies investigate longer sample periods, though they are limited in the number of transition countries analysed.
3. The Barro and Lee dataset provides educational attainment data for 146 countries in five-year intervals from 1950 to 2010. The educational attainment of the adult population over age 15 and over age 25 is provided at seven levels of schooling, from no formal education up to complete tertiary. The Penn World Tables provide an index of human capital per person, which is related to the average years of schooling and the rate of return to education; the average years of schooling are taken from the Barro and Lee dataset, while the assumed rate of return to education is based on Mincer equation estimates around the world.
4. The rule of law index captures perceptions of the extent to which agents have confidence in and abide by the rules of society, in particular, the quality of contract enforcement, property rights and the courts, as well as the likelihood of crime and violence. The regulatory quality captures perceptions of the ability of the government to formulate and implement sound policies and regulations which permit and promote private sector development.
5. Still, most studies on the stock market-growth nexus rarely include data from after the GFC and usually use data for only several CEE countries.

Bibliography

Acemoglu D, Aghion P, Zilibotti F (2003) Distance to frontier, selection and economic growth. NBER Working Paper, No. 9066

Acemoglu D, Zilibotti F (1997) Was Prometheus unbound by chance? Risk, diversification and growth. J Polit Econ 105:709–775

Acemoglu D, Johnson S, Robinson JA (2001) The Colonial Origins of Comparative Development: An Empirical Investigation. Am Econ Rev 91(5):1369–1401

Acemoglu D, Johnson S, Robinson JA (2002). Reversal of Fortune: Geography and Institutions in the Making of the Modem World Income Distribution. Q J Econ 118: 1231–1294

Agénor PR, Canuto O, Jelenic M (2012) Avoiding Middle-Income Growth Traps. Economic Premise, No. 98, World Bank. https://openknowledge.worldbank.org/handle/10986/16954

Aghion P, Dewatripont M, Rey P (1999) Competition, financial discipline and growth. Rev Econ Stud 66:825–852

Aghion P, Howitt P (1992) A Model of Growth Through Creative Destruction". Econometrica 60 (2):323–351

Aghion P, Howitt P (1998) Endogenous Growth Theory. MIT Press, Cambridge, MA

Akimov A, Wijeweera A, Dollery B (2009) Financial development and economic growth: evidence from transition economies. App Financ Econ 19(12): 999–1008. https://doi.org/10.1080/09603100701857880

Alfaro L, Chandab A, Kalemli-Ozcanc S, Sayekd S (2004) FDI and economic growth: the role of local financial markets. J Int Econ 64:89–112. https://doi.org/10.1016/S0022-1996(03)00081-3

Allen F, Gale D (1997) Financial markets, intermediaries and intertemporal smoothing. J Polit Econ 105: 523–546

Arcand JL, Panizza U, Berkes E (2015) Too much finance?. J Econ Growth 20(2):105–148. https://doi.org/10.1007/s10887-015-9115-2

Arellano M, Bond S (1991) Some Tests of Specification for Panel Data: Monte Carlo Evidence and an Application to Employment Equations. Rev Econ Stud 58 (2):277

Arestis P, Chortareas G, Magkonis G (2015) The financial development and growth nexus: a meta-analysis. J Econ Surv 29(3):549–565. https://doi.org/10.1111/joes.12086

Atje R, Jovanovic, B (1993) Stock Markets and Development. Eur Econ Rev 37(2–3):632–40

Barajas A, Chami R, Yousefi SR (2013) The Finance and Growth Nexus Re-Examined: Do All Countries Benefit Equally? IMF Working Paper, No. 13/130

Barro RJ, Sala-i-Martin XI (2003) Economic growth. MIT press, Boston

Beck T (2008) The Econometrics of Finance and Growth. World Bank Policy Res Working Paper Series 2(April):1–51

Beck T (2013) Finance for Development: A Research Agenda. DEGRP research report

Beck T, Berrak B, Rioja F, Valev NT (2012) Who gets the credit? And does it matter? Households vs firms across countries. B.E. J Macroecon 12(1):1–46. https://doi.org/10.1515/1935-1690.2262

Beck T (2011) The Role of Finance in Economic Development: Benefits, Risks, and Politics. Center Discussion Papers, No. 141

Bencivenga VR, Smith BD (1993) Some Consequences of Credit Rationing in an Endogenous Growth Model. J Econ Dyn Control 17:97–22

Berglof E, Bolton P (2002) The Great Divide and Beyond: Financial Architecture in Transition. J Econ Persp 16(1):77–100. https://doi.org/10.1057/9780230374270_4

Bevan AA, Estrin S (2004) The determinants of foreign direct investment into European transition economies. J Comp Econ 32:775–787. https://doi.org/10.1016/j.jce.2004.08.006

Blackburn K, Hung VTY (1998) A theory of growth, financial development and trade. Economica 65:107–124

Blundell, RW, Bond, SR (1998) Initial Conditions and Moment Restrictions in Dynamic Panel Data Models. J Economet 87:115–143. https://doi.org/10.1016/S0304-4076(98)00009-8

Bolton P, Santos T, Scheinkman J (2011). "Cream Skimming in Financial Markets." National Bureau of Economic Research Working Paper 16804

Borensztein E, De Gregorio J, Lee JW (1998) How does foreign direct investment affect economic growth?. J Int Econ 45:115–135. https://doi.org/10.1016/S0022-1996(97)00033-0

Boyd JH, Smith BD (1992) Intermediation and the equilibrium allocation of investment capital: implications for economic development. J Monetary Econ 30:409–432

Boyd JH, Smith BD (1994) How good are standard debt contracts? Stochastic versus nonstochastic monitoring in a costly state verification environment. J Bus 67:539–562

Bruno V, Hauswald R (2014) The real effects of foreign banks. Rev Financ 18:1683–1716. https://doi.org/10.1093/rof/rft041

Buch CM, Kokta RM, Piazolo DM (2003) Foreign direct investment in Europe: Is there redirection from the South to the East? Comp Econ 31:94–109. https://doi.org/10.1016/S0147-5967(02)00013-6

Buch CM, Toubal, F (2003) Economic Integration and FDI in Transition Economies: What Can We Learn from German Data? Vierteljahrshefte zur Wirtschaftsforschung 72(4):594–610. https://doi.org/10.3790/vjh.72.4.594

Caporale GM, Rault C, Sova AD, Sova R (2015) Financial Development and Economic Growth: Evidence from 10 New European Union Members. Int J Financ Econ 20(1):48–60. https://doi.org/10.1002/ijfe.1498

Carkovic M, Levine R (2002) Does Foreign Direct Investment Accelerate Economic Growth? Mimeo University of Minnesota

Carp L (2012) Can Stock Market Development Boost Economic Growth? Empirical Evidence from Emerging Markets in Central and Eastern Europe. Procedia Econ Financ 3:438–444

Carstensen K, Toubal F (2004) Foreign direct investment in Central and Eastern European countries: a dynamic panel analysis. J Comp Econ 32: 3–22. https://doi.org/10.1016/j.jce.2003.11.001

Chee YL, Nair M (2010) The Impact of FDI and Financial Sector Development on Economic Growth: Empirical Evidence from Asia and Oceania. Int J Econ Financ 2 (2):107–119

Cheng S, Ho CC, Hou H (2014) The Finance-growth Relationship and the Level of Country Development. J Financ Serv Res 45:117–140. DOI https://doi.org/10.1007/s10693-012-0153-z

Čihák M, Demirgüç-Kunt A, Feyen E, Levine, R (2012) Benchmarking Financial Systems around the World. World Bank Res Policy Working Paper, No. 6175

Claessens S, Laeven L (2003) Financial Development, Property Rights, and Growth. J Financ 58(6):2401–2436

Claessens S, Demirgüç-Kunt A, Huizinga H (2001) How does Foreign Entry Affect Domestic Banking Markets?. J Bank Financ 25 (5):891–911. https://doi.org/10.1016/S0378-4266(00)00102-3

Claessens S, Van Horen N (2014) Foreign banks: trends and impact. J Money Credit Bank 41(1): 295–326. https://doi.org/10.1111/jmcb.12092

Compton RA, Giedeman DC (2011) Panel evidence on finance, institutions and economic growth. Appl Econ 43(25):3523–3547. DOI: https://doi.org/10.1080/00036841003670713

Dawson PJ (2003) Financial development and growth in economies in transition. App Econ Lett 10(13):925–929. https://doi.org/10.1080/1350485032000154243

de Haas RTA, van Lelyveld IPP (2006) Foreign banks and credit stability in Central and Eastern Europe. A panel data analysis. J Bank Financ 30:1927–1952. https://doi.org/10.1016/j.jbankfin.2005.07.007

De La Fuente A, Marin JM (1996) Innovation, bank monitoring and endogenous financial development. J Monetary Econ 38:269–301. https://doi.org/10.1016/S0304-3932(96)01277-9

de Mello LR (1999) Foreign Direct Investment-Led Growth: Evidence from Time Series and Panel Data. Oxford Econ Papers, No. 51(1), Symposium on Trade, Technology, and Growth

Demetriades, P, Rousseau P (2016) The changing face of financial development. Econ Lett 141(C): 87–90. https://doi.org/10.1016/j.econlet.2016.02.009

Diamond DW (1984) Financial intermediation and delegated monitoring. Rev Econ Stud 51: 393–414

Diamond DW (1991) Monitoring and reputation: the choice between bank loans and directly placed debt. J Polit Econ 99:689–721

Diamond DW, Verrecchia RE (1982) Optimal managerial contracts and equilibrium security prices. J Financ 37:275–287

Eichengreen B, Park, D, Shin, K (2011) When Fast Growing Economies Slow Down: International Evidence and Implications for China, NBER Working Paper, No. 16919

Eichengreen B, Park, D, Shin, K (2013) Growth Slow Downs Redux: New Evidence on the Middle-Income Trap. NBER Working Paper, No. 18863

Eicher TS, Leukert A (2009) Institutions and Economic Performance: Endogeneity and Parameter Heterogeneity. J Money Credit Bank 41(1):197–219

Eller M, Haiss PR, Steiner K (2005) Foreign Direct Investment in the Financial Sector: The Engine of Growth for Central and Eastern Europe? Vienna University of Economics and B.A., Europainstitut Working Papers, No. 69. https://doi.org/10.2139/ssrn.875614

Fink G, Haiss P, Vuksic G (2009) Contribution of Financial Market Segments at Different Stages of Development: Transition, Cohesion and Mature Economies Compared. J Financ Stabil 5(4):431–455. https://doi.org/10.1016/j.jfs.2008.05.002

Gaffeo E, Garalova P (2014) On the finance-growth nexus: additional evidence from Central and Eastern Europe countries. Econ Change Restruct 47(2):89–115. https://doi.org/10.1007/s10644-013-9143-x

Gale D, Hellwig M (1985) Incentive-compatible debt contracts: the one-period problem. Rev Econ Stud 52:647–663

Galetovic A (1996) Specialization, intermediation and growth. J Monetary Econ 38:549–559. https://doi.org/10.1016/S0304-3932(97)84693-4

Giannetti M, Ongena S (2005) Financial Integration and Entrepreneurial Activity: Evidence from Foreign Bank Entry in Emerging Markets. ECB Working Paper, No. 498.

Goldsmith RW (1969) Financial structure and development. Yale University Press, New Haven CT

Greenwood J, Jovanovic B (1990) Financial development, growth and the distribution of income. J Polit Econ 98:1076–1107

Greenwood J, Smith BD (1997) Financial Markets in Development, and the Development of Financial Markets. J Econ Dyn Control 21(1):145–181

Grossman SJ, Stiglitz J (1980) On the impossibility of informationally efficient markets. Am Econ Rev 70:393–408

Handa J, Khan SR (2008) Financial development and economic growth: a symbiotic relationship. Appl Financ Econ 18(13):1033–1049. DOI: https://doi.org/10.1080/09603100701477275

Harrison P, Sussman O, Zeira J (1999) Finance and growth: theory and evidence. Mimeo. Federal Reserve Board, Washington DC

Hassan MK, Sanchez B, Yu JS (2011) Financial development and economic growth: new evidence from panel data. Q Rev Econ Financ 51(1):88–104. https://doi.org/10.1016/j.qref.2010.09.001

Herzer D (2012) How Does Foreign Direct Investment Really Affect Developing Countries' Growth?. Rev Int Econ 20(2):396–414. DOI:https://doi.org/10.1111/j.1467-9396.2012.01029.x

Holmstrom B, Tirole J (1993) Market liquidity and performance monitoring. J Polit Econ 101:678–709

Jensen M, Meckling WR (1976) Theory of the firm, managerial behavior, agency costs and ownership structure. J Financ Econ 3:305–360

Jensen M, Murphy K (1990) Performance pay and top management incentives. J Polit Econ 98:225–263

King RG, Levine R (1993a) Finance, Entrepreneurship and Growth. J Monetary Econ 32(3):513–42.

King RG, Levine R (1993b) Finance and Growth. Schumpeter Might Be Right. Q J Econ 108:717–738

Koivu T (2002) Do Efficient Banking Sectors Accelerate Economic Growth in Transition Countries. BOFIT Discussion Paper, No. 14/2002, Bank of Finland

Kyle AS (1984) Market structure, information, future markets, and price formation. In: Storey GG, Schmitz A, Sarris AS (ed) International Agricultural Trade: Advanced readings in price formation, market structure and price instability. Westview, Boulder CO

Laeven L, Levine R, Michalopoulos, S (2015) Financial innovation and endogenous growth. J Financ Intermed 24:1–24. https://doi.org/10.1016/j.jfi.2014.04.001

Lensink R, Murinde V (2006) Does foreign bank really stimulate gross domestic investment?. Appl Financ Econ 16(8):569–582. https://doi.org/10.1080/09603100600649701

Lensink R, Hermes N (2004) The short-term effects of foreign bank entry on domestic bank behaviour: Does economic development matter?. J Bank Financ 28(3):553–568. https://doi.org/10.1016/S0378-4266(02)00393-X

Léon F (2018) Convergence of credit structure around the world. Econ Model 68:306–317. https://doi.org/10.1016/j.econmod.2017.07.021

Levine R (1991) Stock markets, growth, and tax policy. J Financ 46:1445–1465

Levine R (2005) Finance and Growth: Theory and Evidence. In: Aghion P, Durlauf SN (ed) Handbook of Economic Growth. Volume 1A, chapter 12, Elsevier, North Holland

Levine R, Loayza N Beck, T (2000) Financial Intermediation and Growth: Causality and Causes without Outliers. J Monetary Econ 46(1):31–77. https://doi.org/10.1016/S0304-3932(00)00017-9

Levine R, Zervos, S (1998) Stock Markets, Banks, and Economic Growth. Am Econ Rev 88:537–558

Mankiw G, Romer D, Weil DN (1992) A Contribution to The Empirics Of Economic Growth. Quat J Econ 408–437

Mehl A, Winkler, A (2003) The finance-growth nexus and financial sector environment: new evidence from southeast Europe. Paper Presented at The Ninth Dubrovnik Economic Conference on Banking and the Financial Sector in Transition and Emerging Market Economies. Croatian National Bank

Morales MF (2003) Financial intermediation in a model of growth through creative destruction. Macroecon Dyn 7:363–393. https://doi.org/10.1017/S1365100502020138

Petkovski M, Kjosevski J (2014) Does Banking Sector Development Promote Economic Growth? An Empirical Analysis for Selected Countries in Central and South Eastern Europe. Econ Res-Ekonomska Istraživanja 27(1):55–66

Philippon T (2010) Financiers versus Engineers: should the financial sector be taxed or subsidized?. Am Econ J- Macroecon 2(3):158–82

Popov A, Udell G (2010) Cross-Border Banking and the International Transmission of Financial Distress during the Crisis of 2007–2008, ECB Working Paper, No. 1203

Popov A (2017) Evidence on Finance and Economic Growth. ECB Working Paper Series No.2115

Rioja F, Valev N (2014) Stock markets, banks and the sources of economic growth in low and high income countries. J Econ Financ 38(2):302–320. https://doi.org/10.1007/s12197-011-9218-3

Rodrik D (2000) How far will international economic integration go?. J Econ Perspect 14(1):177–186. DOI: https://doi.org/10.1257/jep.14.1.177

Rodrik D (2011) The Future Of Economic Convergence. NBER Working Paper, No. 17400

Rousseau P, Wachtel P (2011) What is Happening to the Impact of Financial Deepening on Economic Growth?. Econ Inq 49(1):276–88. https://doi.org/10.1111/j.1465-7295.2009.00197.x

Rousseau PL, Wachtel P (1998) Financial Intermediation and Economic Performance: Historical Evidence from Five Industrialized Countries. Journal Money Credit Bank 30(4):657–78.

Sahay R, Čihák M, N'Diaye P, Barajas A, Bi R, Ayala D, Gao Y, Kyobe A, Nguyen L, Saborowski C, Svirydzenka K Yousefi SR (2015) Rethinking financial deepening: stability and growth in emerging markets, SDN 15/08, International Monetary Fund, Washington

Sassi S, Gasmi A (2014) The effect of enterprise and household credit on economic growth: new evidence from European Union countries. J Macroecon 30:226–231. https://doi.org/10.1016/j.jmacro.2013.12.001

Scharfstein D (1998) The disciplinary role of takeovers. Rev Econ Stud 55:185–199

Shan J (2005) Does financial development 'lead' economic growth? A vector autoregression Appraisal. Appl Econ 37(12):1353–1367. DOI: https://doi.org/10.1080/00036840500118762

Sirri ER, Tufano P (1995) The economics of pooling. In: Crane DB et al (ed) The global financial system: a functional approach. Harvard Business School Press, Boston MA

Solow RM (1956) A Contribution to the Theory of Economic Growth. Q J Econ LXX, p 65–94

Soussa F (2004) A Note on Banking FDI in Emerging Markets: Literature Review and Evidence from M&A Data, Working Paper, https://www.bis.org/publ/cgfs22gb.pdf

Stein JC (1988) Takeover threats and managerial myopia. J Polit Econ 96:61–80

Sussman O (1993) A theory of financial development. In: Giovannini A (ed) Finance and Development: issues and experience. Cambridge University Press, Cambridge

Tennant D, Abdulkadri A (2010) Empirical exercises in estimating the effects of different types of financial institutions' functioning on economic growth. Appl Econ 42(30):3913–3924. DOI:https://doi.org/10.1080/00036840802360252

Valickova P, Havranek T, Horvath R (2015) Financial Development and economic growth: a meta-analysis. Econ Surv 29(3):506–526. https://doi.org/10.1111/joes.12068

Wu JL, Hou H, Cheng SY (2010) The dynamic impacts of financial institutions on economic growth: Evidence from the European Union. J Macroecon 32(3):879–891. https://doi.org/10.1016/j.jmacro.2009.09.003

Yu JS, Hassan MK, Sanchez B (2012) A re-examination of financial development, stock markets development and economic growth. Appl Econ 44(27):3479–3489. https://doi.org/10.1080/00036846.2011.577019

CHAPTER 7

Concluding Remarks: Who Is the Winner of Foreign Banks' Presence?

Małgorzata Iwanicz-Drozdowska

In Chaps. 3, 4, 5, and 6 we presented the results of our comprehensive study on banking sectors and economic development in the CESEE countries over the 1995–2015 period. We first tackled the question of why international banks decided to go abroad and to enter post-communist economies. In the case of CESEE, it was not the "follow your customer" approach as in many well-developed countries, which large global corporations follow. We find, instead, that reasons to enter the CESEE markets were high-profit expectations along with the "follow your competitor" strategy. One of the first international banks that entered the region was Austrian Raiffeisen Bank (it was a greenfield entry). Such a decision may be linked to historical links with many Central and Southern European countries. The mode of entry was mainly through acquisition of local banks which were privatized or which faced some financial difficulties. The preference for takeovers stemmed from the fact that foreign banks wanted to focus on the retail segment, which is less risky and, in most of the cases, more profitable than the corporate segment. The growth of the banking sectors in CESEE is to a large extent attributable to foreign-owned banks. However, we cannot identify significant differences in the financial position, including profitability, of foreign-owned banks and their domestic-owned peers. Therefore, we can conclude that the banking business was operated in a similar manner in both groups

M. Iwanicz-Drozdowska et al.,
Foreign-Owned Banks, Studies in Economic Transition,
https://doi.org/10.1007/978-3-030-01111-6_7

of banks. Domestic-owned banks were fairly easily able to catch-up with foreign-owned subsidiaries in many respects. In our opinion, this is a win-win situation. However, in order to obtain a complete picture of the foreign-owned banks' operations in the host countries, one should analyse at least some other important issues, such as transfer prices applied between parent banks and its subsidiaries and the cost of the borrowed funds between them. This information is not publicly available and therefore we were not able to expand our analysis. These two things may have an impact on the profitability achieved by parent banks out of this investment.

In the second step, we analysed bank credit growth and its procyclicality. We find that favourable macroeconomic conditions stimulate credit growth in banks with different owners. Bank-specific traits show similar impact across different groups of banks, except for banks located in the VI countries. An important finding is that credit activity of foreign-owned banks is immune to crisis events in the host country, while a crisis in parents' home countries destimulates credit growth. The situation was different, however, in the VI countries. The high amplitude of bank credit cycles underlines the significance of cyclicality of bank credit in the CESEEs. The differences in the cyclicality of credit provided by domestic- and foreign-owned banks are not very high, especially after the global financial crisis. Being a winner depends on the occurrence of a crisis event. If there is no crisis, all banks go on the same boat. In the case of a local crisis, the host country economy may be regarded as a winner, since the credit supply channelled by foreign-owned banks is stable. In this way, foreign-owned banks may increase their market share. While the crisis occurs in a home country, the host country loses because credit activity of foreign-owned banks is reduced. At the same time, the parent bank may rely on profits of its subsidiaries, which are supporting financial results of the international (or even global) banking group.

Our research cannot clearly support either positive or negative impact of foreign-owned banks on the banking sector stability in the CESEEs. The results show that it is the host country's macroeconomic conditions that affect the stability of banking sectors, including foreign-owned banks, meaning that foreign-owned banks react to local conditions and their success is the same as the host country's success. We find that banks' stability in CESEEs is more dependent on the banks' balance sheet structures and their lending policies, rather than just on the type of the owner. It is more likely that foreign ownership indirectly affects financial stability via the credit policy channel. If aggressive, it may damage financial stability. Moreover, robust economic growth in the CESEE countries incentivizes the expansion and aggressive credit policies of both domestic- and foreign-owned banks, which contributes to boom-bust cycles. Therefore, we are inclined to find it as win-win or loss-loss situation, depending on the type of credit policy.

While the unsustainable credit boom is unlikely to reoccur in the CESEEs anytime soon, many new post-GFC challenges emerged and will continue to shape the banking landscape in the CESEEs. Yet the foundations for financial stability in the CESEEs have been strengthened along with the establishment of national macroprudential frameworks and improvement of banking regulatory standards, all of which will most likely be put to the test in the years to come.

Last, but not least, we investigated the link between foreign bank penetration in the CESEEs and economic growth of the region. The enormous changes and transformations we witnessed in the last 25 years in the real economy and in the institutional setting do not seem to be driven nor facilitated by development of the banking sector. We find that the finance-growth nexus in the region is at best weak if not negative and foreign-owned banks do not seem to have delivered positive effects on financial innovation and development and, ultimately, on economic growth. For future research on finance-growth nexus, one should take into account at least the composition of the credit portfolio (households vs businesses), which may play a role (Sassi and Gasmi 2014) for the impact the bank credit has on economic growth. One could observe foreign-owned banks' preference to provide credit mostly to households due to better risk diversification and higher profitability. To date, data on credit portfolio composition for the CESEEs have not been sufficient to carry out this kind of analysis. Who seems to be the winner then from the perspective of economic development? Not the CESEEs real economies, but the banking sector, which generates profits regardless of the ownership structure.

To sum up, we have identified win-win situations for the development, performance, and stability of domestic-owned and foreign-owned banks, and the feedback between the home and host countries in the case of crisis events for the credit stability. However, for economic development the activity of the banking sector was not identified as growth-enhancing. We claim that the banking sector itself in general is a winner in this part of the game.

Bibliography

Sassi S, Gasmi A (2014) The effect of enterprise and household credit on economic growth: new evidence from European union countries. J Macroecon 39(A):226–231. https://doi.org/10.1016/j.jmacro.2013.12.001

Index[1]

[1]Note: Page numbers followed by 'n' refer to notes.

M. Iwanicz-Drozdowska et al.,
Foreign-Owned Banks, Studies in Economic Transition,
https://doi.org/10.1007/978-3-030-01111-6

V

Z

FSC
www.fsc.org
MIX
Papier | Fördert gute Waldnutzung
FSC® C083411

Kolibri 360 GmbH
Ferdinand-Jühlke-Straße 7
99095 Erfurt, Deutschland
produktsicherheit@kolibri360.de